MEDIATION

PRINCIPLES AND PRACTICE

By

Kimberlee K. Kovach

Assistant Professor of Clinic Studies
South Texas College of Law

WEST PUBLISHING CO.
ST. PAUL, MINN., 1994

COPYRIGHT © 1994 By WEST PUBLISHING CO.
610 Opperman Drive
P.O. Box 64526
St. Paul, MN 55164–0526
1–800–328–9352

Library of Congress Cataloging-in-Publication Data
Kovach, Kimberlee K., 1955–
    Mediation : principles and practice / by Kimberlee K. Kovach.
       p.   cm. — (Misc. series)
    Includes index.
    ISBN 0–314–04053–6
    1. Mediation—United States.   2. Dispute resolution (Law)—United
States.   I. Title. II. Series.
KF9084.K68   1994
347.73 ' 9—dc20   94–21618
[347.3079]   CIP

ISBN 0–314–04053–6

 TEXT IS PRINTED ON 10% POST CONSUMER RECYCLED PAPER    PRINTED WITH SOY INK™

Dedication

For all mediators past, present, and future. And for my special mediator, my love, colleague, and husband, Eric.

*

Preface

This book was written in an effort to combine the theory, law, and practice of mediation into one work. It is primarily intended for use in skill based courses; consequently, the coverage of both theory and legal principles is not exhaustive. Hopefully, it is sufficient, however, to provide the reader with an adequate background in these subjects for beginning the practice of mediation.

My goal was a work which could be used in teaching and training the general principles of the mediation process. It is also intended to serve as a quick reference for both novice and experienced mediators. I attempted to present a variety of views about the mediation process, and struggled to not strongly advocate my personal views. It is my belief that as teachers of mediation, we also have a duty to empower students of mediation to come to their own decisions about the myriad of issues facing the "profession".

The materials have been organized in the manner in which I teach them. I deliberately mixed them so that there is a blend of activity throughout the semester. Each chapter, however, can stand alone, and I support flexibility in the use of this book.

As the problems and exercises were designed to be used in a number of ways, I urge experimentation with them.

*

Acknowledgements

My warmest gratitude goes to Larry Ray and Scot Dewhirst, who were the first to realize and acknowledge mediator-like tendencies in me. Not only did Larry, Scot and I enjoy working together in the Night Prosecutor's Program in Columbus, Ohio but more importantly, we have remained friends and colleagues throughout the years. An acknowledgement goes to the Capital University School of Law which was farsighted enough to provide mediation opportunities for students twenty years ago. Capital, and in particular its Center for Dispute Resolution, continues to be a leader in the field. I warmly thank the 1979–80 Houston Bar Association Neighborhood Justice Committee, led by Hon. Frank G. Evans, Hon. Eric Andell, and Joe Bart for their hard work in bringing ADR to Texas. Judge Evans' vision and energy is a true inspiration. And warmest gratitude to Janet Pignataro Evans, who dedicated hundreds of hours as a member of that committee. Janet assured that the committee ran smoothly, to the point of unloading my U-Haul when I arrived in Houston, and today remains one of my closest and dearest friends.

I would also like to recognize the work of Melinda Ostermeyer, who while in Houston set a high standard for administration of ADR programs, and who continues to be a good friend and training partner. And a special acknowledgement to Hon. Margaret Garner Mirabal, who set a superior example of dedication to mediation and ADR while engaged in the practice of law, and later as a member of the judiciary.

Of course without the foresight of South Texas College of Law this book would not have been written. A special thanks to Professor R. Hanson Lawton, a mentor, friend, and colleague, who continues to provide support and enthusiasm each day. I am especially grateful for the wisdom of Professor Catherine G. Burnett in realizing the importance of ADR to the future of the justice system. It was a result of Cathy's initiative that the Mediation Clinic was established. And thanks are in order for Dean William Wilks and Associate Dean Sandra DeGraw, for providing the assistance and support in the implementation of our ADR curriculum. I also acknowledge all of my fellow faculty, who on a daily basis provide me with support and encouragement. I am especially grateful to Michael Wheeler for his kind and affable support. (And in particular those who were brave enough to participate in the mediation trainings I conducted.)

I would also like to thank all of the law students who have provided me with an education. And similar appreciation to all of those mediators who have participated in my trainings over the years. You truly make the world a better place. And deepest appreciation to my very good friend Lanelle Montgomery, my co-chair of the 1991-92 State Bar of Texas ADR Committee and the 1992-93 ADR Section. Lanelle truely personifies collaboration and made the work a delightful experience. Warmfelt gratitude to all my friends and colleagues on the Council of our State Bar ADR Section. Special thanks go to the staff and council of the ABA Dispute Resolution Section. And warmest gratitude to former ABA staffer Prue Kestner. I also acknowledge all of the wonderful mediators whom I have met in my travels. It is because of colleagues like you that this field is so exciting, stimulating, and special.

And a very, very special thanks to those who commented on the drafts of this work, Dean James Alfini, Professor Catherine G. Burnett, Larry Ray, Prue Kestner and Eric Galton.

This book would have been impossible if it were not for all of the hard work of research assistants Judy Meeh and Jeri Weschler. Thanks to all of the secretaries who contributed to this effort, and my utmost gratitude to Teresa Elizondo for seeing this project through to completion.

And on a personal note, I want to thank my parents, Mike and Mary Kovach and my sister, Karol Wilson, who have continually provided love and support in all my efforts. And special gratitude to my friends Sherry Ferrell, Janet Pignataro Evans, Pam Price Finnerman, Marta Bourke and Joanne McCarthy who are my Houston family and remained my friends even though I rarely talked with them.

And finally I thank each individual who contributes to the effort of a peaceful world.

"Let mine be a voice for peace" — Dan Fogelberg

Summary of Contents

*

Table of Contents

———

MEDIATION

PRINCIPLES AND PRACTICE

*

Chapter One

OVERVIEW OF THE
ADR UNIVERSE

A. INTRODUCTION

People resolve disputes everyday. Some are better at it than others. Yet, conflict resolution is a discipline that is rarely formally taught. In fact, analysis of the origin and nature of disputes and conflict rarely occurs. Admittedly, discussion and debate about the content of conflict are common. But these discussions infrequently turn to the examination of the skills involved in resolving disputes. The *process* of dispute resolution is virtually ignored. Conflict resolution is not part of our secondary or higher education systems. We constantly search for ways to resolve conflict. But unfortunately we rely upon some sort of "automatic pilot" or "knee jerk" approach, instead of a more analytical, process-oriented method. Due to hectic schedules, discomfort, or ignorance, avoidance is often the response to conflict. At the more unfortunate end of the continuum, some opt for violence. Fortunately, many options for conflict resolution exist somewhere between the two.

Many professionals deal with conflict resolution on a daily basis. These include diplomats, police officers, lawyers, and judges. However, most professionals are not educated in skills vital to the constructive resolution of conflict. This text will explore a rather old, yet traditionally under-utilized method of dispute resolution: Mediation.

Mediation, as a process of resolving conflict, has gained recent [1] popularity and acceptance. This has been primarily as part of the trend to explore, particularly in legal or quasi-legal disputes, alternatives to formal, expensive litigation. Such exploration of alternatives has been a direct result of the often voiced frustration and disappointment associated with the use of our justice system as a means of dispute resolution. This criticism, at least in part, explains the development of the Alternative Dispute Resolution (ADR) movement.

Alternative Dispute Resolution procedures do not ignore the fact that disputes exist; rather, ADR focuses on new and creative methods to

---

1. Acknowledging that the term *recent* is relative, it is used in this context to refer to the last fifteen years, specifically in the United States.

1

resolve disputes. Such an approach often includes an examination of the underlying causes of conflict. This chapter will provide an overview of the ADR universe. It should be immediately noted that this universe is not static; rather, it continues to grow and expand as society continues to investigate the nature and causes of disputes.

B. WHAT ARE DISPUTES?

Many words may be used to describe disputes: arguments, disagreements, challenges, contests, debates, conflicts, quarrels, lawsuits, fights, altercations, controversies, feuds, wrongs, combat, and war. A detailed analysis of the differences in these terms and the specific instances in which one may evolve into another is beyond the scope of this text.[2] However, because the work of the mediator necessarily involves intervention in a dispute, some consideration of the disputing process is necessary. Since the mediator's job is to assist in the resolution of conflict,[3] it is important that she[4] have an understanding of the many forms and functions of conflict.[5]

The word conflict is derived from the Latin *con* (together) and *fligere* (to strike). Conflict is defined as "an encounter with arms, a fight, a battle, a prolonged struggle."[6] Additional definitions include a mental or spiritual struggle within a man; the clashing or variance of opposed principles, statements, or arguments.[7] It has been suggested that conflict exists when there are incompatible activities.[8] Conflict has also been defined as a set of divergent aims, methods, or behavior.[9] Some even go so far as to declare that conflict has its own life cycle.[10] We have all observed that conflict varies in intensity and duration. It is crucial that the mediator, as an intervenor in another's conflict, be aware of the variety of factors affecting conflict.

When we initially think of conflict or disputing, what usually comes to mind is manifest conflict. In other words, that conflict which we can observe. Yet in most situations, where there is such overt conduct, underlying conflict also exists. This is the implicit, often hidden or denied, conflict. And, it is the latter which may truly drive the conflict. In order to achieve a complete or final resolution of a dispute, the underlying conflict must be identified and resolved. These underlying issues are often referred to as the "hidden agenda". One goal of the

---

2. For analysis of disputes, see William L. F. Felstiner, et al., *The Emergence and Transformation of Disputes: Naming, Blaming, Claiming*, 15 L. & Soc'y. Rev. 63 (1980–81).

3. This is but one of the many descriptions of the work of a mediator. The role is examined in detail in Chapter 2, Sec. D, infra.

4. Gender will be systematically alternated.

5. For an in depth study of conflict, see Joyce L. Hocker & William W. Wilmot, Interpersonal Conflict, 3rd Ed. (1991).

6. The Oxford English Dictionary 713 (2nd Ed. 1989).

7. Id.

8. Morton Deutsch, The Resolution of Conflict 10 (1973).

9. Jay Folberg & Alison Taylor, Mediation: A Comprehensive Guide to Resolving Conflicts Without Litigation 24 (1984).

10. Id. at 22.

mediation process is to uncover the underlying motivations of the parties.

Another significant aspect of conflict is that it exists internally. This is termed "intrapersonal conflict," i.e., conflict existing within one's self. These intrapersonal conflicts range from difficulty in choosing between a health conscious meal and a favorite but high calorie dinner, to choices between career and family. While some of the dispute resolution principles set forth in this text may apply to intrapersonal conflict, such conflicts are better treated by those within the psychology or social work fields.[11] Therefore, this work will deal primarily with the disputes or conflict between individuals or groups, i.e., interpersonal conflict. The mediator should nonetheless be aware of intrapersonal conflict, and appreciate that it may impact the interpersonal dispute, or vice versa.

Conflict consists of a number of variables. We know that overt conflict takes many forms, ranging from a slight look of exasperation to a pistol shot. Further, the intensity of conflict varies. In some instances, conflict, if left unresolved, will escalate. In other situations, time and space may act to minimize the dispute. There is also variation in what conflict affects. It can range from a slight influence on only two parties in dispute, to the complete destruction of a social structure or nation.

The communication process is an integral part of conflict. The exchange of both verbal and nonverbal messages is the most significant part of disputing. How conflict is viewed can depend on the participants' method of communication. The manner in which individuals dispute can also depend upon factors such as the culture, history, and relationship of the parties. In fact, it has been observed that disputing can, in fact, define the relationship.[12] A mediator must be cognizant of the disputing process, and its attendant characteristics.

Conflict appears to have escalated in the United States. The response has been more police, more courts, even more violence. With this approach has come a view of conflict that is primarily negative. Historically disputes were battles to be won, usually by force. Consequently, resolution of disputes in America is often seen as a win-lose proposition, with conflict perceived as necessarily carrying negative consequences. Yet conflict can be positive. In some instances conflict can be an exciting and inspiring experience. Conflict may lead to a closer examination of issues, and assessment of situations.[13] Conflict can result in creative and new resolutions. Relationships can be established or strengthened. And in fact, conflict is at the root of personal and social change.[14] While mediation has as its philosophical basis the creative and

---

11. See for example, Deutsch, supra note 8, Chapter 3.

12. Jerald S. Auerbach, Justice Without Law 16 (1983).

13. Stephen Worchel & Sharon Lundgren, The Nature of Conflict and Conflict Resolution in Community Mediation 17 (Karen Grover Duffy, et al. eds., 1991).

14. Deutsch, supra note 8, at 9.

constructive means of dispute resolution, this has not been a traditional approach to conflict.

C. TRADITIONAL MEANS OF RESOLVING DISPUTES

If conflict is viewed as a struggle, then it is not surprising that traditional means of resolution include fight, force, or coercion. These responses have resulted in the win-lose perspective of conflict resolution. An often used alternative to force is the flight or avoidance mechanism. But, to ignore the conflict in most instances is to not resolve it. Other traditional responses to conflict include compromise or splitting down the middle; decision making by an individual outside of the dispute; a gamble or chance method of determining the outcome; and counseling.[15] Each of these more traditional means of resolving disputes has merit as well as drawbacks which will be briefly mentioned.

When conflict is encountered, the initial means of dispute resolution usually considered is the win-lose approach. This is essentially the violence or fight response which has been used throughout history, as well as on the street today. In many instances, an individual's survival instinct probably leads to the use of this alternative. The response becomes automatic in many people. The media, sports, and even the courts assist in perpetuating this method. The underlying theory is that in order to effectuate a resolution, one side must win and the other must lose. Seen in the best light, the loser then goes away. The worst, and too often played out, case scenario results in elimination of the loser; that is, his death.

Avoidance is also a common response to conflict. Even when faced with it directly, many people continue to ignore conflict. In some cases, this can be an appropriate response. Where the dispute is not of great significance to one or all of the parties, or for some reason the dispute is, or becomes, of low priority, it may fade away. This is more likely to occur where the disputing parties will have no future relationship. However, psychologists tell us, and we know from personal experience, that if conflict is unresolved, more often than not it lingers. The manifest conflict may no longer be apparent, but the underlying conflict remains intact. Most likely it intensifies. This is particularly true where there is an ongoing relationship between the parties in conflict. In order to resolve the conflict, it must be disclosed. If the matters in dispute are not out on the table and resolved, it is very likely that the dispute will recur, or simply manifest itself in another manner.

In using compromise as a means of resolution, all parties move from their initial positions in nearly equivalent increments until the middle ground is reached. Seen initially as a cooperative style of negotiation, compromise has disadvantages. The movements toward the middle may

15. It is acknowledged that this list is not exhaustive, but rather only suggestive as to traditional methods of response to conflict.

not be of equal magnitude. Resentment is then felt by one of the parties, and it lingers. Moreover, important underlying interests or needs are not identified, let alone met.

Another method of dispute resolution is to voluntarily relinquish responsibility for the conflict. This is accomplished by turning it over to chance. Chance may consist of a third party who has no interest in the conflict, or it may be an object (such as dice or a lottery drawing). Chance intervenes and makes the decisions for the parties. Today in the United States this method can be observed in the court system. The third party, either the judge or the jury, determines the outcome of the dispute for the parties. Individuals can avoid responsibility for their disputes by relying on these outside entities. If the result is unsatisfactory to a party, the system can be blamed. At least in part, this attributes to what has been termed the "litigation explosion". Admittedly, in some instances it is important that a neutral party make the decision. Litigation and arbitration are viable options for dispute resolution. However, in many instances the parties have more information and understanding about the dispute. Therefore, decisions made by the parties on their own would likely be better than those made by outsiders. While each of the previous methods of dispute resolution are used every day, more creative methods of resolving conflict are needed. Each of the preceding processes is appropriate in some instances. Each also has drawbacks which limit its use.

Another characterization of how disputes are resolved places the emphasis on choices the disputing parties may make. These are: 1) to reconcile underlying interests; 2) to determine who is right; and 3) to conclude who is more powerful.[16] Each is appropriate in different circumstances. The choice may depend upon how the parties relate to one another and the nature of the dispute. Previous experience is also a key ingredient in selection of these alternatives. Determining rights and making power plays are currently the commonly known methods of resolving disputes.

It is suggested that the most effective system of dispute resolution consists of a method which increases the reconciliation of interests. If the primary goal of reconciling interests is not successful, then a rights determination should be next, leaving a power resolution as the last resort.[17]

As we, as individuals and as a society, grow and evolve, so should our means of dispute resolution. We have observed a shift in the methods used to resolve conflict. A number of alternatives have developed which employ neutral third parties to resolve disputes. The degree of influence which the third party has over the final result varies with each process. But this is only the beginning. The ADR Universe is clearly in its infancy.

16. William L. Ury, et al., Getting Disputes Resolved: Designing Systems to Cut the Costs of Conflict 4 (1993).

17. Id. at 18.

D. THE VARIETY OF ADR DEVICES

In general, Alternative Dispute Resolution (ADR) is the term which identifies a group of processes through which disputes, conflicts, and cases are resolved outside of formal litigation procedures. The development of ADR in the United States has been primarily as an adjunct to our legal system. ADR procedures include negotiation, mediation, arbitration, case evaluation techniques, and private judging. These processes have been designed and developed to assist those involved in a dispute to arrive expeditiously at a mutually satisfactory resolution of a matter.

At the basis of alternative dispute resolution is the negotiation process. But, for a number of reasons, direct negotiations do not always result in satisfactory settlements.[18] Often, when direct negotiations break down and do not produce a resolution, a neutral third party can provide assistance. All ADR processes, as developed, involve a third party neutral [19] who facilitates a resolution to a dispute. When selecting an ADR device, an examination of the factor which will most likely move the case toward a resolution is necessary.

The type of assistance provided to the dispute depends largely on the neutral's role. That role determines the effect the neutral has on the negotiation. In fact, what the third party neutral does to assist in settlement defines the process. The following provides a closer examination of the more common ADR processes. They can be categorized into three primary types: adjudicative, evaluative, and mediative.

1. ADJUDICATIVE

In adjudicatory dispute resolution processes, the neutral adjudicates, or makes a decision. Adjudication is the basis of the legal system. When a case is submitted to the court or a jury, someone other than the parties makes the decision. Many times this is necessary because the parties clearly want or need an outside decision maker. Arbitration and private adjudication, or private judging, are the ADR procedures most similar to formal court proceedings. While traditional adjudication is always binding, arbitration can be varied. Non-binding or advisory decisions are possible.

Arbitrations are generally conducted by a sole arbitrator or a panel of three.[20] In the arbitration process, arbitrators listen to a typically adversarial presentation of all sides of the case, and thereafter render a decision, usually termed an award. The arbitration procedure is generally conducted with more formality than the other dispute resolution

---

18. An in depth look at the negotiation process, including a brief examination of negotiation problems, is provided in Chapter 9, infra. See also, Robert Mnookin, *Why Negotiations Fail: An Exploration of Barriers to the Resolution of Conflict,* 8 Ohio St. J. On Disp. Resol. 235 (1993).

19. Although the term is used here in the singular, in many dispute resolution processes the *neutral party* may be two or more individuals.

20. For simplicity, the plural form will be used in this discussion.

devices which will be described. More often than not attorneys are involved. The attorneys make the presentations to the arbitrators. Often live testimony is presented and actual evidence may be submitted. Experts may be involved, and in some cases the arbitrators may visit the actual site of the dispute, e.g., a construction area. Post-hearing briefs may be submitted. Thereafter, the arbitrators take a period of time, usually thirty days, to deliberate and render their decision. Arbitration awards may be binding upon the parties if previously agreed upon or ordered by the court.

In the cases where the arbitration is conducted by a three person panel, the common practice is for each side to choose an arbitrator. The two arbitrators then select the third, usually the chair. This individual is essentially the real "neutral". While the better practice requires that a consensus among all three arbitrators be reached to support an award, some procedures allow for the award to be issued upon a majority decision.

The process for appeal from a binding arbitration differs significantly from the normal court appellate process. In many instances there are very limited rights of appeal, which are often provided by statute. Of course, where the arbitration award is non-binding or advisory the parties may disregard it. For instance, mandatory court arbitration programs are of an advisory nature. If however, parties in a dispute voluntarily agree to participate in arbitration by either contract or stipulation, the award is often binding.

There are a number of other variables which should be considered when employing the arbitration process. These include determination of the rules of procedure, if any, which will be followed; the appropriate time during the life of the dispute for the use of arbitration; the amount of discovery to be completed prior to the arbitration; and the background of the arbitrators. Arbitration may be used before suit is filed, during discovery, and as a substitute for trial or appeal. Most of these decisions may be made by the participants, except for those cases involved in a court-annexed program.

Over the long history of the use of arbitration, a number of modifications of the process have occurred. Two of the more common variants are high-low arbitration and final offer arbitration. In high-low arbitration, the parties in a monetary dispute minimize risk by choosing the parameters of the arbitration award. In advance of the arbitration, two figures are determined, a high number which is automatically awarded if plaintiff prevails, and a low number, the award if there is a finding for the defendant. In final offer arbitration, each party submits, usually in confidence, a final offer to the arbitrators. The final award must be one of the submitted offers. Consequently, parties tend to submit reasonable offers.

Arbitration is most effective in cases where the parties cannot agree on the facts, or where the dispute is purely monetary. Arbitration is also appropriate where the matter is highly complex or technical, and an expert decision is needed. In many instances, arbitrators, who are not necessarily attorneys, have expertise in the subject matter of the dispute.[21]

Another distinct ADR tool falling within the adjudicatory sphere is known as private or special judging. With this option, the parties hire a retired or former judge to hear the case and render a decision. In several states, courts can order a referral of a civil or family case to this procedure, or the parties themselves can agree to take the matter to the private judge, also known as "rent-a-judge". The judge, also termed a referee, can either decide all issues or just a portion of the case. Because this is essentially the retention of a special judge for a fee, this type of procedure has been criticized as private justice, only for the wealthy.[22] However, with time, cost and other savings resulting from the use of this procedure, in the long run, private judging may be more economical than traditional litigation. A recent California study indicates that while the preceding criticisms were valid, because of the infrequent use of the process no actual abuses were found. Close monitoring of the process by court rules were recommended.[23]

Several states have statutes outlining the specific procedures to be followed in the use of this process.[24] Although some of the statutes do not mandate that the private judge have judicial experience,[25] as a practical matter, at least in California, retired judges are used. Use of a private judge is probably most useful in cases where a dispute of both law and fact is the impediment to settlement. The parties see a need for the decision-maker to possess judicial expertise, and therefore select a former judge.

Neutral fact-finding is another adjudicatory process. In this process, the neutral third party, after gathering information from all parties, makes a determination of the facts. This determination is then made public. Recommendations for final resolution of the matter may also be included in the fact-finder's report. Neutral fact-finding, used primarily in the resolution of public sector labor relations disputes, is seen as only quasi-adjudicatory in that the recommendations of the neutral are not final.[26]

2. EVALUATIVE

Case evaluation consists of providing the lawyers and the litigants with feedback as to the merits of the case. Case evaluation may be

21. For further detail on the arbitration process, see John S. Murray, et al., Processes of Dispute Resolution, (Chapter Four) (1989).

22. For example, see David S. Shapiro, *Private Judging in the State of New York: A Critical Introduction*, 23 Colum. J.L. & Soc. Probs. 275, 293 (1990).

23. 4 World Arb. & Med. R. 108 (1993).

24. See, for example, West's Ann. Cal. Civ. Proc. Code §§ 638–645, N.Y.–McKin-

ney's Civ. Prac. L. & R. §§ 4301–4321 (1963 & Supp. 1989). V.T.C.A., Civ. Prac. & Rem. Code § 151.001 et. seq. (1992).

25. West's Ann. Cal. Civ. Proc. Code §§ 638–645, N.Y.–McKinney's Civ. Prac. L. & R. §§ 4301–4321 (1963 & Supp. 1989).

26. Leonard Bierman, *Factfinding: Finding the Public Interest*, 9 Rutgers–Camden L.J. 667, 668 (1978).

defined as a process whereby advocates present their version of the case to one or more third party neutrals, who then evaluate the strengths and weaknesses of each. In particular, the primary purpose of neutral case evaluation is to provide an objective, non-binding, confidential, evaluation of the case, which may be used by the lawyers and clients in further settlement negotiations.[27] Depending on the dispute and type of evaluation sought, feedback can be provided by peers, professionals, experts, or lay persons.

a. Peer Evaluation

Peer evaluation in a confidential setting has been the phrase used to describe the Moderated Settlement Conference.[28] The Moderated Settlement Conference (MSC), a process designed in Texas, utilizes a panel of three neutral, experienced attorneys who listen to a presentation consisting of both factual and legal argument by counsel for each party. The panel then questions the attorneys as well as the clients who are present throughout the entire process. After deliberation, the panel renders an advisory, confidential evaluation of the strengths and weaknesses of the case and often provides a range for settlement. The evaluation is non-binding upon the parties and is to be used as a basis for further settlement negotiations.

A very similar, almost identical process is "Michigan Mediation".[29] In both the MSC and Michigan Mediation, the neutral panel consists of three attorneys, and those coordinating the process are careful to mix the expertise of the panel members. For instance, the panel in a personal injury case will be made up of a plaintiff's attorney, a defense attorney, and a neutral, such as a lawyer whose expertise is commercial or family law.

Peer evaluation may be adapted to better assist the litigants in achieving resolution of the case. Modification of the panel in either the MSC or Michigan Mediation may result in peer evaluation for both the attorneys and one or both of the parties. For example, in a pilot program for medical malpractice cases in El Paso County, Texas, the three moderator panel consisted of two attorneys and one physician.

One of the most common evaluative processes is termed "neutral evaluation," or "neutral case evaluation".[30] This process uses only a singular individual, an attorney serving as the evaluator. This method of neutral case evaluation has been used informally, where a magistrate

27. Kimberlee K. Kovach, Neutral Case Evaluation, St. Mary's Alternative Dispute Resolution Institute at C–8 (1989).

28. R. Hanson Lawton, The Dynamics and Mechanics of ADR, St. Mary's Alternative Dispute Resolution Institute at C–13 (1988).

29. Although it is termed *mediation*, the process used in Wayne County, Michigan state courts is case evaluation. For a detailed report, see Kathy L. Shuart, et al., *Settling Cases in Detroit: An Examination of Wayne County's "Mediation" Program*, 8 Just. Sys. J. 307 (1983). Michigan Mediation has two additional components to the process. First the panel makes a specific recommendation for settlement. If the parties choose to go to trial, and their position is not improved by at least ten percent, a penalty is assessed.

30. These are the most common generic terms used to describe the process.

or colleague provides feedback to the attorneys about their case. However, there are now court programs which provide a more structured process. The first court to institute the process was the Northern District of California. The process was termed Early Neutral Evaluation (ENE).[31] In the ENE procedure, the attorney evaluator is hand-selected by the court. The process takes place very early in the life of the case, usually upon the filing of the response. The initial goals of the process included the following: to force the parties to confront their case as well as that of the opponent; to identify the actual matters in dispute; to develop an efficient discovery process; and to obtain an assessment of the case. Settlement was later added as an explicit goal.[32] In practice the process often became a settlement conference, and more than one-third of the cases were settled.[33] Many neutral case evaluation procedures in other jurisdictions do have settlement of the case as an explicit and primary goal. But even if a settlement is not reached, the parties will have established a time-line for administration of the case including discovery practices, which is an effective method of expediting the resolution of the case.[34] A variety of modifications of neutral case evaluation is possible.

b. Lay Evaluation—The Summary Jury Trial

Many litigants want their day in court—they have a right to a trial by a jury of peers, and will not be satisfied with anything less. To provide one in a summary fashion saves time and dollars for the parties and the court. For this reason, the summary jury trial (SJT) procedure was developed.[35]

During the summary jury trial, the attorneys present an abbreviated version of their evidence to an advisory jury usually selected from the regular jury pool. Some courts will inform the jurors in advance that their verdict is only advisory, while others argue that the SJT will be more effective if the jurors return a "true" verdict.[36] After making an opening statement, each attorney summarizes in a narrative manner what the evidence would show if the case went to trial. In about fifty percent of the cases, the court will permit live testimony. However, testimony is often limited to one witness per side, usually the primary party to the dispute. These individuals are able to tell the jury their "story" in their own words. In most cases, each presentation is limited to one half day in duration. The lawyers also present closing argu-

31. David I. Levine, Early Neutral Evaluation: A Follow–Up Report, 70 Judicature 236 (1987).

32. David I. Levine, *Early Neutral Evaluation: The Second Phase*, J. Disp. Resol. 1 (1989).

33. Id. at 41.

34. Id. at 47.

35. This procedure was first designed by the Hon. Thomas Lambros of the District Court for the Northern District of Ohio.

He found that a trial normally taking six to eight weeks could be condensed to one or two days. See, Thomas Lambros, *The Summary Jury Trial—An Alternative Method of Resolving Disputes*, 69 Judicature 286 (1986).

36. Richard A. Enslen, *ADR: Another Acronym, or a Viable Alternative to the High Cost of Litigation and Crowded Court Dockets? The Debate Commences*, 18 N.M.L. Rev. 1, 13 (1988).

ments. In most cases, all details of the SJT are worked out at a pre-trial conference.[37] After the presentation is complete, the jury, usually a panel of six, deliberates and returns a non-binding, advisory verdict. The parties and their attorneys may then poll and question the jurors to gain feedback about the case. The information gained from this process can then be used as a basis for further settlement negotiations.

The summary jury trial is utilized when the parties or the court feel that a preview of what a jury may do would be helpful to better assess the case for purposes of settlement. This procedure is typically more adversarial than peer review since each side is trying to persuade the jurors to return a verdict in their favor.

As with all ADR devices, the summary jury trial can be modified to provide the parties the feedback which will assist in settlement. In some cases, the procedure has been conducted with two juries, who simultaneously watch the case presentation, but who deliberate separately. It is also possible for parties to stipulate in advance that the jury's verdict will be binding. The parties may also submit only part of the case; for example, a summary jury trial may be held on the liability issue only.

c. *Judicial Evaluation*

In some instances, the knowledge, experience and temperament a retired judge can bring to a case can be quite helpful in assisting the parties reach a settlement.[38] In contrast to private judging where the judge actually decides the case, in a case evaluation process the judge will merely point out to the lawyers and litigants the strengths and weaknesses of the case. This assessment is based, in part, upon past judicial experience. As with other types of case evaluation, the parties may engage in dialogue to gain additional feedback. They are then free to accept or reject the evaluation. Judicial evaluation may also take place in a less formal setting, such as when the judge presides over a pre-trial conference during a pending case.

d. *Specialist or Expert Evaluation*

Many cases turn on a technical issue which is sometimes beyond the understanding of the court, the lawyers, and the jury. By providing an independent, neutral, expert evaluation of such an issue, a resolution may be achieved in a case which would otherwise take months to try. Examples include matters of construction, computer design, securities, or biomedical technology. As long as all parties agree to the selection of the neutral expert, the results are generally accepted as definitive. The expert evaluation can apply to the entire case or only a single issue.

3. MEDIATIVE

In the mediative processes, the neutral does not render a decision or an evaluation. Rather the neutral provides facilitation in reaching an

37. Id.

38. This was the theory behind the creation of Judicial Arbitration and Mediation Service (JAMS) which was founded by Retired Judge, Hon. Warren Knight in 1979 in Orange County, California.

acceptable agreement.   Three common mediative processes are mediation, conciliation, and consensus building.

Mediation is the process where the third party neutral, whether one person or more, acts as a facilitator to assist in resolving a dispute between two or more parties.[39]   Mediation is the least adversarial approach to conflict resolution and encourages the parties to communicate directly.   The role of the mediator includes facilitating communication between the parties, assisting in identifying the real issues of the dispute, and generating options for settlement.   The goal of mediative processes is that the parties themselves arrive at a mutually acceptable resolution of the dispute.

As with all types of ADR, the mediation process is flexible.   Primary variables affecting the process include the type of dispute, the style of the mediator and the relationship of the parties.   While mediators may come from all walks of life, most litigation cases are handled by attorney mediators.   An exception is in the family law area, where a combination of mediators, generally an attorney and a therapist, is used.

Mediation is appropriate in all types of cases, and it is effective even at the appellate level.   Mediative processes are of particular value in those instances where the parties want to maintain the relationship, whether personal or professional, or where there are issues underlying the dispute which need to be identified and resolved.

While historically the terms mediation and conciliation have been used interchangeably, there are some differences worth noting.   Usually, mediation, while quite an informal process, maintains more structure than pure conciliation.   For instance, it may be possible to achieve conciliation over the telephone, whereas telephonic mediation is rarely used.   Moreover, the term conciliation usually denotes that the disputing parties have been reconciled, and the relationship has been mended.   In mediation, although maintenance of the relationship is an important factor, often resolution of a case will occur without an actual reconciliation between the disputants.

Consensus building is another process which is mediative in nature. Consensus building may be thought of as an extended mediation, with large groups, which involves a number of conflicts.   Unlike traditional mediation which is, by design, usually a one time, one day intervention, the consensus building process takes place over a more extended period of time.   Additionally, because there are a number of individuals within groups, it is unlikely that everyone attends the process.   Each group will have representatives who then must obtain ratification of any decision reached at the consensus building session.

4.   COMBINED PROCESSES AND HYBRIDS

It is also possible to design a specific ADR procedure.   This may be accomplished by blending processes to create a completely new device

---

39. As the remainder of the text is concerned with these processes, only a brief   explanation is provided here.

termed a hybrid. This is how some of the processes previously mentioned were invented.[40] Additionally, ADR devices may be used in conjunction with one another. This mixture of the primary processes is known as combined processes. For instance, if, after presentation of the evaluation in a neutral case evaluation, the parties are unable to settle, utilization of a mediator for facilitation, or an arbitrator for a rendition of an award, may be appropriate. In other cases, if, after a summary jury trial the parties agree on liability, but cannot reach an agreement on damages, a mediator or arbitrator can assist with the remaining issues. The most common combined process is Med–Arb, which combines the mediation and arbitration processes. In fact, it has been applied in so many instances that modifications have resulted. There are currently three different versions of the Med–Arb process.[41]

A hybrid which is used primarily in large corporate litigation is the Mini–Trial. This is a hybrid of negotiation, mediation, and case evaluation. Used primarily in business, the mini-trial has as its philosophical basis the realization that mutual benefit may be gained by each corporation or company in resolving disputes short of protracted litigation. Continued business dealings will enhance each company's profitability. Therefore, preservation of the business relationship is a key element in the resolution. It is imperative that a high level corporate decision-maker attends the process. The attorneys and corporate executives meet with an expert, third party neutral advisor and all sides present their "best case". Direct negotiation by the corporate executives, usually without the attorneys or the neutral present, follows. If unsuccessful after a predetermined amount of time, the expert advisor provides a non-binding opinion or evaluation regarding the merits of the case. Thereafter, the executives, armed with this additional information, negotiate again. If a resolution is not reached, the neutral may act as a mediator.

Another recently developed hybrid process is the jury-determined settlement. It is a blend of the summary jury trial and arbitration. In the jury determined settlement (JDS) proceeding, the jury is empaneled, and the trial proceeds similar to a summary jury trial. However, at the conclusion of the JDS, the jury provides a binding settlement rather than a verdict.[42] Moreover, the parties are more directly active in the process, and set limits of the settlement in advance through the use of a high-low agreement.[43]

E. USE OF ADR

The ADR processes described above are designed to assist disputing parties in reaching a final resolution of a matter. But each process

---

40. For example, the summary jury trial can be seen as a hybrid of two more traditional processes: the jury trial and a settlement conference.

41. Med–Arb will be examined in greater detail, as will all mediative combinations and derivatives, in Chapter 17, infra.

42. Neil Vidmar and Jeffrey Rice, *Jury–Determined Settlements and Summary Jury Trials: Observations About Alternative Dispute Resolution in an Adversary Culture*, 19 Fla. St. U.L. Rev. 89, 98 (1991).

43. Id. at 99.

differs in exactly how that is accomplished. How does one determine, then, which process to select off of this diverse ADR "menu"—a menu with many entrees. A specific, scientific means for choosing the most appropriate process has not been established. Determining the type of assistance needed to reach resolution of a case is a helpful first step. However, it is often difficult to precisely identify in advance the barriers to settlement. Cases, as well as clients, differ, and the exact nature of both is relevant in selecting which device is most advantageous in a given case. Perhaps it is only with continued use that the answers will become clear.

However, current informal reports indicate that there are no bad choices; that is, most procedures have been successful in effectuating a settlement in a variety of cases. The ADR menu is still expanding and guided by flexibility. Therefore, modification of ADR procedures may be appropriate. For example, the litigants might stipulate beforehand that the panel's evaluation in a moderated settlement conference be binding. Likewise, the parties may agree to accept the summary jury's verdict as final. Perhaps only part of a case may receive ADR treatment. Thus, in most situations, after consideration of the client's objectives and an analysis of the available dispute resolution devices, it is likely that an appropriate procedure can be either found or designed. As ADR programs and procedures develop, they will do so in relation to variations inherent in particular jurisdictions. Although in a few jurisdictions ADR use has been integrated within the courts, in most locations, ADR processes are still developing.

Reservations have been expressed about the use of ADR;[44] yet its growth in less than two decades has been phenomenal. And, although once debated, it is now widely acknowledged that ADR is a permanent part of our system of justice. In fact, many of these *American* ADR processes have not only been recognized, but are beginning to be implemented in courts and communities around the world. When observing this explosive nature of ADR growth, one may question just what it is about these procedures that accounts for such a trend. The answer most likely lies in a combination of factors. The saving of monetary, time and emotional costs are the most often cited reasons for ADR use. And while these are very important factors, others such as confidentiality and party participation should not be overlooked. Courts are limited in the types of resolution they can provide. When the actual disputants are involved in the process, often they can be creative and fashion relief particular to the matter. By having a part in the decision-making process, the litigants are able to generate settlements with which they are pleased and will comply. The benefits of ADR use which are rarely attainable through traditional court processes certainly account for its ever increasing use.

44. See, for example, Owen M. Fiss, *Against Settlement*, 93 Yale L.J. 1073 (1984). See also Chapter 15 § H, infra which examines more closely some criticisms of mediation.

There has been, and continues to be, debate about whether these processes should be part of the legal system—or separate from it. As will be more fully described, much of the initial work in the area was done apart from the courts; to be seen as truly alternative. Now, however, rather than viewing these processes as a threat, more lawyers are utilizing them to their benefit. Lawyers are finding that these processes can be "tools of the trade". Moreover, as the business world realizes the benefits of ADR use, corporations are demanding that legal counsel be educated in its use. ADR has begun to enhance, rather than restrict, the lawyer's practice. But as these processes are placed in the lawyer's toolbox, other issues emerge.

A recent concern is whether these ADR processes have become too "legalized".[45] As the use of ADR processes within the court system increased, legal issues surrounding such use were raised. ADR developed as an "alternative" to litigation. Yet it appears that as this ADR universe became integrated with our legal system, ADR became legalized. Adversarial approaches were taken and legal questions encompassing ADR use were encountered. The "law" of ADR is now in its developmental stages.[46] As we endeavor to identify and create additional dispute resolution options which become part of our system, we continue the evolution process.

45. See Carrie Menkel–Meadow, *Pursuing Settlement in an Adversary Culture: A Tale of Innovation Co–Opted or "The Law of ADR"*, 19 Fla. St. U.L. Rev. 1 (1991).

46. Id. at 2.

Chapter Two

THE MEDIATION PROCESS

A. OVERVIEW

Mediation is facilitated negotiation. It is a process by which a neutral third party, the mediator, assists disputing parties in reaching a mutually satisfactory resolution. At first glance, the definition of mediation appears simple. Yet over the last few years, especially within the ADR field, very few items spark more controversy than the definition of mediation. In fact, it has been alleged that the term "mediator" is now used so loosely that no one may safely presume that a speaker intends its original meaning: helping people to reach their own settlement.[1] Of course debate about the "original" definition of mediation is also possible.

The term mediate is derived from the Latin "mediare", which means "to be in the middle".[2] Certainly the mediator finds himself in the middle of a dispute. But mediation involves much more than placement of the mediator. A variety of definitions for the term "mediation" exist. While these definitions differ, and are subject to debate, most people agree on the purpose of the process: to assist people in reaching a voluntary resolution of a dispute or conflict. Definitional debates primarily surround the specifics of how the assistance is actually provided.

Some of the more basic definitions of mediation include:

• The broad term describing the intervention of third parties in the dispute resolution process.[3]

• A process in which a third party facilitates and coordinates the negotiation of disputing parties.[4]

• The intervention into a dispute or the negotiation process by an acceptable impartial and neutral third party who has no authoritative

---

1. Linda Singer, Settling Disputes 21 (1990).

2. Merriam Webster's Collegiate Dictionary 722 (10th ed. 1993).

3. John S. Murray, et al., Processes of Dispute Resolution 247 (1988).

4. Roberta S. Mitchell & Scot E. Dewhirst, The Mediator Handbook 13 The Center For Dispute Resolution, Capital University Law and Graduate Center (1990).

decision-making power. This individual will assist disputing parties in voluntarily reaching their own neutral acceptable settlement of the issues in dispute.[5]

• A process where third parties not involved in the controversy assist disputing parties in their negotiations.[6]

• A private, voluntary, informal process where a party-selected neutral assists disputants to reach a mutually acceptable agreement.[7]

• Mediation is a process by which a third party neutral, whether one or more, acts as a facilitator to assist in the resolving of a dispute between two or more parties. It is a non-adversarial approach to conflict resolution where the parties communicate directly. The role of the mediator is to facilitate communication between the parties, assist them on focusing on real issues of the dispute, and generate options for settlement. The goal of this process is that the parties themselves arrive at a mutually acceptable resolution of the dispute.[8]

• A voluntary process where an impartial mediator actively assists disputants in identifying and clarifying issues of concern and in designing and agreeing to solutions.[9]

• A forum in which an impartial person, the mediator, facilitates communication between parties to promote reconciliation, settlement, or understanding among them.[10]

• A process in which a neutral third party assists the parties in developing and exploring their underlying interests (in addition to their legal positions), promotes the development of options and assists the parties toward settling the case through negotiations.[11]

• In its simplest term, mediation is trying to get two people to do that which they least want to do—talk to each other.[12]

The number and variety of definitions demonstrate that the mediation process is a flexible one. Although there is a structure to the mediation process, it is not rigid, but rather fluid in nature. Many other definitions of mediation are subject matter specific and often dictate diverse approaches. Since the mediation process deals with human behavior and motivation, it must also be adaptable to individual differences.

There is little doubt that the use of the mediation process has grown tremendously and will continue to do so. Much of this growth can be

5. Christopher W. Moore, The Mediation Process: Practical Strategies for Resolving Conflict 6 (1984).

6. Nancy H. Rogers & Craig A. McEwen, Mediation: Law, Policy, Practice 1 (1990).

7. Alternative Dispute Resolution: An ADR Primer (Standing Committee on Dispute Resolution 3d ed., 1989).

8. Kimberlee K. Kovach, *ADR–Does It Work?*, South Texas College of Law, Advanced Civil Litigation Institute, (1989).

9. Ill. Rev. Stat. § 852 (1993).

10. V.T.C.A. Civ. Prac. & Rem. Code § 154.023(a) (Supp. 1993).

11. Civ. Just. Reform Act Plan, W.D. Mo. (1992).

12. *Comment*, J. Disp. Resol. 307, 309 (1991).

attributed to the process itself rather than the mediator.[13]   The process which is our focus is not new.   In fact, the process is deep rooted, having developed over a long period of time.

B.   HISTORICAL PERSPECTIVES

When looking for a historical reference to the initial use of mediation, commentators often quote the Bible.   Yet it can be argued that mediation was used long before recorded history, particularly in the broad context where a third party neutral served several functions.   This brief historical perspective will primarily focus on the mediator in a role close to the term as we currently know it.   It should be remembered, however, that because it is a flexible process, mediation has varied over its long history, influenced in part by the circumstances of its use.

1.   INTERNATIONAL SPHERE

Use of mediation, similar to that which we see today, can be traced back several hundreds, even thousands of years.[14]   Mediation was used in China and Japan as a *primary* means of conflict resolution.   The mediative approach was not an alternative to fighting or adversarial approaches to problem solving.   Rather, mediation was the first choice for dispute settlement.   Those cultures placed emphasis on peace-making and peace-keeping.   A win or lose approach was not an acceptable means of resolution.   For instance, China's principle use of mediation was a direct result of the Confucian view of natural harmony and dispute resolution by morals rather than coercion.[15]   Chinese society therefore placed emphasis on the mediative or conciliatory approach to conflict. This has continued throughout history within that culture.   Chinese mediation boards or committees are made up of several individuals from each local community and resolve more than 80 percent of all civil disputes.   Today the mediation boards in China, termed People's Mediation Committees (PMCS) are the dominant institution for mediation and resolve over 7.2 million disputes per year.[16]   They assist in maintaining peace and social control throughout both urban and rural communities.

In Japan, conciliation was historically the primary means of resolution with village leaders serving as mediators.[17]   Current Japanese negotiation style still places an emphasis on the relationship and is often regarded as a purely conciliatory style.[18]   In a negotiation, particularly in

---

13.   In fact, mediators often refer to themselves as mere *caretakers* of the process.

14.   Use of mediation has been documented in ancient China over two thousand years ago.   See, for example, Jerome Alan Cohen, *Chinese Mediation on the Eve of Modernization*, 55 Cal. L. Rev. 1201, 1205 (1966).

15.   Jay Folberg & Alison Taylor, Mediation: A Comprehensive Guide to Resolving Conflicts Without Litigation 2 (1984).

16.   Donald C. Clark, *Dispute Resolution in China*, 5 J. Chinese L. 245, 270 (1991).

17.   Folberg & Taylor, supra note 15, at 49.

18.   A number of books have been recently published on Japanese negotiation style.   See, for example, Edward T. Hall, Hidden Differences: Doing Business with Japanese (1987), Chi Nakan, Japanese Society (1970); and *generally*, U.S. Department of State, National Negotiating Styles (Hans Binnendijk, ed., 1987).

the business world, time is spent on building the relationship, without which a final agreement may not occur.

Informal dispute resolution was used in many other cultures as well. For example, Scandinavian fishermen, African tribes, and Israeli Kibbutzim all valued peace and harmony over conflict, litigation and victory.[19] The use of mediation in a historical perspective can also be seen in attempts at resolution of matters between disputing nations.[20] Some of the principles of informal dispute resolution, or mutual satisfaction in settlement rather than conceding power, made their way to the United States.

2. UNITED STATES

The history of current mediation use in the United States has two distinct paths, neither of which is within the formal legal system. One course by which mediation developed was as a method of providing community justice. Disputes in the labor arena was the other area of historical development. It is only very recently that the courts have considered the use of mediation.

Often overlooked, however, is the application of mediative approaches to conflict by both Native Americans and colonists. In the Native American culture, peacemaking is the primary method of problem solving. More conciliatory than mediation, peacemaking is concerned with sacred justice. Disputes are handled in a way which deals with underlying causes of conflict, and mends relationships.[21] Native Americans continue to use peacemaking today.[22]

Upon settlement in the United States, various groups within the colonies placed a major emphasis on maintenance of peace. The very close proximity of living arrangements, along with the need for joint efforts in survival against the crown, contributed to peacekeeping endeavors.[23] The cultural priority of community consensus over an individual adversarial approach to conflict served as the basis for the use of mediation and other informal means of dispute settlement.[24] In addition, many colonists had developed a negative view of the legal profession, and consequently the use of litigation as a means of dispute settlement was explicitly discouraged. Accordingly, these settlers went about settling their own disputes.[25]

However, by the end of the seventeenth century, use of these non-legalistic dispute resolution methods was in decline. A number of

19. Jerold S. Auerbach, Justice Without Law 8 (1983).

20. Jacob Bercovitch, *The Structure and Diversity of Mediation in International Relations*, in Mediation in International Relations 2 (Jacob Bercovitch and Jeffery Z. Rubin eds., 1992).

21. For more detail on Native American peacemaking, see generally *Special Issue*, 10 Mediation Q. 327 (1993).

22. Diane LeResch Editor's Notes, 10 Mediation Q. 321 (1993).

23. Susan L. Donegan, *ADR in Colonial America: A Covenant For Survival*, 48 Arb. J. 14 (1993).

24. Auerbach, supra note 19, at 20.

25. Id. at 23.

factors accounted for this. The population increased, and with growth and mobility, the sense of community dissipated. Moreover, the development of commerce and industry resulted in more complex dealings, use of documents, and the need for commercial laws. A large portion of common law, initially avoided, was then seen as practical and acceptable, though not in all respects.[26] Competitiveness replaced a cooperative approach to problem solving, and overt conflict increased. Litigation took a greater role in assisting in the resolving of disputes by providing a framework for order and authority.[27]

The other distinct area in which mediation was historically used was in the labor industry. In the early industrial United States, when disputes occurred within business, quick resolutions were imperative. This was particularly important where the conflict was between labor and management, and if left unresolved, could lead to strikes and a shut down of industry. As labor became unionized and disputes were common, Congress reacted in 1913 by creating the Department of Labor, and providing that the Secretary of Labor act as mediator.[28] Mediation was used so that disputes could be settled expeditiously, and strikes avoided. A speedy resolution promoted the ongoing relationship between the factions, which was very important to the continued economic development of the United States. As the area of labor relations developed,[29] and need for mediation increased, Congress in 1947, created the Federal Mediation and Conciliation Service (FMCS).[30] An independent federal agency, FMCS has jurisdiction over disputes in industries which engage in interstate commerce, private non-profit health facilities, and agencies of the federal government.[31] The Federal Mediation and Conciliation Service is still quite active today, primarily focused on mediating in labor disputes.[32]

For the general population, courts became the primary dispute resolvers, replacing communities and churches. Yet, dissatisfaction with the courts was expressed. This dissatisfaction primarily centered on issues of expense and time, although there was some concern with the complete legalization of disputes [33] as well as the relinquishing of decision making to outside parties. This dissatisfaction served as the catalyst for the current ADR movement. While the current use of mediation has some of the colonial and labor characteristics and philosophy, its primary focus is serving as an option, or adjunct, to the courts.

3. CURRENT "MOVEMENT"

The current ADR movement is most often regarded as beginning

26. Paul S. Reinsch, English Common Law in the Early American Colonies 6 (1898).

27. Auerbach, supra note 19, at 71.

28. See William E. Simkin, and Nicholas A. Fidandis, Mediation and the Dynamics of Collective Bargaining 25 (2d ed. 1986).

29. For a complete perspective of mediation in the labor area, see Id.

30. Id. at 38.

31. Deborah M. Kolb, The Mediators 7 (1983).

32. Id.

33. Auerbach, supra note 19, at 120.

with the Pound Conference in 1976.[34] Prior to that, however, there existed several programs, a few of which originally came about as a response to the conflict surrounding the civil rights movement. Others originated as an alternative method of community justice. For example, the American Arbitration Association (AAA)[35] was active in setting up pilot mediation projects funded by the Ford Foundation in the late sixties. These projects were an attempt to ease social tensions through the use of mediation. In the early seventies, the American Arbitration Association also established Dispute Resolution Centers in Philadelphia and Rochester. Cases were referred to the centers from the local court system.[36]

In 1971, through a grant from the United States Department of Justice, Law Enforcement Assistance Administration (LEAA), the Columbus, Ohio City Prosecutor's Office established a mediation program for citizens' disputes. This was the first court system sponsored dispute resolution program. It utilized law students who served as mediators to help resolve disputes involving minor criminal actions. In 1977, the program was designated by LEAA as exemplary, and its replication throughout the country was encouraged.[37] In 1975 the Institute for Mediation and Conflict Resolution opened in New York City, which pioneered mediation program development on the East coast. While these programs introduced mediation to the legal system and the community, it was only in these select locations. There was no systematic development or coordination of these mediation programs until the Pound Conference.

The Pound Conference was called to commemorate the 70th anniversary of Dean Roscoe Pound's dissertation on the public's dissatisfaction with the American legal system.[38] It was at this Conference that the current "movement" was actually born. Conference attendees included federal judges, court administrators, and legal scholars in the American Bar Association who wanted to take a closer look at exactly why people were so dissatisfied with the way justice was administered in the United States. One focus was on the often criticized, overcrowded, and costly court system. The conference consisted of a series of discussions and debates, and a follow-up task force was established.

One result of the conference was a pilot project, consisting of the

---

34. See Warren E. Burger, *Isn't There a Better Way*, 68 ABA Journal 268 (1982).

35. The AAA, a not for profit corporation, is one of the oldest private providers of arbitration services in the United States.

36. Paul Wahrhaftig, *Non–Professional Conflict Resolution* in Mediation: Contexts and Challenges 49 (Joseph E. Polenski and Harold M. Launer, eds., 1986).

37. Id. at 50.

38. Roscoe Pound, *The Causes of Popular Dissatisfaction with the Administration of Justice*, (1906), reprinted in 20 J. Am. Jud. Soc'y. 178 (1936) and as Appendix B in The Pound Conference: Perspectives on Justice in the Future (A. Leo Levin et al. eds., 1979). It is interesting to note that in 1994 the ABA will be holding a Pound Two Conference. The role of ADR therein has yet to be determined.

creation of three Neighborhood Justice Centers (NJC).[39] These centers were to be located in Kansas City, Los Angeles, and Atlanta, and were designed to determine if the mediation process could assist in resolving "minor disputes". Funding for the creation of these pilot centers and their evaluation was obtained from the Law Enforcement Assistance Administration (LEAA) Division of the Department of Justice. Each center proved to be successful in bringing about timely and inexpensive resolutions of disputes.[40] Cases were referred to the centers from local courts. Trained volunteers served as mediators, and in most instances the services were offered at no cost to the disputants. Party satisfaction with the process was high.[41] Based partially upon the results from these three centers, additional experimental centers were established. Today, there are over 400 centers throughout the country. While the centers were designed to provide a form of community justice, most were related to the legal system, by either court or local bar associations sponsorship.[42] Many centers have expanded to handle more than "minor" matters, and are not located in the neighborhoods. Hence, most have been renamed Dispute Resolution Centers. There is at least one in every state, and many states have a system wide network of centers.[43]

The work of these centers led to the development of ADR use in the court system. There are a number of reasons which account for this transition. First, many of the centers were located in or near the courthouse. Second, since the programs were often sponsored by bar associations, many of the individuals who worked as center volunteers were attorneys and judges. These lawyers and judges observed firsthand the benefits of mediation and recognized that ADR processes were successful in resolving many problems. Those involved began to believe that if these processes work well in smaller matters, perhaps they would be helpful in larger ones as well.[44] The applicability of ADR in pending lawsuits became clear.

Simultaneously, the idea of a "multi-door" courthouse began to surface. This concept, which was first articulated by Professor Frank Sander at the Pound Conference,[45] basically consists of a process by which an individual can locate the most appropriate method of resolving

39. Griffen B. Bell, Report of Pound Conference Follow-up Task Force, August 1976.

40. Royer F. Cook, et al., Neighborhood Justice Centers Field Test: Final Evaluation Report (1980).

41. Id.

42. One exception is the San Francisco Community Boards Program which is *independent* of either a court or bar association.

43. Public Services Division of the American Bar Association, Section of Dispute Resolution, 1993 Dispute Resolution Program Directory (1993).

44. When alternatives to the courthouse were initially developed, only *minor* cases were to be handled. When the ABA created its first committee on this subject, it was termed the *Special Committee on the Resolution of Minor Disputes*. As the movement grew, so did the status of the committee and its work. Soon there was the *Standing Committee on Dispute Resolution*, and 1993 saw the birth of the *ABA Dispute Resolution Section*.

45. Professor Sander of Harvard Law School initially outlined the concept in a paper he presented at the Pound Conference: Frank E. Sander, *Varieties of Dispute Processing* in The Pound Conference: Perspectives on Justice in the Future (A. Leo Levin et al. eds., 1979).

a dispute. There is one building, or courthouse, where individuals can go to obtain a multitude of services. The individual seeking assistance would first see an interviewer, called an intake specialist, who would help assess the problem. Thereafter, the party would be directed to the most appropriate "door" for resolution of the problem. Behind these doors an individual could find a number of processes including mediation, arbitration, litigation and social services.

In the mid-eighties, the ABA Standing Committee on Dispute Resolution sponsored and assisted in the establishment of experimental multi-door centers in three cities: Tulsa, Houston, and Washington, D.C. Additional multi-door courthouses have been created in Burlington, New Jersey and Middlesex County, Massachusetts. The design of this experiment, with the location of these "doors" within the courthouse, led many to realize the applicability of ADR processes to disputes even after a lawsuit was filed. Judges heard about these processes, and realized that most cases settle, but do so very late in the case. Judges realized that by referring a matter to a dispute resolution process early, a settlement could occur more expeditiously—with generally more satisfied participants. By the late eighties, experimentation with ADR in pending litigation was on-going. Today, in many courts, both state and federal, ADR is an integral part of pre-trial procedure.

C. DISSECTION OF THE MEDIATION PROCESS

Discussions about what mediation is are plentiful. Because of its inherent flexibility and wide application, mediation is an art, not a science. Debate occurs about whether, as an art, it can be learned. While many purport that mediators are born, not made, mediation training occurs every day. And although the mediator may be seen as an artist with attendant creativity, the process itself is subject to some technical analysis.

1. GENERALLY: TRADITIONAL MODELS

Mediation has been given many definitions, the broadest being simply the facilitation of a settlement between individuals. The intermediary or mediator basically serves as a go-between for individuals or groups with different opinions, outlooks, ideas, and interests. Over the years of mediation's growth, a variety of outlines or views of the process have developed. Once individuals became familiar with the fundamentals of mediation, a number of modifications took place. However, it is important to first become familiar with the basics of each stage of the mediation process. A variety of authors and trainers have enumerated the stages or segments of mediation. These may range from a four or five stage model to one with ten or more stages. The majority of these set forth the same basic concepts, and recognize the inherent fluidity of the process.

For educational purposes, the process can be separated into nine stages, all of which should be present in nearly every mediation. In addition, there are four components of the process which are considered optional. While these stages are often part of the mediation process, they frequently occur as part of another stage. Resolution may also be reached without involvement of these steps. The optional stages are listed in parenthesis, close to where, if used, they would occur. Employment of these optional stages will depend upon the parties, the nature of the matter, and the mediator's style. The basic model is as follows:

Preliminary Arrangements

Mediator's Introduction

Opening Statements by Parties

(Ventilation)

Information Gathering

Issue Identification

(Agenda Setting)

(Caucus)

Option Generation

(Reality Testing)

Bargaining and Negotiation

Agreement

Closure

While each of the preceding stages will be examined in detail throughout the remainder of the text, the following provides a brief introductory description of each.

The preliminary arrangement stage encompasses everything that happens prior to beginning the actual mediation session. This includes matters of referral, getting to the mediation table, selection of the mediator, the determination of who should attend, issues of fees, settlement authority issues, timing and court orders. Moreover, from the standpoint of the mediator, this stage also includes items such as gathering or gaining information from the parties or their attorneys, as well as dissemination of information about the mediator and mediation process to the parties. Selection of the location, the room or rooms to be used, and arrangement of furniture are also part of the preliminary arrangements stage of the process. Because it is the first stage, initial decisions about the process are made as part of preliminary arrangements. The impact on the process is considerable, and the importance of preliminary matters should not be overlooked.

The mediator's introduction, is just that. The mediator introduces himself, the parties, and their representatives; describes the process; and sets out any ground rules that will be followed. By doing this, the mediator provides time for the parties to become comfortable. Goals and objectives from mediator's standpoint may be set out here, as well as any housekeeping details. This introduction sets the stage for the remainder of the mediation.

In the opening statements, the parties and/or their representatives are invited to make an uninterrupted presentation of their view of the case or dispute. It is important that each side be given this opportunity, and not be interrupted by either the other party or the mediator. The opening statement stage is the time for parties to fully express and explain to the mediator, and more importantly, to each other, in their own words, how they view the dispute. Ideally, there should be little restriction placed on the opening statements. However, in complex, multi-party cases, it may be necessary to establish time limits.

If the parties' opening statements do not provide a clear or complete picture of what the dispute is about, as often they do not, the mediator will engage the parties in an information gathering process. In most instances additional information is necessary, and the mediator should ask open-ended questions. During either the opening statements or during the information gathering process, the disputing parties may need to express their feelings. This is termed venting or ventilation. It is important to afford individuals an opportunity to ventilate their frustration, anger, and emotions. Often, if such emotions are not expressed, the dispute cannot be resolved.

Once it appears that sufficient information about the case has been exchanged, the mediator will attempt to identify exactly what issues are in dispute. This may or may not be similar to identifying the underlying interests of the parties.[46] Once the mediator has the issues identified, he will move the parties toward generating ideas, options or alternatives which might resolve the case. It is usually during these two stages (identifying issues and underlying interests and option generation) that the mediator may meet privately with each party. This is also termed caucusing. It is advisable, however, that some attempt at issue identification take place while the parties are together so that there is an agreement between the disputing parties and the mediator as to the actual issues in dispute. In complex cases, the mediator may also want to set an agenda, that is, determine which issues will be dealt with in a specific order. There are a variety of strategies with regard to agenda setting.

Once the potential options or alternatives for settlement have been identified by the parties and the mediator, the negotiation process begins. This is the "give and take" part of the mediation, where the mediator assists the parties in their bargaining. As part of this process, the mediator may also engage in "reality testing", that is, checking out with each side the realistic possibility of attaining what he or she is

---

46. Identifying the interests is at the core of *Principled Negotiation,* as set forth by Roger Fisher and William Ury, Getting to Yes (1981).

hoping for. If the parties are in a purely positional bargaining approach,[47] this will also help to move them off of unrealistic positions.

If the negotiations result in an agreement, the mediator will restate it and in many instances, draft either the complete agreement or a memorandum of settlement. If no agreement is reached, the mediator will restate where the parties are, noting any progress made in the process. The final stage of the process is closure, although in some models there is subsequent action on the part of the mediator.

While the process usually consists of these stages, it is designed to be flexible, and often there is a variation in the occurrence of one or more of the stages. Some of the stages may overlap; and many times the mediator must revisit one or more of the stages.

A number of mediation trainers see the stages a bit differently. Moore has described the process as including twelve stages, five of which take place prior to the actual mediation session. These pre-session events include collecting background information, designing a plan for mediation, and building trust and cooperation.[48]

One of the oldest ongoing programs, The Columbus, Ohio Night Prosecutor Program, in conjunction with the Center for Dispute Resolution at Capital University Law and Graduate Center utilizes a seven stage model of mediation. The stages are

- Introduction
- Problem determination
- Summarizing
- Issue identification
- Generation and evaluation of alternatives
- Selection of appropriate alternatives
- Conclusion [49]

Folberg and Taylor also use a seven stage model, which is as follows:

1. Introduction
2. Fact finding and isolation of issues
3. Creation of options and alternatives
4. Negotiation and decision-making
5. Clarification and writing a plan
6. Legal review and processing
7. Implementation, review, and revision

They do acknowledge that not all stages will be completed in every case, and that other authors and practitioners may divide the stages

47. The various types of negotiation are explored in Chapter 9, infra.

48. Moore, supra note 5, at 33–34.

49. Mitchell and Dewhirst, supra note 4, at 15.

differently or use different labels.[50]   Compared with most models, this model is "bottom heavy"; the majority of models do not focus on activity after an agreement is reached.

2. RECENT ADAPTATIONS AND MODIFICATIONS

It is beyond this work to belabor the discussion about the use of the more traditional model, also labeled purist or classic, versus recent adaptations and modifications. Even where the process is traditional, the mediator possesses a great amount of control in how it is conducted. The ability to adapt and modify the mediation process is a primary benefit of its use. Yet some argue whether "true" mediation exists, or whether it should be called something else. For instance, one well known critique was that once the court systems and lawyers got into mediation, it was the end of "good" mediation.[51] It is true that some of the most dramatic changes have been within the legal field. Even at this early stage of mediation use, there is great diversity in practice. Some lawyers have simplified the process and divided it into three primary segments or stages: joint session, caucus and conclusion. From a learning or descriptive standpoint, this is too simple and does not provide any indication about what is going on in terms of the problem-solving process. The focus is on where the parties and mediator meet, rather than on the phases which take place, and how those factors lead to settlement or resolution.

Other modifications have occurred as well. With the increased use of mediation in a greater variety of cases, it has become clear that the basic one-time intervention model may not work in all cases. As mediation was originally designed, particularly by those outside of the labor field, it was viewed as a single intervention. The mediator sat down with the parties and either an agreement was eventually reached that day or it was not. Only in rare instances where another individual or additional information was needed, would the mediation session be rescheduled. However, in some cases, due to the number of parties involved, and the complexity or the nature of the dispute, modification of the single mediation session approach was appropriate.

The first and most prevalent of these areas was in family law. Mediation in family cases is quite different and will be examined in more detail in Chapter 16. However, because of the emotional issues involved and the nature of the dispute between the parties, many of the original divorce mediation practitioners felt that the mediation sessions should be broken down over a period of weeks. Time was needed for adjustment to the renegotiated relationship of the parties, as well as for thinking through these major life changes. Consequently, sessions were limited to approximately an hour, and took place once a week until all matters were settled.

50. Folberg and Taylor, supra note 15, at 22.

51. Statement of Albie Davis, in James J. Alfini, *Styles of Mediation: Trashing,* *Bashing and Hashing It Out: Is this the End of "Good Mediation"?* 19 Fla. St. U. L. Rev. 47 (1991).

Another arena in which mediation takes place over an extended period of time is that of public policy matters.[52] In cases involving public policy, there are a number of people with a variety of interests. It is often impossible to get everyone together at one time, in one place, with all issues on the table. Therefore, the mediation may take place in stages. Likewise, in some complex commercial disputes, the mediator may choose to resolve only portions of the case at a time. Fortunately, the mediation process has proven to be adaptable and has successfully been used in all of these instances.

D. THE ROLE OF A MEDIATOR

We have looked at the mediation process, but just what a mediator does with it is often a key to its effectiveness. What, then, is the role of this person? How does he move the parties through these stages? Compiling a complete list of the different hats that a mediator must wear can be an extensive exercise. A mediator has sometimes been called a traffic cop, particularly in directing the communication. The simplest description of the mediator's role is that of a facilitator. But how one facilitates differs. A conductor of the negotiation is another role that the mediator plays. Throughout the process the role of the mediator changes. Sometimes the mediator will have to supervise, even parent, the parties. Other times, the mediator will be a teacher, not only in assisting the parties to learn the subject matter of their dispute, but also in teaching the process. At other times the mediator is a clarifier. The mediator can also serve in the role of an advocate. Not for the parties, but for the process and settlement. A devil's advocate may also be a role the mediator assumes. Attorney mediators seem to adopt this role. Certainly few would argue with the role of the mediator as a catalyst, moving the parties in the direction of resolution. Mediators have also been designated as orchestrators, deal makers,[53] and as translators of comments and proposals.[54]

The foregoing roles are descriptive of the many facets of the mediator's work, and usually do not meet with controversy. However, an in-depth examination provides a conceptual framework for the mediator's role which has led to much debate.[55] Specifically, what is it that should be expected of this neutral intervenor? There is concern about the degree of influence the mediator should have on the outcome of the case. For instance, the mediator's role can be viewed as promoting an agreement—at whatever cost, thereby achieving efficiency in settlement.[56]

52. These cases will also be examined in greater detail in Chapter 16, infra.

53. Kolb, supra note 31, at 23.

54. Joseph B. Stulberg, *Training Interveners for ADR Processes*, 81 Ky. L.J. 977, 987 (1992–93).

55. The role of the mediator in light of fairness, neutrality and ethical consider-ations is also examined in Chapters 7 and 14, infra.

56. Robert A. Baruch Bush, *Efficiency and Protection, or Empowerment and Rec-ognition?: The Mediator's Role and Ethical Standards in Mediation* 41 Fla. L. Rev. 253, 260 (1989).

The goals of saving time and perhaps money for the parties may be actualized. Alternatively, the mediator's role may be to protect rights by assuring that the agreements reached in mediation are based upon informed consent.[57] Some even go a step or two further and expect the mediator to assure that the agreements are fair and stable.[58] Others want the mediator not only to ensure that the agreement is fair, but also is one which a court would enforce.[59]

If the mediator is a neutral, before, during and after the mediation, and must refrain from making judgments, how can he assume these roles? How can we be sure that the parties even want their rights protected or their agreements fair? If self-determination by the parties is an overriding feature of the mediation process,[60] then the mediator's role may be to empower the parties to make their own judgments. It has been claimed that the mediation process and the mediator, as conductor of that process should promote self-determination and empowerment. But what should the mediator do in assuring that the parties make their own decisions?

The most important thing to remember about the mediator's role is that the mediator is in control of the process. Mediation works in resolving disputes because of the process, not the person. That, of course, is not to say that a skillful mediator will not be more effective than one possessing less skill. But more often it is the procession through the stages of the process that leads parties to a mutually satisfactory resolution. The role of the mediator then, is to safeguard, maintain, and control the process. This must be distinguished from control of the content matter of the dispute—that is up to the parties. Regardless of the subject matter of the dispute, the process remains the same. **The parties are responsible for the content; the mediator is responsible for the process.**

EXERCISES

2–1. Write down all of the distinct tasks that might encompass the mediator's role. Put the list away. Pull your list out for review upon completion of your tenth mediation.

2–2. When observing a mediation session, either live or simulated, focus on the variety of roles the mediator assumes, noting each role change.

(a) What were the causes of the changes?

(b) Was the mediator more effective in some roles than others?

(c) Were any roles assumed by the mediator inappropriate?

---

57. Id. at 261.

58. Lawrence Susskind, *Environmental Mediation and the Accountability Problem* 6 Vt. L. Rev. 1, 18 (1981).

59. Leonard L. Riskin, *Toward New Standards for the Neutral Lawyer in Mediation* 26 Ariz. L. Rev. 329, 354 (1984).

60. Bush, supra note 56 at 270.

Chapter Three

MEDIATOR SKILLS

As the use of mediation increased, and more individuals were educated and trained in the process, a closer examination of just what a mediator did was warranted. As the preceding chapter has alluded to, there is little specific agreement about proper mediator conduct. Much depends on when and where mediation is used, as well as the mediator's personal style. There is recognition, however, that a wide variety of skills is necessary. Some individuals come to the mediation table with innate skills. Others must learn them. In most mediation training programs, skill development is a major portion of the educational process. These skills include communication, analytical ability, and patience. Some mediators have been very detailed in describing what it takes to mediate.

For instance, former Federal Mediation and Conciliation Service Director William E. Simkin lists sixteen characteristics which a potential mediator ought to possess:

1. the patience of Job
2. the sincerity and bulldog characteristics of the English
3. the wit of the Irish
4. the physical endurance of the marathon runner
5. the broken field dodging abilities of a halfback
6. the guile of Machiavelli
7. the personality-probing skills of a good psychiatrist
8. the confidence-retaining characteristic of a mute
9. the hide of a rhinoceros
10. the wisdom of Solomon
11. demonstrated integrity and impartiality
12. basic knowledge of and belief in the negotiation process
13. firm faith in voluntarism in contrast to dictation
14. fundamental belief in human values and potential, tempered by ability to assess personal weaknesses as well as strengths

15. hard-nosed ability to analyze what is available in contrast to what might be desirable

16. sufficient personal drive and ego, qualified by willingness to be self-effacing.[1]

Another labor mediator has noted that one characteristic may transcend the previous lists; that the mediator must be master of the alternative. The mediator should be capable of eliciting acceptable alternatives to the unobtainable positions of the disputing parties.[2] Just how mediator skills and qualities are assessed have historically presented concerns in the labor field. In fact, it was quickly recognized that all the listed characteristics are not to be found in one person, and are not subject to objective assessment.[3] The main difficulty is that many of these skills are purely subjective and can be demonstrated only by performance. These issues now face the general mediation population.[4]

Each mediator is an individual with a variety of life experiences and a personality that must be used in conjunction with the mediation process. Therefore, after initial training in the process, each trainee is encouraged to develop a personal style, depending on those personal characteristics.[5]

Mediation is, to be sure, an interdisciplinary field. Mediators come from all walks of life. Yet uniform skills are necessary. Often questioned is what specific skills are involved in mediating, and whether those skills are innate or can be learned. While many within this field are currently examining issues such as these, no definitive answer has emerged. If mediation is an art, and not a science, then a variety of combined skills is needed.

Because any dispute resolution or problem solving activity involves communication, certainly one of the most important skills for a mediator is the ability to communicate. Not only does the mediator communicate directly with each of the parties, she also facilitates communication between the parties. In fact, styles of problem solving have been defined in terms of communication. A cooperative approach to conflict is characterized by an open and honest transmittal of information; whereas, the competitive mode consists of either misleading or a lack of communication.[6] Most of the activity which takes place during a mediation involves sending and receiving information, both verbal and nonverbal. In fact, it has been observed that mediation is a communication process, and that the solving of legal problems is a mere byproduct.[7] We often

1. William E. Simkin & Nicholas A. Fidandis, Mediation and the Dynamics of Collective Bargaining 43 (1986).

2. Walter A. Maggiolo, Techniques of Mediation 73 (1985).

3. Simkin & Fidandis, supra note 1, at 44.

4. An in depth examination of these dilemmas is provided in Chapter 15, infra.

5. Some identifiable styles of mediation are reviewed in Chapter 15, infra.

6. Morton Deutsch, The Resolution of Conflict 29 (1973).

7. [Panel Discussion Series. Topic 3—1983] *Alternative Dispute Resolution: Mediation and the Law: Will Reason Prevail?* 48 Special Committee on Dispute Resolution, Public Services Division, American

take communication, and specifically listening, for granted. With practice however, these skills can be improved.

A. COMMUNICATION

Communication consists of both sending and receiving messages. Some hold that the most important part of the mediator's role is that of a listener or recipient of a message [8]. Although this is certainly a major role of the mediator, it should be recognized that feedback or sending a message is actually part of the listening process. While the primary focus of our study is on the communication process during the mediation, it actually begins earlier. Information or messages are conveyed prior to the session. This should not be overlooked, and will be discussed in greater detail in Chapter 5. Once at the mediation session, the primary focus is on direct interpersonal, or face to face, communication. The mediator must be cognizant of the constant exchange of messages which takes place during the mediation session.

1. VERBAL

Interpersonal communication can take at least four forms, as shown by the following diagrams:

```
         A                                    B
Conversation (2 way              Listening (primarily 1 way
          communication)                   communication)
(1) S ————> R                    (2) S ————> R  Passive
    R <———— S                    (3) S ————> R  Active
                                     <· · · · · ·
                                 (4) S ————> R  Interactive
                                     <— — — — —

S – Sender        R – Receiver
```

In diagram A, which depicts a two-way conversation, there is a continuous exchange of information. Both parties in this interpersonal communication take turns sending and receiving information or messages. Diagram B represents the various information exchanges which are more illustrative of the listening process that the mediator will initially engage in. When examining how people listen, it is helpful to think in terms of one person designated as the sender of the message or information, and the other as the receiver. Because listening is a continual process, the various roles may alternate.

In the initial stages of the mediation process, the sender (S) is one of the disputing parties or their representative, attorney, or otherwise. The receiver of the message (R) is the mediator. In example number (2),

Bar Association (Larry Ray, et al. eds., 1983).

8. See Nancy H. Rogers & Richard A. Salem, A Student's Guide to Mediation and the Law 12 (1987).

the pattern is identified as passive listening. Here the sender sends a message and receives no feedback from the listener. Examples of such purely passive listening include receiving information from television and radio. In an interpersonal situation, an example might be a lecture in a large hall, where the speaker fails to receive any response, including direct eye contact.

The third example illustrates the active listening mode. When the sender transmits information, there is feedback provided from the listener. A message is imparted back to the sender that informs the sender that the information has been received. Examples of active listening include the nod of a head or a mere one or two word acknowledgment that lets the individual know that the message has been heard. Verbal acknowledgements include: "oh"; "I see"; "uh-huh"; and "really". Non-verbal messages such as nods, direct eye contact, and various facial expressions can also be very effective in providing feedback to the sender to signify that the message has been received.

In an interactive listening mode, as illustrated by the fourth example, the amount of information in the message from the listener going back to the sender has increased. Interactive listening techniques include brief restatements or parroting of the last few words of the speaker; summations; reflective statements; and paraphrasing. This provides even more feedback to the sender, and allows the listener to check with the speaker about the accuracy of the message. Asking follow-up questions is also an extension of the listening process, but this element of the communication process will be covered in a later chapter.[9]

It is very important for the mediator to be a good listener for a number of reasons. First, most individuals with a problem or dispute are very interested in feeling that they have been heard. Often the mediation is the only opportunity that disputing parties will have to voice their concern or explain to anyone what the conflict is about. The mediation session is, in essence, their "day in court." The mediator then provides them with the opportunity to be heard. Second, in order to competently assist in the problem solving process, a mediator must have sufficient information about the dispute. It is only with acute listening skills that the mediator will be able to gather the information necessary to identify issues, interests, and alternatives. Third, by demonstrating good listening skills, the mediator not only gathers information, but simultaneously provides feedback which encourages the speaker to provide additional information.[10] However, some parties have a tendency to ramble during the mediation, and the mediator must utilize a technique such as close-ended questioning or restating to terminate the information gathering process. Yet, in most instances, encouragement is appropriate.

As a listener, the mediator should also model good listening behavior for the parties. Disputes often exist because people have failed to

---

9. See Chapter 6, infra.

10. Most individuals, realizing that someone is listening, will continue to talk.

communicate with each other, or if they communicate, it is not accurate. If one disputing party observes the mediator listening intently when the other is discussing the problem, the first may, in turn, be encouraged to mirror this behavior. By doing so, the party may more accurately hear another view of the matter. This often can act as a catalyst to move individuals off of positions by increasing understanding, which leads to increased opportunities for settlement.

2. NON-VERBAL MESSAGES

Most of the discussion thus far has focused on verbal communication. It is also important that the mediator pay attention to the non-verbal communication that occurs. Non-verbal communication takes place through three primary channels of expression: proxemics, kinesics, and paralinguistics.[11] Proxemics include the spatial relationships and their influence on communication. Examples include office design; the type and style of furniture; the seating arrangements; and physical distance of all parties. Kinesics is essentially body language. This is what most often is termed non-verbal communication, and includes all physical movement. The paralinguistics portion of non-verbal communication is the vocal portion of the message other than the actual words. These include the pace, pitch, tone, and volume of the message.[12]

All three of these methods of nonverbal communication are important to a mediator analyzing the messages sent by the parties. Proxemics can effect the message in the way it is initially directed. This is the one aspect of communication over which the mediator may have initial control. The mediator can influence proxemics by arranging the time and place of the mediation, as well as seating arrangements of all participants.[13]

Body language, or kinesics, of the parties can affect the message in a number of ways. In fact, some believe non-verbals control the message. Studies have shown that the percentage of communication which is non-verbal varies anywhere from about a 50–50 split, to a 93% non-verbal portion.[14] Often the physical movements of the speaker, or body language, will accent or emphasize part of a message. In other instances, one may substitute a non-verbal communication for the verbal message. A non-verbal communication can also contradict the message conveyed by the content of the spoken words.

The paralinguistics portion of speech patterns may also have influence on the message. Voice tone and pitch may accent the content. In other cases these factors may contradict it. The pace and volume of speech also provide a great amount of information about the message. It is imperative that the mediator pay close attention to all of these elements of a message. The skillful mediator will soon learn that it is

11. Robert M. Bastress & Joseph D. Harbaugh, Interviewing, Counseling and Negotiating 132 (1990).

12. Id.

13. See also Chapter 5, § A infra, which will examine this in detail.

14. Roberto Aron, et al., Trial Communication Skills 27 (1986).

only by attentiveness to all aspects of a message that the most accurate information will be gathered. And the more accurate the information about the matter is, the better the opportunity for understanding, and hence resolution.

The mediator, in the role of listener, must be certain to listen to the two-parts of a message; that is, the content or substantive part of the message as well as the affective or feeling part of the message. Most messages have both a content and a feeling portion, although it is rare that these are evenly split. In some instances where the parties are in need of venting and expressing their feelings, the content portion is small. In other situations, it is the substantive information which is the most important. The primary emphasis of the message will usually be evident from the manner of communication, but the mediator should always be aware of both parts of the message.

A word of caution. While in interactive communication, the mediator, as a listener, should acknowledge the individual's feeling, or affective part of the message, she must be careful not to focus so much on the feeling or emotional part of the message that the mediation becomes, in essence, a therapy session.

Although it is imperative for the mediator to be a good listener and ascertain the entirety of each person's message at the mediation, her role differs from that of other individuals in the problem solving process. The mediator does not make a decision as to the truth or veracity of anything that is stated. Therefore, although it is important to listen, the mediator must do so without regard to the need to determine the facts or who is telling the truth. Moreover, it is important that when the mediator is listening, that it is done in an objective fashion. Part of the mediator's role is to assist the parties in looking at the dispute in a more neutral fashion. Therefore, the mediator must be nonjudgmental in the listening process.

B. NOTE–TAKING AND ORGANIZATION

Even though the mediator is busily paying attention to all parts of the messages conveyed, she will most likely also need to be taking notes. Note-taking during listening varies from individual to individual. In complex cases it is very important that notes be taken. It is often the job of the mediator to keep the information straight and to refocus the parties on the main issues. On the other hand, if the mediator is too intent on writing everything down, there is little time or ability to pick up on any of the non-verbal communication. Moreover, one of the most important elements of non-verbal communication is eye contact. The mediator may find it difficult to maintain eye contact with the speaker when taking copious notes. The use of phrases and abbreviations in note-taking can be very helpful.

There is much debate on the amount of note-taking, and finding the right balance is critical. In many other interview situations, the use of a tape recording device is suggested.[15] However, due to the confidential nature of mediation, audio or videotaping is strongly discouraged. Moreover, many individuals become reluctant to open up if a video or audio recording device is used.

Individuals react differently to note-taking. Some perceive that if someone is writing down what they are saying, then it is more important or relevant than items mentioned which were not recorded. In response, they will emphasize that portion of the discussion even more. On the other hand, there are those who perceive if direct eye contact is made, then what is being stated is of importance. These matters are then stressed by the speaker. To prevent the parties' inaccurate placement of emphasis on the mediator's note-taking behavior, the mediator should include in her introductory remarks an explanation of note-taking. She should explain that the purpose of taking notes is only to assist the mediator in maintaining accuracy.

Data organization is also part of the information gathering and note-taking process.[16] The manner in which the mediator arranges the information can help the parties focus on the primary issues of the dispute, particularly in complex cases or in the family arena where the mediation occurs over a period of time. By her organization, the mediator assists the parties in looking at the dispute in a systematic manner, which can produce a fresh view of the case. Many parties are then better able to enter the problem-solving process.

How to proceed in note-taking and organizing the data, like many elements of the mediation process, will be individual decisions for the mediator. However, as with all mediator skills, one will find that as she progresses in the process, experimentation with different methods will assist in finding the right balance.

C. COUNSELING AND CALMING SKILLS

Just as the role of a mediator is not to be an advocate for a party in a legal dispute, so should she refrain from therapeutic intervention.[17] However, this is not to say that some skill and knowledge in counseling cannot be helpful. General empathetic understanding is essential if the mediator is to establish rapport and trust with the parties. Demonstrating awareness of the feelings of those in dispute can provide a positive environment for the exchange of information which will pave the way toward resolution. Providing a safe environment where the parties feel comfortable venting their feelings is also part of the mediator's role. However, the mediator must not allow ventilation to become uncontrollable.

15. David A. Binder, et al., Lawyers as Counselors: A Client–Centered Approach 195 (1990).

16. Jay Folberg & Alison Taylor, Mediation: A Comprehensive Guide to Resolving Conflicts Without Litigation 125 (1984).

17. While some divergence of opinion exists, most mediators contend that providing *any type* of professional advice by the mediator is generally not advised. See Chapters 14 and 15, infra.

In cases where conflict is overt, the mediation session itself can be a very stressful situation for the participants, as well as the mediator.[18] Often the subject matter of the mediation is a highly emotional topic. It is common for disputants to experience emotions such as frustration, anger, sadness, and grief during the process. Basic calming skills, such as softening of the voice, providing tissue, and a light touch on the arm are all useful techniques to employ when a party demonstrates overt emotions. The mediator must be comfortable dealing with these emotional aspects of the mediation. In fact, it has been suggested that an important part of becoming a mediator is sensitization to the feeling of others as well as self.[19] Specific counseling techniques employed by the mediator will often depend upon the nature of the emotion expressed by the party. It is imperative however, that the mediator refrain from becoming emotionally involved in the matter. Although a demonstration of empathetic understanding is appropriate, the mediator must remain objective and neutral.

D.　HUMAN BEHAVIOR AND MOTIVATION: THE MEDIATOR'S ROLE

A complete, or even incomplete, analysis of human behavior and motivation is beyond the scope of this work. Likewise, such analysis is beyond the parameters of the mediator's role. Yet, to achieve mutual resolution of a matter, much of the mediator's work will involve motivating human behavior. While the mediator will not actively attempt to influence the specific resolutions of the parties, she should be aware of human decision-making behavior. A variety of psychological theories about motivation exist, none of which is strongly advocated as a basis for the mediator's work. However, in general terms, a mediator should remember that people are motivated by needs. Individuals will likely choose a course of action by which needs can be met. Ascertaining these needs, or interests, is part of the mediator's role. This is very similar to identification of interests which is examined in Chapter 8.

Group dynamics also play a significant role in the behavior of the participants in a mediation. A mediation, particularly when structured in a collaborative problem-solving format, is a collective enterprise, and as a consequence group dynamics must be considered.[20] Even apart from the mediation process, individuals involved in a dispute, and particularly those in a lawsuit, can clearly be identified as a *group*. A group is defined as two or more individuals who have at least one characteristic in common; form a distinguishable identity; are aware of positive interdependence of goals; interact; and pursue goals together.[21] As time passes, the group develops norms which guide interaction along

---

18. Mediator *mental health* is a virtually unexplored aspect of mediation practice.

19. Folberg & Taylor, supra note 16, at 87.

20. For an in-depth examination of group dynamics, see Deborah G. Ancona, et al., *The Group and What Happens on the Way to "Yes,"* 7 Negotiation J. 155 (1991).

21. Deutsch, supra note 6, at 49.

with roles composed of specific activities, obligations, and rights.[22] It is likely that the longer the duration of the dispute, the more firmly established these behavioral patterns become. The mediator must first determine what they are. Thereafter, she may need to decide whether these patterns are constructive or destructive with regard to resolution of the matter. If destructive to the group, the mediator may try to influence the group behavior and effect change in the patterns of conduct.

There may also be subgroups within the larger group. For instance, an ongoing group may exist prior to the mediation where the lawyers for the parties have worked together in the past. Specific behavior may have been previously established as the group norm. There may already be a designated leader of the group. It is important for the mediator to pay attention to these dynamics, and recognize what elements of the group are able to be changed as well as those which are not subject to modification.

EXERCISES

3–1. The next time a friend or colleague engages you in conversation, pay special attention to the non-verbal parts of the message. Afterwards ask if you may check back the accuracy of your perceptions.

3–2. Experiment with your friends and colleagues in both giving and receiving messages. Vary the non-verbals and the paralinguistics, while keeping the content the same. Note how the message and subsequent reaction can change.

3–3. You are mediating a dispute between several neighbors in a subdivision. The dispute involves ambiguous deed restrictions. The parties, composed of about ten different families, have been embroiled in this conflict for nearly two years. The first group, essentially comprised of seven couples, is intent on a strict construction of the restriction providing that residences are only for residential purposes. They contend that any hint of commercial use is a violation of the restrictions. Their goal is to enforce these restrictions against the Tuens, who offer piano, voice, and guitar lessons out of their home. Two other homeowners support the Tuens in the enterprise, and maintain that the intent of the drafters of the restrictions was to allow flexibility in their application. While actual full-time businesses and shops should be prohibited, activities such as occasional music lessons do not violate the restrictions.

After about three hours of mediation, it appears clear to you that the first group is led by Patti Smith, one of two individuals in the first group who is not employed outside of the home. You, as the mediator, have concluded that this dispute has become Smith's "career". It appears that she has developed a leadership role with the group. Fur-

22. Id.

thermore, based upon general comment, you feel that if Ms. Smith were to be more open to alternatives, the entire matter could be settled.

How will you approach this problem? What behavior dynamics will you need to take into consideration?

Chapter Four

GETTING TO THE MEDIATION TABLE

Mediation is a positive, creative dispute resolution process which offers many benefits which other procedures do not. But how do individuals or groups involved in conflict gain access to the process? A number of questions surround this issue. What are the ways by which a dispute or conflict finds its way to the mediation process? When a dispute or conflict occurs, how do we know if, and when, mediation is appropriate? Who should attend the mediation? Should a party be forced to go? Where do the participants sit? What cases are inappropriate? Is it ever too early for mediation? Too late? What will it cost? How long will it take? These are a sampling of the questions which surround the use of the mediation process.

A. GENERAL APPROPRIATENESS

The development of mediation as a viable alternative to litigation was due, largely, to its overt benefits; that is, mediation saves time and money. Clearly in those cases where it is important to the parties to save time and money, mediation is indicated. But there are other factors which also signify that mediation is appropriate. The specific factors which indicate that a case or matter is appropriate for mediation are numerous. An illustrative listing includes:

- there is an ongoing relationship that the parties wish to maintain;
- the parties hope to establish an ongoing relationship through the mediation;
- avoidance of a legal precedent;
- need for assurance of confidentiality about the nature of the dispute, the agreement or both;
- need for assistance in communication and information exchange;
- an inability to identify common interests;
- the parties and/or their advocates need assistance with the negotiation;

- need for creativity in resolution;
- desire for self-determination;
- one or both parties (or their counsel) has made an unrealistic assessment of the case; and
- despite differences, there is a mutual superordinate goal of a mutually satisfactory resolution.

Most topical literature as well as anecdotal research supports this list, rendering a detailed analysis of the specific issues unnecessary.[1] The more difficult determination is whether there exist cases where mediation should not be used. Many lawyers, judges, and parties contend that mediation is appropriate in nearly every case, conflict, or dispute,[2] at least as a first step. If mediation assists the parties in resolving a matter short of litigation, should it not be made available to all parties?

Some have attempted to determine which instances are inappropriate for mediation. It has been hypothesized that mediation may be inappropriate in the following situations: the decision-maker will not attend this session; a case involves governmental and political issues; budgetary constraints may obstruct settlement; and a settlement had been previously reached but broken.[3] However, it was recognized that even within the preceding categories, cases could be successfully mediated.[4]

Others have identified a longer list of cases where mediation is inappropriate. These include matters in which:

- the client cannot effectively represent her best interest and is not represented by counsel;
- the client seeks to establish legal precedent;
- a significant person is unable to be present;
- a party is entitled by statute to attorney's fees;
- there is strong business competition between the parties in concentrated markets;
- there is a threat of criminal action;
- one party wants to delay a resolution;
- there is likelihood of bankruptcy;
- discovery is needed;

1. For additional detail, see Nancy H. Rogers & Richard A. Salem, A Student's Guide to Mediation and the Law, (Chapter 3) (1987). Also Nancy H. Rogers & Craig A. McEwen, Mediation: Law, Policy, and Practice, (Chapters 3, 4, and 5) (1989 & Supp. 1993).

2. This has been argued in several instances. See, Robert A. Baruch Bush, *Me-*

diation and Adjudication, Dispute Resolution and Ideology: An Imaginary Conversation, 3 J. Contemp. Legal Issues 1 (1989); Eric R. Galton, Representing Clients in Mediation (1994).

3. Galton, supra note 2, at 5.

4. Id.

- enforcement of the outcome will be necessary.[5]

However, continued research and experimentation have failed to evidence with any precision the validity of these factors. It has been suggested that perhaps this list is the beginning, rather than the end, of the analysis.[6] Many, if not all, cases with these types of difficulties have been successfully mediated.

In cases of threatened or even actual criminal action, the mediation process has been successfully used, particularly where the parties know each other. One of the oldest mediation programs, the Columbus, Ohio Night Prosecutor's Program,[7] involves cases where there have been allegations of criminal activity, albeit misdemeanors. Many other programs, including those in Dispute Resolution Centers have been established within, or in conjunction with, prosecutors' and district attorneys' offices. Moreover, some police officers are learning the mediation process, and mediate on the spot in neighborhood disputes. Mediation in the criminal sphere also takes place in terms of the mediation of restitution issues between victims and offenders. Mediation has also been used to successfully resolve disputes within a prison system.[8]

Litigants in cases where attorneys' fees are provided by statute should not be dissuaded from the use of mediation. The attorneys' fees can be a factor in the negotiation. While admittedly problems are presented by a waiver of attorneys' fees which are provided by statute,[9] fee waiver can be a problem in any type of case. Cases involving statutorily provided attorneys' fees are now settled through negotiation and mediation on a regular basis.

As the business world has become educated about the benefits of collaborative problem solving, the number of commercial disputes resolved through mediation has increased. Many companies, large and small alike, now require their attorneys to use ADR processes before proceeding with formal legal action. Therefore, it is not unrealistic to see parties who are business competitors use mediation, particularly where a speedy resolution is beneficial to all parties.

While it is often hypothesized that one of the major factors in reaching a mediated resolution is the parties' willingness to do so, it has been documented that even the most unwilling party, once forced to the mediation table, will not only participate, but will walk away with a settlement and a satisfactory experience with the procedure.[10] It appears that initial unwillingness to participate in mediation is not an accurate indicator of inappropriateness.

---

5. Rogers & Salem, supra note 1, at 57–58.

6. Id. at 59.

7. See generally discussion of *NPP*, Chapter 2, § B,2, supra.

8. For further details of the application of mediation in *criminal matters*, see Chapter 16, § I, infra.

9. This was the argument set forth in Rogers and Salem, supra note 1, at 58.

10. See Janice A. Roehl & Royer F. Cook, *Mediation in Interpersonal Disputes: Effectiveness and Limitations* in Mediation Research: The Process and Effectiveness of Third Party Intervention (Kenneth Kressel & Dean G. Pruitt, eds. 1989).

The entire bankruptcy process is essentially a supervised negotiation.[11] The mediation process is facilitated negotiation. Use of mediation to assist in resolving disputes in the bankruptcy process has long been advocated by a few individuals.[12] Although many bankruptcy courts and practitioners hesitated in joining the ADR bandwagon, there has recently been some discussion of projects urging the bankruptcy courts to use the mediation process.

In some situations, the litigants want to delay the court process or are in need of formal discovery. It is inappropriate to use the mediation process to achieve such goals. However, in the case of discovery needs, one option is to postpone the mediation until after information has been exchanged. Another is to use the mediation to structure the discovery process. In cases where a party merely wants to delay the court process, it is nevertheless possible to achieve settlement once at the mediation. These situations also relate to the matter of proper timing of mediation.

In those cases where the decision-makers in the dispute are not present, or are present but unwilling to make a decision, mediation should not be utilized. The lack of settlement authority accounts for the most difficult situation presented to the mediator.[13] However, in some instances, particularly where organizations such as large corporations or political subdivisions have a hierarchal distribution of authority, it may be impossible to have the ultimate decision-maker present. Yet, an ability to reach a final decision does exist. Perhaps the mediation can proceed until a tentative settlement is reached. Subsequent ratification to finalize the agreement is then possible. In other cases, the mediator may telephone the final decision-maker and convey the options. This particular form of "telephonic" or long distance mediation is strongly discouraged, since a very crucial part of the mediation process is the presence of all parties at the table, listening to one another. Nevertheless, it must be recognized that in the real world this form of mediation does take place. Remember—mediation is a flexible process. In essence, mediation is probably appropriate in nearly every case. Its use has been documented, although more by anecdotal data than empirical. Nonetheless this premise is a good place to start.[14]

B. THE REFERRAL PROCESS

The nature or type of case may directly affect the referral to mediation. And certainly the method of referral impacts the mediation process. There are a number of ways by which cases find their way to

11. For full exploration of this issue, see J. Bradley Johnson, *The Bankruptcy Bargain,* 65 Am. Bankr. L.J. 213 (1990) and Theodore Eisenberg, *Commentary on the Nature of Bankruptcy: Bankruptcy and Bargaining,* 75 Va. L. Rev. 205 (1990).

12. I personally am one of those individuals.

13. Based upon numerous comments from practicing mediators.

14. However, compare statements of those who oppose the settlement of any case, and hence have the view that mediation is *inappropriate* in every case. For example, see Owen M. Fiss, *Against Settlement,* 93 Yale L.J. 1073 (1984) (see also, Bush, supra note 2.)

the mediation table. Along a continuum, these range from the parties' completely voluntary desire to attend mediation and resolve the case to a mandatory, over both parties' objection, court referral. While in the majority of cases the referral process of pre-litigation matters and pending lawsuits are similar, because of the intervention of the court system, the two will be examined separately.

1. PRE–LITIGATION MATTERS

In this instance, assume that no lawyers are directly involved in the dispute and no lawsuit has been filed. If individuals involved in the dispute decide to voluntarily go to mediation, they could merely do so. Parties may also participate in mediation prior to litigation in accordance with a contract provision. In either of these instances, locating mediation services merits consideration.

a. *Voluntary*

Many individuals find themselves at dispute resolution centers. At these centers, mediation services are provided at little or no charge to the parties, and the focus is primarily on smaller cases; those cases in which the amount in controversy is not great.[15] Although those within the ADR field are continuously educating the general public, the use of mediation has not reached the point where most individuals involved in a dispute immediately think of this alternative. The process by which many individuals dispute often discourages disputants from entering mediation spontaneously or voluntarily.[16] Moreover, the character of conflict, along with the cultures and social relationship involved contribute to the need for pressured mediation.[17] Therefore, it is often necessary to utilize a different avenue to allow or encourage disputing individuals to access the mediation process. One such method is referral via a citizen complaint center.[18]

In many of these disputes, the individuals are unrepresented. Questions then arise as to whether, by direct referral to mediation, a different form of justice is provided to these disputing parties. For instance, in a pending lawsuit, most jurisdictions have a variety of options, including mediation, available. In a pre-litigation matter, where the individuals are not represented by counsel, most agencies such as dispute resolution centers provide only the mediation alternative. There is some concern that these individuals are deprived of other options such as arbitration or a hybrid process. A second issue for consideration is whether the individuals truly understand the mediation process. There is no representation by counsel because the amount in controversy does not warrant such, or the parties' income level prohibits it. In many cases,

---

15. It is recognized that these cases are just as important, or more important, to some individuals, than multi-million dollar cases. It is for descriptive purposes only, that the word *small* is used.

16. Craig A. McEwen & Thomas W. Milburn, *Explaining a Paradox of Mediation*, 9 Negotiation J. 23, 34 (1993).

17. Id. at 26.

18. These centers are often an adjunct of prosecutors' offices.

participation in mediation might be the only viable alternative for these individuals other than self-help or avoidance. So they enter into the mediation process, not knowing exactly what that means. These concerns have been raised primarily on a theoretical basis. As a practical matter in most instances, those who participate in mediation through a dispute resolution center though unrepresented, are very satisfied with the process. This is true even if no final agreement is reached.[19]

b. Contractual

In cases where mediation is contracted for in advance, the parties are less hesitant about the process, and usually are easily able to locate a mediator. In fact, the mediator may be identified in the mediation clause. Moreover, the parties are at least vaguely familiar with the process. It is also likely that since the parties voluntarily agreed to the mediation clause, they will comply with it. It is advisable though, to include in the clause matters which may be subject to disagreement at the time a dispute arises. These matters include the time, place, and cost of the mediation, the identification of the mediator and who will attend the mediation. With these items agreed to, chances for voluntary compliance are increased.[20]

In the instance where one of the disputing parties refuses to participate in the mediation, questions arise about enforceability of the mediation clause. Can reluctant parties be compelled to mediate in accordance with mediation clauses included in contracts or other documents such as wills or trusts? While the number of cases are slight, it currently appears that most courts will enforce voluntary mediation clauses.[21]

DeVALK LINCOLN MERCURY, INC. v. FORD MOTOR CO.

United States Court of Appeals, Seventh Circuit, 1987.
811 F.2d 326.

Automobile dealer and its owner and manager brought action against manufacturer following termination of dealership.

* * *

Plaintiffs believe they fulfilled the first alleged purpose of the mediation clause by writing four letters to Ford detailing DLM's grievances. Plaintiffs argue these letters gave Ford all the notice it needed of the claims with which plaintiffs were concerned.

As for the second alleged purpose of the mediation clause, plaintiffs contend they presented Ford with ample opportunity to settle their claims prior to litigation. The negotiations between plaintiffs and Ford's

---

19. See Roehl & Cook, supra note 10.   **21.** Id. at 61.
20. Rogers & McEwen, supra note 1, at 63.

representatives spanned over eight months. Both Ford and plaintiffs effectively articulated their respective positions during these negotiations. Plaintiffs argue this negotiation process fulfilled the purpose of allowing Ford to attempt to settle its claims with DLM.

Although it is true that "Michigan follows the substantial performance rule," P & M Construction Co. v. Hammond Ventures, Inc., 3 Mich.App. 306, 142 N.W.2d 468, 473 (1966) (citation omitted), and that in Michigan "the extent of nonperformance [is] viewed in relation to the full performance promised," Gordon v. Great Lakes Bowling Corp., 18 Mich.App. 358, 171 N.W.2d 225, 228–29 (1969), we cannot agree with plaintiffs' contention.

* * *

[12] The mediation clause here states that it is a condition precedent to any litigation. As a result, the clause takes itself outside the sphere of influence of the substantial performance rule. Because the mediation clause demands strict compliance with its requirement of appeal to the Dealer Policy Board before the parties can litigate, plaintiffs' substantial performance arguments must fail.

2. WAIVER OF MEDIATION CLAUSE

Undaunted, plaintiffs argue that even if the mediation clause operates as a condition precedent to litigation, Ford waived the requirements of that clause by its conduct following the final date on which an appeal could be taken to the Dealer Policy Board. The mediation clause requires the dissatisfied dealer to appeal its claims to the Dealer Policy Board "within one year after the termination or nonrenewal has become effective." Ford accepted DLM's resignation and DLM ceased operations in October 1979. Therefore, any continuing negotiations between DLM and Ford after October 1980, plaintiffs argue, constitute a waiver by Ford of the requirements of the mediation clause....

* * *

Specifically, the conduct giving rise to an interference of waiver may take the form of continued performance by the breaching party without any attempt by the non-breaching party to call a halt to the performance.... ("[A] party standing silent while the other party to the contract fails to perform a condition will be estopped from later asserting the condition.")

In this regard, plaintiffs point us to the law of arbitration clauses as closely analogous area of contractual agreement by which we should be guided. The Supreme Court of Michigan has held that an insurer "may waive the compulsory arbitration provision of its insurance policy by its conduct." Bielski v. Wolverine Insurance Co., 379 Mich. 280, 150 N.W.2d 788, 790 (1967). That court also explained:

"A clause in an insurance policy providing for arbitration or appraisal of the loss or damage as a condition precedent to a suit by the policyholder to recover insurance is inserted wholly for the protec-

tion of the insurer and may be waived by it. Such waivers need not be expressed in terms, but may be implied by the acts, omissions, or conduct of the insurer or its agents authorized in such respect."
Id. (quoting 29A American Jurisprudence Insurance § 1617 (1960)); Capital Mortgage Corp. v. Coopers & Lybrand, 142 Mich.App. 531, 369 N.W.2d 922, 924 (1985).

[14] Superficially, it appears that Ford's conduct after the time expired for an appeal to the Dealer Policy Board possibly constitutes a waiver. And we might find persuasive plaintiffs' arguments in this regard were it not for Ford's response, with which we agree, that Michigan's courts uphold anti-waiver clauses. Because DLM agreed in paragraph 27 of the Sales Agreements that implied waivers of Sales Agreements' provisions would not be permitted, plaintiffs' waiver argument cannot stand.

3. REPUDIATION FOR MATERIAL BREACHES OF CONTRACT

In a final effort to skirt the requirements of the mediation clause, plaintiffs argue that Ford's alleged material breaches of the Sales Agreements relieved DLM of any duty to appeal its grievances to the Dealer Policy Board.

[15] Ford argues, however, that plaintiffs did not raise this repudiation argument in the district court and they thus waive it on appeal. Our review of the record, and plaintiffs' failure in their reply brief to counter Ford's charge, persuade us that indeed this argument was not raised in the district court. It is thus waived on appeal. See Zbaraz v. Hartigan, 763 F.2d 1532 (7th Cir.1985); Textile Banking Co. v. Rentschler, 657 F.2d 844, 853 (7th Cir.1981).

IV. Conclusion

Even after drawing all the reasonable inferences in favor of plaintiffs' positions on this appeal from an adverse grant of summary judgment, we cannot find any genuine issues of material fact. Because there are no such issues, the judgment granted to defendants by the district judge as a matter of law is

AFFIRMED.

2. PENDING CASES: PUBLIC OR PRIVATE SECTOR MEDIATION

Where a lawsuit is pending in a court, there are a number of ways through which the suit may find itself in mediation. Although currently rare, certainly the urging of mediation by the parties is an appropriate avenue to mediation. There may have been a previous contractual provision which either advises or mandates participation in mediation in an attempt to settle a case before a lawsuit may be formally pursued. Although these cases technically fall within the voluntary prelitigation cases, in some instances the mediation will not occur until after suit is filed. Lawyers may suggest mediation to one another, or the court may prompt mediation use.

Lawsuits are settled on a regular basis; however, this often occurs late in the case. If the parties avail themselves of the assistance of a mediator, they may speed up the settlement process. Many courts have become active in referring pending lawsuits to a variety of ADR processes, including mediation. This activity has raised concerns about a court's authority to make such referrals, along with the parties' right to object and demand a trial. Cost considerations are another issue for examination in this context.

a. Mandatory Referral

When examining issues of mandatory referral, it is very important to first distinguish between public or private sector mediation. Public mediation covers those situations in which the mediation process is provided in a public forum [22] at very little or no charge. In these cases the mediator or mediators are either employed by, or volunteers with, the court system in which the case is pending.[23] In private sector mediation, the mediator is in business for a profit and will provide mediation services for a fee. There is little debate about whether individuals, with or without counsel, may voluntarily avail themselves of the private sector mediator for whatever cost they determine appropriate; in essence, the free market principle. However, in instances in which the court compels or mandates participation in a private mediation, substantial concerns arise.

Before addressing these matters, the initial issue is whether an individual in a dispute or with a claim can be compelled to go to mediation. That is, whether the court has the inherent authority to mandate referral, particularly over the objection of one of the litigants. There are a number of attributes associated with our public justice system, which include equal access for all, openness to public scrutiny, and neutrals not handpicked by the disputing parties. Should individuals, against their will, be forced to participate in a system of justice that does not afford these alleged safeguards? Most state courts which routinely refer cases to mediation rely upon statutory authority. The number of statutes which have a mediation referral scheme for courts is increasing. Some require a determination on the part of the court as to appropriateness of the case for mediation, while others are given carte blanche to any referral. The federal courts, in referring cases to other forms of ADR often relied upon their inherent authority to manage cases or Rule 16 of the Federal Rules of Civil Procedure, which produced conflicting results.[24] Now however, federal courts in response to a Congressional mandate[25] have enacted plans and new local rules which

---

22. *Public*, here meaning, accessible by all, not open in terms of nonconfidential.

23. *Examples* include court based California Mandatory Custody Mediation and the Multi–Door Dispute Resolution Division of the Superior Court of the District of Columbia.

24. See Strandell v. Jackson County, 838 F.2d 844 (7th Cir.1987) and In re NLO 5 F.3d 154 (6th Cir.1993).

25. The Civil Justice Reform Act of 1990, 28 U.S.C.A. §§ 471–482 (1993).

embrace, and even mandate the use of ADR.[26]

KEENE v. GARDNER
Court of Appeals of Texas, Dallas, 1992.
837 S.W.2d 224.

* * *

MEDIATION SANCTIONS

In its seventh and eighth points of error, Keene complains that the trial court erred in ordering mediation and imposing sanctions against Keene for not participating in the mediation proceeding.

* * *

Pertinent Facts

On another defendant's motion, the court ordered all parties to participate in mediation beginning on the morning following the court's order. The order required that an executive officer from each corporate defendant, with authority to negotiate a settlement, attend the mediation. Keene explained to the court that its predetermined settlement policy permitted only the company's president to negotiate a settlement. Keene's president was in New York and could not be in Dallas on twenty-four hours' notice. The court maintained that someone with settlement power would have to attend.

The next morning, Keene requested the statutory ten days to file written objections to the court's referral order. The court overruled Keene's request and oral objection. Keene sent a representative without settlement authority to the mediation proceeding. After the representative restated Keene's position, the mediator excused Keene's representatives from further attendance.

Appellees moved for sanctions for Keene's not participating in the mediation. The court conducted a hearing on appellees' motion and ordered that Keene pay all costs of mediation.

Applicable Law

The Texas Civil Practice and Remedies Code authorizes courts to refer a pending dispute to an alternative dispute resolution procedure at any point in the trial or appellate process. *Downey v. Gregory*, 757 S.W.2d 524, 525 (Tex.App.—Houston [1st Dist.] 1988, no writ); *see* Tex.Civ.Prac. & Rem.Code Ann. § 154.021 (Vernon Supp. 1992). The statute also provides a procedure for notice of an objection to the court's referral:

(a) If a court determines that a pending dispute is appropriate for referral under Section 154.021, the court shall notify the parties of its determination.

26. Since each federal court has designed its own individual plan, each plan must be reviewed to determine if mediation has been implemented.

(b) Any party may, within 10 days after receiving the notice under Subsection (a), file a written objection to the referral.

(c) If the court finds that there is a reasonable basis for an objection filed under Subsection (b), the court may not refer the dispute under Section 154.021. Tex.Civ.Prac. & Rem.Code Ann. § 154.022 (Vernon Supp. 1992).

Application of Law

[22] Section 154.022 allows parties ten days to file objections once the trial court determines that alternative dispute resolution is appropriate. The trial court required Keene to participate in mediation on twenty-four hours' notice. Keene specifically requested ten days to file objections as provided in the statute.

The statute's stated intent is "to encourage the peaceable resolution of disputes . . . and the early settlement of pending litigation through *voluntary* settlement procedures." Tex.Civ.Prac. & Rem.Code Ann. § 154.002 (Vernon Supp. 1992)(emphasis added). Keene requested, and the court denied, ten days to file written objections under the applicable statutory provision. This mediation proceeding was neither voluntary nor in accord with the required statutory procedures.

Although the trial court has an interest in expediting the resolution of pending litigation, it cannot force the parties to follow an unreasonable timetable. If the trial court can force a resisting party to participate in alternative dispute resolution without regard to the ten-day objection period, it renders a portion of the statute meaningless. While the trial court has discretion in determining whether alternative dispute resolution is appropriate [1], it has no authority to ignore the statute's intent and wording. We sustain points of error seven and eight.

CARMICHAEL v. WORKERS' COMPENSATION COURT OF THE STATE OF MONTANA
Supreme Court of Montana, 1988.
234 Mont. 410, 763 P.2d 1122.

HARRISON, JUSTICE.

Hoagy Carmichael petitioned this Court for a writ of supervisory control challenging the 1987 amendments to the Workers' Compensation Act concerning dispute resolution and mediation, §§ 39–71–2401 and –2406 through –2411, MCA. We granted the writ for the purpose of determining whether these statutes are constitutional as applied to cases where the injury occurred before the effective date of the amendment

* * *

Because we determine the nonbinding mediation requirements unconstitutionally impair a contractual obligation when applied to the facts of this case, we need not go beyond an analysis of the first issue.

---

1. See Tex.Civ.Prac. & Rem.Code Ann. §§ 154.02(a), 154.022(c); *Downey,* 757 S.W.2d at 525.

Generally, Carmichael's argument is based on the fact that his injury occurred prior to the time the legislature enacted the nonbinding mediation requirements.

* * *

Carmichael demonstrates a substantial impairment of his contractual rights and there is insufficient evidence to demonstrate the mediation statutes achieve their purpose as applied to claimants injured prior to the effective date of the statute....

WEBER, JUSTICE, dissents as follows:

* * *

In my opinion, there has been no showing that the mediation requirement substantially impairs any contractual right. The requirement does not affect Mr. Carmichael's right to workers' compensation payments; it only presents the possibility of a delay in his receiving compensation, provided that he shows he is entitled to it.... I therefore disagree with the theory set forth in the majority opinion that the delay presented by mediation is an "additional delay" not existing on the date Mr. Carmichael was injured....

* * *

Mr. Carmichael argues that the mediation requirement violates his due process rights. He has not cited any authority that a delay in reestablishing a right which has been unchallengedly taken away is a deprivation of due process. Further, under the former statutes, there was no right to a decision by the Workers' Compensation Court within any particular time....

* * *

West's Annotated Calif. Code (1994)

§ 3170. Mediation proceedings; setting matter for mediation

If it appears on the face of a petition, application, or other pleading to obtain or modify a temporary or permanent custody or visitation order that custody, visitation, or both are contested, the court shall set the contested issues for mediation.

(Added by Stats.1993, c. 219 (A.B.1500), § 116.87.)

———

Mandatory mediation can be described in a number of ways. Discussions about what specifically is mandated by participation in mediation are numerous. A closer look provides a more detailed manner of approaching the issue. The types of participation which may be required include: a good faith participation; an exchange of position papers and other information; minimal meaningful participation; attendance with settlement authority; and an obligation to pay a mediator's fee.[26]

———

26. Edward F. Sherman, *Court–Mandated Alternative Dispute Resolution: What* *Form of Participation Should be Required?* 46 SMU L. Rev. 2079, 2089 (1993).

DECKER v. LINDSAY

Court of Appeals of Texas, Houston, First District, 1992.
824 S.W.2d 247.

OPINION

SAM H. BASS, JUSTICE.

We are faced with two questions today: (1) Can a party be compelled to participate in an alternative dispute resolution (ADR) procedure despite its objections?, and (2) Have relators established their right to mandamus relief?

John and Mary Decker, relators, seek mandamus relief against respondent, Judge Tony Lindsay, who signed an order on October 18, 1991 referring their suit against Jordan Mintz,[1] the real party in interest, to mediation under Tex.Civ.Prac. & Rem.Code Ann. § 154.021(a), 1 (Vernon Supp.1992).

Judge Lindsay's mediation order was made on her own motion, without any hearing. She consulted with neither party before entering her order. See Tex.Civ.Prac. & Rem.Code Ann. § 154.021(b) (Vernon Supp.1992). However, only relators objected to the referral (timely, on November 1, 1991), and they submitted their objections for a ruling without oral argument.

The October 18, 1991, order requires the parties to agree on a mediation date "within the next 30 days," or by November 18, 1991. If no agreed date is scheduled, the order provides that the mediator will select a date within the next 60 days, or by December 18, 1991. The order also reads, "TO BE MEDIATED PRIOR TO TRIAL SETTING OF 1–20–92."

We are concerned primarily with the following provisions of Judge Lindsay's order:

> Mediation is a *mandatory but non-binding settlement conference*, conducted with the assistance of the Mediator.... Fees for the mediation are to be divided and borne equally by the parties unless agreed otherwise, shall be paid by the parties directly to the Mediator, and shall be taxed as costs. *Each party and counsel will be bound by the Rules for Mediation printed on the back of this Order*
> ....
>
> Named parties shall be present during the entire mediation process.... *Counsel and parties shall proceed in a good faith effort to try to resolve this case* ....
>
> Referral to mediation is not a substitute for trial, and the case will be tried if not settled.

(Emphasis added.)

---

1. Decker v. Mintz, No. 90–46678 (Dist.   Texas).
Ct. of Harris County, 280th Judicial Dist. of

Two of the Rules for Mediation, affixed to the order, are relevant to our discussion:

2. Agreement of the Parties. Whenever the parties have agreed to mediation they shall be deemed to have made these rules, as amended and in effect as of the date of the submission of the dispute, a part of their agreement to mediate. . . .

6. Commitment to Participate in Good Faith. While no one is asked to commit to settle their dispute in advance of mediation, all parties commit to participate in the proceedings in good faith with the intention to settle, if at all possible.

* * *

Relators assert Judge Lindsay's order is void and constitutes a clear abuse of discretion for the following reasons, which they also stated in their objection to mediation filed with the trial court: (1) the lawsuit arises out of a simple rear-end car collision, where the only issues are negligence, proximate cause, and damages; (2) trial is likely to last for only two days; (3) it is relators' opinion that mediation will not resolve the lawsuit, and they have not agreed to pay fees to the mediator; (4) mediation may cause relators to compromise their potential cause of action under the Stowers [2] doctrine; (5) the law does not favor alternative dispute resolution where one of the litigants objects to it and when the litigants have been ordered to pay for it; and (6) court-ordered mediation, over the relators' objection and at their cost, violates their right to due process under the fifth and fourteenth amendments to the United States Constitution and article I, section 13 of the Texas Constitution.

The real party in interest disputes relators' contention that the lawsuit and its issues are simple. The real party in interest has raised the defense of unavoidable accident and asserts that the parties have wide-ranging disagreement over Mr. Decker's claimed economic and medical damages.

Relators contend that trial will last for only two days. Consequently, it will take only slightly more time than the mediation ordered. However, the proposed joint pretrial order, signed by counsel for the relators and counsel for the real party in interest, provides an estimated trial time of three to four days.

While relators assert that mediation will not resolve the lawsuit, the real party in interest suggests that in a day invested in mediation, where communication between the parties is facilitated, relators may change their evaluation of the lawsuit.

Under Tex.Civ.Prac. & Rem.Code Ann. § 154.054(a) (Vernon Supp. 1992), the court may set a reasonable fee for the services of an impartial

---

2. G. A. Stowers Furniture Co. v. American Indem. Co., 15 S.W.2d 544 (Tex.   Comm'n App. 1929, holding approved).

third party appointed to facilitate an ADR procedure. Unless otherwise agreed by the parties, the court must tax the fee as other costs of the suit. Tex.Civ.Prac. & Rem.Code Ann. § 154.054(b) (Vernon Supp.1992). No fee was ever set for the mediation in this case. On December 6, 1991, after this proceeding was filed, the mediator advised the parties that she waived her fee in the case.

We cannot say that Judge Lindsay abused her discretion in impliedly finding the first three reasons advanced by relators were not reasonable objections to court-ordered mediation. Mediation may be beneficial even if relators believe it will not resolve the lawsuit. The statute certainly allows a reasonable fee to be charged, and relators never challenged the reasonableness of the fee, but now the fee issue is moot.

Concerning relators' remaining objections, Texas law recognizes that an insurer has a duty to the insured to settle a lawsuit if a prudent person in the exercise of ordinary care would do so. *G.A. Stowers Furniture Co.*, 15 S.W.2d at 547; *American Centennial Ins. Co. v. Canal Ins. Co.*, 810 S.W.2d 246, 250 (Tex.App.—Houston [1st Dist.] 1991, writ granted). If an ordinarily prudent person would have settled the lawsuit, and the insurer failed or refused to do so, it is liable to the insured for the amount of damages eventually recovered in excess of the policy limits. *American Centennial Insurance Co.*, 810 S.W.2d at 251. Relators assert that an insured, for example the real party in interest here, frequently assigns to the plaintiff his *Stowers* rights against his insurer, in return for a covenant that the plaintiff will not execute on the insured's personal assets. Therefore, relators contend that by ordering them to mediation, Judge Lindsay is interfering with their right to preserve a potential cause of action against the liability insurer of the real party in interest.

First, relators have no *Stowers* rights against the liability insurer of the real party in interest. *See American Centennial Ins. Co.*, 810 S.W.2d at 250–51. Second, there has been no trial; there has been no judgment; there has been no assignment of the real party in interest's *Stowers* rights to relators; there has been no determination that a reasonably prudent person would have decided, at the time relators made their offer, to settle the litigation for the policy limits. A *Stowers* cause of action does not accrue until the judgment in the underlying case becomes final. *Street v. Second Court of Appeals*, 756 S.W.2d 299, 301 (Tex.1988, orig. proceeding). We cannot say that Judge Lindsay abused her discretion in impliedly finding that court ordered mediation would not cause relators to compromise a potential cause of action under *Stowers*.

Relators rely on *Simpson v. Canales*, 806 S.W.2d 802 (Tex.1991), for their contention that the law does not favor alternative dispute resolution procedures where one of the parties objects to it and when the parties are compelled to pay for it. Relators' reliance on *Simpson* is misplaced. In *Simpson*, the supreme court found that the trial court abused its discretion in appointing a master to supervise all discovery because the "exceptional cases/good cause" criteria of Tex.R.Civ.P. 171 had not been met and the blanket reference of all discovery was unjustified. 806 S.W.2d at 811–12. Although the supreme court commented that the parties had been ordered to pay for resolution of discovery issues by a master that other litigants obtained from the court without such expense, the matter of expense was not a basis for the court's decision. *See* 806 S.W.2d at 812.

Relators also argue that chapter 154 of the Texas Civil Practice and Remedies Code presents a "voluntary" procedure, and that mandatory referral to a paid mediator is not within its scope.

Section 154.002 expresses the general policy that "peaceable resolution of disputes" is to be encouraged through "voluntary settlement procedures." Tex.Civ.Prac. & Rem.Code Ann. § 154.002 (Vernon Supp. 1992). Courts are admonished to carry out this policy. Tex.Civ.Prac. & Rem.Code Ann. § 154.003 (Vernon Supp.1992). A court cannot force the disputants to peaceably resolve their differences, but it can compel them to sit down with each other.

Section 154.021(a) authorizes a trial court *on its motion* to refer a dispute to an ADR procedure. However, if a party objects, *and there is a reasonable basis* for the objection, the court may not refer the dispute to an ADR procedure. Tex.Civ.Prac. & Rem.Code Ann. § 154.022(c). The corollary of this provision is that a court may refer the dispute to an ADR procedure if it finds there is no reasonable basis for the objection. A person appointed to facilitate an ADR procedure may not compel the parties to mediate (negotiate) or coerce parties to enter into a settlement agreement. Tex.Civ.Prac. & Rem.Code Ann. § 154.023(b) (Vernon Supp.1992). A mediator may not impose his or her own judgment on the issues for that of the parties. Tex.Civ.Prac. & Rem.Code Ann. § 154.023(b) (Vernon Supp. 1992).

Therefore, the policy of section 154.002 is consistent with a scheme where a court refers a dispute to an ADR procedure, requiring the parties to come together in court-ordered ADR procedures, but no one can compel the parties to negotiate or settle a dispute unless they voluntarily and mutually agree to do so. Any inconsistencies in chapter 154 can be resolved to give effect to a dominant legislative intent to compel referral, but not resolution. *See, e.g., Southern Canal Co. v. State Bd. of Water Eng'rs*, 159 Tex. 227, 318 S.W.2d 619, 624 (1958).

However, Judge Lindsay's order does not comport with the scheme set forth in chapter 154. Her order, and the mediation rules that are a part of it, do more than require the parties to come together; they require them to "negotiate" in good faith and attempt to reach a settlement.

Finally, relators object to Judge Lindsay's order on the constitutional grounds of due process and open courts.

Relators' brief does not contain any argument or authorities supporting their contention that their due process rights under the fifth and fourteenth amendments to the United States Constitution and article I, section 13 of the Texas Constitution have been violated. Therefore, they have not demonstrated their entitlement to mandamus relief on this ground. *See Wood v. Wood*, 159 Tex. 350, 320 S.W.2d 807, 813 (1959). They have not brought forth contentions that chapter 154 is in and of itself unconstitutional.

Relators contend that under the "capable of repetition yet evading review" doctrine, the constitutionality of the mediator's fee under the open courts provision should be addressed. They argue that subsequent litigants attempting to challenge the "mediation for pay" orders being issued by trial courts should not be forced to expend substantial sums in filing petitions for writ of mandamus in filing petitions for writ of mandamus only to have challenged mediators waive their fees.

The Texas Supreme Court has characterized the "capable of repetition yet evading review" doctrine as an exception to the mootness doctrine. *General Land Office v. Oxy U.S.A., Inc.*, 789 S.W.2d 569, 571 (Tex.1990); *State v. Lodge*, 608 S.W.2d 510, 912 (Tex.1980). It is applied where the challenged act is of such short duration that the appellant cannot obtain review before the issue becomes moot and where there is a reasonable expectation that the same complaining party would be subject to the same action again. *Spring Branch Indep. School Dist. v. Reynolds*, 764 S.W.2d 16, 18 (Tex.App.—Houston [1st Dist.] 1988, no writ). The doctrine has been used to challenge the unconstitutionality (1) of mental commitments after the complaining party has been released, (2) of juvenile delinquency adjudications, and (3) of restraints on speech. *See Reynolds*, 764 S.W.2d at 18. Perhaps the most famous application of the doctrine was in *Roe v. Wade*, 410 U.S. 113, 93 S.Ct. 705, 35 L.Ed.2d 147 (1973).

Relators do not claim that assessment of mediators' fees is of such short duration that it evades appellate review, particularly by the route of mandamus. Nor do they assert that they may be subject to court ordered mediation again. The doctrine does not apply.

However, in one very important respect, Judge Lindsay's order violates the open courts provision. It requires relators' attempt to negotiate a settlement of the dispute with the real party in interest in good faith, when they have clearly indicated they do not wish to do so, but prefer to go to trial. As we noted above, the order does more than refer the dispute to an ADR procedure; it requires negotiation. Chapter 154 contemplates mandatory referral only, not mandatory negotiation.

Having reviewed the arguments of relators, which do not attack the statute, but only the order of referral, and those of the real party in interest and the documents submitted to us, we conclude that Judge Lindsay's order is void insofar as it directs relators to negotiate in good faith a resolution of their dispute with the real party in interest through mediation, despite relators' objections.

We conditionally grant the petition for writ of mandamus, and order Judge Lindsay to vacate those portions of her order of October 18, 1991, that require the parties to participate in mediation proceedings in good faith with the intention of settling.

GRAHAM v. BAKER

Supreme Court of Iowa, 1989.
447 N.W.2d 397.

Debtors appealed from an order of the District Court, Warren County, Richard D. Morr, J., which granted creditors' writ of mandamus to force mediation service to issue release.

* * *

Iowa Code section 654A.6 (1987) requires a creditor to request mediation and obtain a mediation release before undertaking forfeiture proceedings. . . .

At that session, Flagg refused to cooperate with the mediator, denying the Henrys any opportunity to put forward their proposals for resolving the situation, and demanding that he be given a mediation release. It was clear that Flagg was hostile to the Henrys, the mediator, and the mediation process. . . .

* * *

Basing its decision on Flagg's behavior, the mediation service refused to issue the Grahams a release, granting instead an extra thirty days to attempt mediation. . . .

* * *

The core of the Henrys' appeal presents us with the question of whether Flagg's behavior at the mediation proceeding constitutes "participation" as that term is intended by the statute. Iowa Code § 654A.11(3). Our review is de novo. . . .

* * *

The single requirement is that the creditor "participate" in one mediation session. Iowa Code § 654A.11(3) (1987).

The word "participate" means "to take part in something (as an enterprise or activity) usu[ally] in common with others." Webster's Third International Dictionary. Participation "means to take part in, to receive or have a part in an activity." Burrell v. Ford Motor Co., 386 Mich. 486, 192 N.W.2d 207, 211 (1971).

The word "participating" has no clear and unmistakable meaning. In its primary sense, it means simply a sharing or taking part with others but when it is applied to a particular situation, it takes on secondary implications that render it ambiguous. Under some circumstances it may denote a mere passive sharing while under other circumstances an implication of active engagement may accompany its use.

Fireman's Fund Indem. Co. v. Hudson Associates, Inc., 91 A.2d 454, 455, 97 N.H. 434 (1952). Given Flagg's attitude during the session, the mediator urged his supervisors not to issue a release, basing his recommendation upon standards for gauging participation formulated by the mediation service itself. His supervisors concurred and no release was issued. By so doing, however, the mediation service arrogated to itself a discretionary function not granted by the statute.... Flagg attended the mediation session as required, and participated to the extent of stating that his position was not negotiable.

The statute does not give the mediation service the power to compel either creditor or debtor to negotiate. It merely attempts to set up conditions in which the parties might find a solution to their problems short of forfeiture or foreclosure....

We find that Flagg's presence at the mediation meeting satisfied the minimal participation required by the statute.

However, there are statutes and case law to the contrary.

Me.Rev.Stat.Ann. (West 1993).

§ 665. Court authority to order mediation

The court may, in any case under this subchapter, at any time refer the parties to mediation on any issues. Any agreement reached by the parties through mediation on any issues shall be reduced to writing, signed by the parties and presented to the court for approval as a court order. When agreement through mediation is not reached on any issue, the court must determine that the parties made a good faith effort to mediate the issue before proceeding with a hearing. If the court finds that either party failed to make a good faith effort to mediate, the court may order the parties to submit to mediation, may dismiss the action or any part of the action, may render a decision or judgment by default, may assess attorney's fees and costs or may impose any other sanction that is appropriate in the circumstances. The court may also impose an appropriate sanction upon a party's failure without good cause to appear for mediation after receiving notice of the scheduled time for mediation.

1983, c. 813, § 4; 1985, c. 396, § 3.

LARRY R. OBERMOLLER v. FEDERAL LAND BANK OF SAINT PAUL
Court of Appeals of Minnesota, 1987.
409 N.W.2d 229.

The trial court denied the application of appellants Larry and Connie Obermoller for a temporary injunction to halt the foreclosure sale of their farm. Appellants argue that the trial court abused its discretion and that they should be allowed to set aside their homestead for a separate sale. Respondent has moved to dismiss the appeal on the grounds of mootness. We address the merits and affirm.

FACTS

Respondent, the Federal Land Bank of Saint Paul, held a mortgage on certain farm land owned by appellants. On February 22, 1986, respondent published notice of a foreclosure sale of this land, to be held April 23, 1986. On March 22, 1986, the Minnesota Farmer–Lender Mediation Act, Minn.Stat. §§ 583.20–.32 (1986), became effective. Appellants attempted to take advantage of this new law by filing a debtor mediation request on April 16, 1986.

Respondent, however, proceeded with the April 23 foreclosure sale on the assumption that the legislation did not apply to proceedings commenced before its enactment. Despite this sale, respondent also participated in mediation in June and July of 1986. In July 1986, this court issued its opinion in Laue v. Production Credit Association, 390 N.W.2d 823 (Minn.Ct.App.1986), holding the farmer-lender mediation act applied even where foreclosure proceedings were already pending on the date the act became effective. Respondent continued to mediate, but also maintained the position that the retroactivity issue was on appeal to the Minnesota Supreme Court and, if Laue was reversed, the April 23 foreclosure sale would be valid.

Appellants and respondent were unsuccessful in mediating a settlement and on September 17, 1986, respondent filed notice of a second mortgage foreclosure sale. This sale was to be held November 25, 1986. On November 12, 1986, appellants served a summons and complaint on respondent, seeking to have both the April foreclosure sale and the upcoming November foreclosure sale declared invalid because respondent had not negotiated in good faith and had not given the requisite notice of mediation rights under Minn.Stat. § 581.05. Appellants also requested damages in excess of $50,000.

* * *

In the present case the trial court refused to issue the temporary injunction primarily because of its assessment that appellants had failed to show bad faith and therefore were unlikely to prevail on the merits in their underlying action which was also based on respondent's bad faith in mediation. Minn.Stat. § 583.27, subd. 1 provides:

> The parties must engage in mediation in good faith. Not participating in good faith includes: (1) a failure on a regular or continuing basis to attend and participate in mediation sessions without cause; (2) failure to provide full information regarding the financial obligations of the parties and other creditors; (3) failure of the creditor to designate a representative to participate in the mediation with authority to make binding commitments within one business day to fully settle, compromise, or otherwise mediate the matter; (4) lack of a written statement of debt restructuring alternatives and a statement of reasons why alternatives are unacceptable to one of the parties; (5) failure of a creditor to release funds

from the sale of farm products to the debtor for necessary living and farm operating expenses; or (6) other similar behavior which evidences lack of good faith by the party. A failure to agree to reduce, restructure, refinance, or forgive debt does not, in itself, evidence lack of good faith by the creditor.

Minn.Stat. § 583.27, subd. 2, sets out a procedure for a mediator to report a party's lack of good faith in mediation by filing an affidavit with the director and the parties. In its accompanying memorandum, the trial court emphasized that the mediator had not filed an affidavit. As the trial court noted, mediation proceedings are unrecorded, and therefore without such an affidavit a determination of bad faith is very difficult.

Appellants claim, however, that an affidavit from the mediator is not necessary to prove their claim of bad faith because there are several aspects of respondent's conduct that prove the claim. First, appellants point to the fact that throughout mediation respondent continued to assert that if the supreme court reversed this court and determined that the mediation laws did not apply where debt enforcement proceedings had already been commenced, the April foreclosure sale would be valid. However, respondent did not use this argument to refuse to enter into mediation but only refused to waive the issue. Maintaining alternative legal positions is not unusual, especially in a case such as this where the law is in flux. Under the circumstances, respondent's approach does not necessarily evidence bad faith.

Appellants also argue that respondent's bad faith was shown because respondent believed it did not have to negotiate, could just wait out the mediation period and then foreclose. What respondent actually asserted at the hearing was that its physical presence was not even required at the mediation sessions and that by being present it had gone beyond what was required. Respondent's assertion is supported by Minn.Stat. § 583.28, subd. 1 (1986), which addresses instances when creditors need not attend mediation sessions. That section provides:

A creditor that is notified of the initial mediation meeting is subject to and bound by a mediation agreement if the creditor does not attend mediation meetings unless the creditor files a claim form. In lieu of attending a mediation meeting, a creditor may file a notice of claim and proof of claim on a claim form with the mediator before the scheduled meeting. By filing a claim form the creditor agrees to be bound by a mediation agreement reached at the mediation meeting unless an objection is filed within the time specified. The mediator must notify the creditors who have filed claim forms of the terms of any agreement.

Respondent's stated positions regarding mediation are not sufficient to demonstrate that the trial court clearly abused its discretion in denying appellants' application for a temporary injunction.

Appellants also challenge the fact that respondent never served a mediation notice on the debtor and the director as required under

Minn.Stat. § 583.26, subd. 1. However, appellants themselves requested mediation under Minn.Stat. § 583.26, subd. 2(c) which provides:

(c) If a debtor has not received a mediation notice and is subject to a proceeding of a creditor enforcing a debt against agricultural property under chapter 580 or 581 * * *, the debtor may file a mediation request with the director. The mediation request form must indicate that the debtor has not received a mediation notice.

The farmer-lender mediation act does not impose a penalty when a creditor fails to serve a mediation notice. In the present case mediation did occur. While respondent did not follow the creditor notice provision of section 583.26, subd. 1, we can discern no prejudice to appellants that would justify granting a temporary injunction to halt the foreclosure sale.

* * *

IN RE STONE
United States Court of Appeals, Fifth Circuit, 1993.
986 F.2d 898.

We are able to conclude, based upon the foregoing, that, subject to the abuse-of-discretion standard, district courts have the general inherent power to require a party to have a representative with full settlement authority present—or at least reasonably and promptly accessible—at pretrial conferences. This applies to the government as well as private litigants. We find no statute or rule that attempts to regulate the court's use of that inherent power. But a district court must consider the unique position of the government as a litigant in determining whether to exercise its discretion in favor of issuing such an order.

* * *

This court, as well, has recognized that the government sometimes must be treated differently. Obviously, high-ranking officials of cabinet agencies could never do their jobs if they could be subpoenaed for every case involving their agency. . . .

In determining whether to require the government (or, for that matter, a private party) to send a representative to a pretrial conference with full authority to settle, a district court should take a practical approach. The court must be permitted to conduct its business in a reasonably efficient manner; it need not allow the parties or counsel to waste valuable judicial resources unnecessarily. On the other hand, the court should recognize that parties have a host of problems beyond the immediate case that is set for pretrial conference. This is particularly true of the government. We have outlined above, in some detail, the peculiar position of the Attorney General and the special problems the Department of Justice faces in handling the government's ever-increasing volume of litigation.

We conclude that the district court abused its discretion in routinely requiring a representative of the government with ultimate settlement authority to be present at all pretrial or settlement conferences. We do not suggest that the district court can never issue such an order, but it should consider less drastic steps before doing so.

b. Cost Considerations

There are a number of issues which surround a court's authority to make referrals which increase costs to the parties who are participating in a public justice system. A primary issue is whether the court can *require* parties availing themselves of a public service to incur additional cost. Because of the courts' sensitivity to the issue of paid mediators and the availability of nonprofit dispute resolution providers, such as dispute resolution centers, there has been little actual litigation surrounding this issue. Looking at the issue in the arbitration process can provide some guidance. When courts were faced with objections to arbitration based upon the additional costs to the parties and attendant constitutional challenges, most resolved the matter in favor of the use of alternatives.[27]

Controversy about fees among providers is significant. For example, a litigant in either Harris or Travis County, Texas, who wishes to file a lawsuit must pay an additional ten dollar sum as part of the filing fee. This ten dollar "surcharge" constitutes the ADR fund for the county.[28] Some then argue that litigants should not have to pay again for a private mediation. A number of lawyers are now making a living mediating court referred cases [29] and want to restrict these litigant-funded centers to providing services for indigent individuals only.

Expenses associated with the mediation process include more than just the cost of the mediator. Penalties or sanctions for non-compliance with a mediation order are possible, albeit remote. Fees for attorney time spent in preparation for, and attendance at, the mediation are additional cost factors. A few of these matters have been raised in court proceedings, and many are discussed regularly by the mediation and legal communities.

c. Voluntary Participation

Parties involved in litigation may voluntarily participate in mediation at any time during the pendency of the lawsuit. Factors which indicate why parties would be willing to do so have been previously enumerated. However, difficulties may arise when one party advocates mediation for a "wrong" reason, such as a disguised opportunity for unstructured discovery. In the instances where the case originally goes to mediation for the wrong reasons, but nonetheless is settled, it is likely that no harm results. However, in those cases where a request, and agreement by the other side, for mediation is made, due to fraudulent reasons, things become more complicated. This situation has not been

27. For detail, see Rogers & McEwan, supra note 1, § 5.5.

28. Tex.Civ.Prac. & Rem.Code Ann. § 152.001 (Vernon Supp. 1993).

29. See Louis J. Weber, *Court–Referred ADR and the Lawyer–Mediator: In Service of Whom*, 46 SMU L. Rev. 2113 (1993).

addressed by the courts. But without an agreement or court order requiring good faith participation, it does not appear that sanctions are available, particularly where there existed an apparent agreement to utilize the mediation process.

C. ISSUES OF TIMING: THE LIFE OF A DISPUTE

While issues of timing, or when to use ADR, are often discussed and debated, there is still little certainty. What is certain is that ADR use, regardless of the time of its intervention in a matter, usually results in a positive outcome. This has been confirmed by both hard or empirical data, as well as soft or commentary information.[30] Although a positive outcome does not necessarily mean a complete final agreement, it does mean that the parties are pleased and satisfied with the process. In other words, there have been demonstrated benefits from ADR use, regardless of the timing. One interpretation is that there is no "wrong" time. Nonetheless, factors to consider when contemplating mediation merit examination.

Many have written of the nature of conflict and disputing, including the premise that "conflict lives". Conflict progresses through relatively predictable stages. Although the stages are distinct and recognizable, the timing or occurrence of each differs in each dispute. Many factors contribute to these differences. In the majority of cases, the parties begin with a recognition that a problem, disagreement, or dispute exists. If an immediate answer or resolution is not attained, the conflict escalates. In fact, the path of conflict has been likened to a snowball rolling downhill. As conflict continues, size and intensity increase. If stopped early, the growth is halted. Premised upon this theory, the sooner a matter is resolved, the better.

Sometimes however, conflict dissipates on its own accord. The intensity of the dispute decreases. Time has intervened, and perhaps the subject of the conflict no longer holds the importance it once did. With time as an intervenor, the parties are better able to rationally examine the matter and work together to find a resolution. It is these two competing theories which contribute to the difficulty of prescribing the best time for mediation.

1. PRE-LITIGATION MATTERS

In those cases where there is an ongoing relationship, whether personal or professional, a conflict or dispute can do harm. If time and energy is devoted to the dispute in a negative or destructive manner, people become more locked into their positions and close their minds to options. Thus in most cases, the sooner the conflict is resolved, the more positive the impact on the relationship. This is especially impor-

---

30. While there is no specific study to establish this, the author reaches this conclusion after numerous discussions with a number of program directors throughout the United States, particularly those in court-annexed programs.

tant when the parties have regular communication or interaction, such as working with each other or living in the same neighborhood.

Therefore, once individuals or entities realize that they are involved in a conflict, attempts at resolution through mediation are appropriate. Moreover, mediation is usually recommended prior to seeking legal assistance. In most cases little harm can result from mediation, even if no settlement is reached. The parties will still have all other options open to them. The only situation where it may be advisable to not adhere to the policy of "the sooner, the better" is where there is such hostility between the parties that any discussion would likely result in physical confrontation. Here, a "cooling off" period is needed.

2. LEGAL DISPUTES

By this phrase, it is meant that lawyers have become involved in representing the parties to a dispute. Of course, the sooner ADR intervention occurs, the greater the amount of monetary savings. These savings can be seen in a number of ways. One direct cost of a legal dispute is attorneys' fees. Another is management cost. In many businesses, time must be spent by key personnel dealing with the dispute. This is time away from managerial roles. Disputing may also cost a company in terms of its employee's productivity. Indirect costs to individuals include emotional costs expended not only in disputing but also in the court process.

Before everyone has become committed to full use of the legal system may be the time to look for creative options. Yet there is some debate about whether it is more conducive to a "better" resolution to attempt to resolve a legal dispute at an early stage. On one hand, if ADR treatment occurs very early, the individuals may still be hostile, and thus unwilling to negotiate. Alternatively, the longer the wait for mediation, the greater the possibility of the parties becoming entrenched in their positions and unmovable. Clearly, each case varies.

When individuals first go to a lawyer, resolution by way of negotiated settlement is not usually one of the options anticipated. Yet, in many instances that is precisely when mediation is appropriate. This is even more true when the parties or entities involved have an on-going relationship—particularly one which depends upon direct communication. Examples include disputes between business partners, construction contracts, and franchise agreements.

After a lawsuit is filed and the defendant has been served, there is usually a period of distrust and hostility between the parties, and sometimes even the attorneys. As the case progresses this may decrease or increase. Through an exchange of information, the parties and their attorneys begin negotiating. If a settlement is not reached, but negotiations have commenced, it is clearly an appropriate time to participate in mediation.

In some matters, the attorneys will allege that discovery is necessary before the case can go to mediation. This may be true. Alternatively, the discovery process may cause the dispute to escalate, especially between the attorneys, which in turn escalates costs. Because mediation has proven to be effective in all these instances, even if discovery is necessary, it may be possible for the participants to informally exchange information prior to the mediation. Moreover, several recent statutes have been enacted which toll the running of discovery deadlines or statutes of limitations. By the time most cases are set for trial, the conflict has decreased and a negotiated resolution is eventually reached. However, costs have been expended, and in some cases the costs are greater than the amount in controversy. Yet mediation has been successfully used even at the time of trial, particularly in those instances where the trial would have taken more than a day or two.

D. THE ROLE OF THE ATTORNEY–ADVOCATE IN THE REFERRAL PROCESS

Issues which surround the attorney's potential duty to advise the client about ADR have just begun to be recognized. Currently there are a few states' supreme courts which strongly recommend, by way of professionalism mandates, that attorneys inform clients of alternative forums for dispute resolution.[31] The subject of the lawyer's duty with regard to ADR has been the subject of a spirited debate.[32] Some clients may be aware of ADR and request it themselves. In some jurisdictions, courts are responsible for an ADR intervention. For instance, the judge may require ADR before setting the case for trial.[33] In other courts, local rules provide that by the time the case has been pending for a certain period, the parties must have participated in an ADR process. However, in the majority of cases, it is still going to be the attorney's role to suggest and discuss the possibility of ADR treatment with her client. In fact, some have argued that the failure to do so constitutes legal malpractice.[34]

The correct time for the attorney to discuss mediation touches upon many of the issues previously discussed. The client may have contacted the attorney because he is ready to fight, not settle. The client may think the suggestion of mediation or settlement is an indication of the attorney's lack of confidence in the case, and become defensive. However, the attorney-counselor must remember that all options for disposition of a case should be discussed with the client.[35] While the initial interview may not be the right time, allowing the client to incur sizeable

---

31. These include *Texas* and *Colorado*.

32. See Frank E.A. Sander & Michael L. Prigoff, *Should There Be a Duty to Advise of ADR Options*, 76 A.B.A.J. 50 (1990).

33. This is known as the carrot approach, where the court induces a party to participate by providing a reward (an early trial setting) for participation.

34. Robert F. Cochran, *Legal Representation and the Next Steps Toward Client*

Control: Attorney Malpractice for the Failure to Allow the Client to Control Negotiation and Pursue Alternatives to Litigation, 47 Wash. & Lee L. Rev. 819 (1990).

35. Id. at 830. See also Mark Spiegal, *Lawyering and Client Decisionmaking: Informed Consent and the Legal Profession* 128 U. Pa. L. Rev. 41 (1979).

legal fees before suggesting mediation is not the best option either. Each case and each client is different. The various factors about each should be considered by the attorney and discussed with the client. The timing of these discussions with the client may be as important as the timing of actual mediation participation, particularly in terms of the client's attitude toward the process.

E. SELECTION OF THE MEDIATOR

A discussion of the most appropriate mediator for each situation can be interesting and educational, at least for some. However, as a practical matter, much of the decision regarding mediator selection will turn on the nature of the mediation community in each jurisdiction. A brief exploration of these considerations follows.

1. MATCHING CASES AND MEDIATORS

Once case characteristics have been identified and prioritized resulting in the parties' referral or agreement to mediation, selection of the mediator is the next step. The process of matching case characteristics with mediator characteristics is not a scientific matter. Sometimes certain factors are obvious, indicating a need for a certain style of mediator. In other situations, the choice will not be as clear.

First and foremost, in many clients' thoughts anyway, is the cost of the mediator. Certainly the client's willingness and ability to pay, in light of the amount in controversy, is a primary consideration. At one end of the range of cost are those programs which offer volunteer mediators such as local dispute resolution centers (DRCs) and court-connected programs. Alternatively, the charge for private mediation service providers range from $100–$300 per hour to $1,500–$2,000 per day, per party or side. Because there is no regulation, the range is quite broad.

In technical or highly complex issues, employment of someone with particular expertise is needed; for example, in patent, engineering, and architectural areas where the discussion may turn on a very specific technical issue. Therefore, in those cases an examination of the mediators' backgrounds to determine if they have specific expertise is the first, and sometimes only, step taken.

In most lawsuits, previous legal experience of the mediator is considered. Some courts focus on attorney-mediators and assert that pending litigation should be mediated almost exclusively by them. However, many experts in the field, as well as some lawyers and clients, feel otherwise and, in fact, steer away from the lawyer-mediator, particularly when the dispute involves primarily non-legal matters.

Personality type is another mediator characteristic that crosses the mind of some litigants and lawyers. This is even more important when considering the personalities and relationship of the lawyers as well as the strengths or weaknesses of the personalities of the disputing parties.

Where the mediation table is surrounded by strong verbose attorneys and parties, the mediator must be able to control the situation. Yet, a mediator must also be able to be quiet, especially at those times when a relaxed approach is more effective.[36] A mediator who primarily allows open discussion will be helpful if parties and lawyers are sophisticated enough to conduct their own negotiation. On the other hand, where the parties are unsophisticated, emotional, or lack familiarity with the bargaining process, then a mediator who is more directive would be appropriate. The background and training of the mediator may also indicate his flexibility. Many mediators can vary styles depending on the matter in dispute and the personalities of the participants.

MEDEIROS v. HAWAII COUNTY PLANNING COMMISSION
Intermediate Court of Appeals of Hawaii, 1990.
8 Hawaii App. 183, 797 P.2d 59.

Property owners appealed from decision of the county planning commission approving permit for drilling of scientific observation holes in geothermal resource subzone established by Board of Land and Natural Resources....

The time constraints in the mediation process were in accord with the dictates of HRS § 205–5.1(e). However, Appellants argue that, although they were required to share the cost of mediation, they were not given a voice in the selection of the mediators. We do not believe it is essential to due process that Appellants participate in naming the mediator or mediators. Appellants' due process rights are protected so long as the selection process and the chosen mediator are unbiased. Appellants do not claim the mediators were biased or prejudiced and do not claim to have been prejudiced by the Commission's selection.

2. FINDING MEDIATORS

There are a number of methods for obtaining information about potential mediators. Several mediator organizations have lists of their members. Many incorporated private providers have brochures describing their services and backgrounds of the affiliated mediators. A number of courts, both state and federal have established approved ADR provider lists.

Many mediators advertise their services. In fact, in many jurisdictions mediators may be found in the yellow pages section of the telephone book. And, as with all service providers, word of mouth can be a helpful source of information about potential mediator selections. One state, Ohio, has published a Consumer's Guide to Selecting a Neutral. It's very likely other states or local mediation programs will produce similar publications.

36. An examination of the variety of mediator *styles* is included in Chapter 15, infra.

Looking for a good mediator is probably much like looking for or finding a good lawyer, a good accountant, doctor or any other professional. Much depends on the specifics of the case, including the people and personalities involved. However, there are some distinct factors about a lawsuit or a dispute that attorneys and their clients may consider when looking for a mediator.

QUESTIONS FOR DISCUSSION

4–1. Since a primary basis for the use of mediation is saving money and time, how is this goal met where the court makes a referral to a private mediator who charges a substantial fee?

4–2. A California resident faced with a custody or visitation issue absolutely refuses to go to mediation. What would you advise? See Trina Grillo, *The Mediation Alternative: Process Dangers for Women*, 100 Yale L.J. 1545 (1991).

4–3. Ruth Suttle sued her employer, Power Driver Tools, for alleged acts of sexual harassment by her immediate supervisor, Joe Caps. The case is pending in the federal district court for the Eastern District of Decree. This court has enacted rules which permit the court to order a case to ADR, including case evaluation, arbitration, and mediation. Defendant has filed its answer two months ago, and the parties are about to initiate the discovery process.

Plaintiff alleges that Power Driver Tools has a specific written policy against sexual harassment which the male supervisors have openly made fun of and "jokingly" violate. Power Driver's C.E.O., Matthew Principle, believes all sexual harassment claims are frivolous and has issued an edict that no such claims will be settled and all such cases shall be tried. Larry Werner, outside counsel in the Suttle case, has been contacted by Sam(antha) Carese, counsel for Ruth Suttle. Sam(antha) asked Larry about the possibility of referring the dispute to mediation, and suggested that mediation will save both sides great expense. It was hinted that Ruth might lower her demands if she had a chance to tell Matthew Principle what is going on at the factory.

Werner has contacted Matthew Principle about the mediation option. Principle's response was "tell them, hell, no."

Carese has, after consultation with Ruth filed a Motion to Refer to Mediation with the court, including a request that Matthew Principle be ordered, as the person with ultimate authority to settle, to attend the entire mediation.

When Principle was furnished a copy of the motion by Werner, Principle roared, "File whatever it takes to oppose this. This is America. No judge can force me to attend a mediation."

Principle has also advised Werner he wants to attend the hearing and "testify and give that civil rights lawyer a piece of my mind."

District Judge Timid Hand has routinely signed agreed orders to mediate. Judge Hand has never been confronted with an opposed motion to Refer.

(a) You are Carese. Prepare a Motion to Refer to Mediation, along with a Brief in support of your Motion. Be prepared for your Oral Argument on this issue.

(b) You are Werner. Prepare a Response to the Motion, along with a Bench Brief supporting your position. Do you take your client to the hearing? Explain.

(c) You are Judge Hand. Upon receipt of the Briefs and hearing the oral arguments of counsel, write your opinion.

Chapter Five

PREPARATION FOR THE MEDIATION

The events leading up to a mediation can have a significant effect on what happens during the session. The mediation process consists primarily of interpersonal communication, and, as such, is not only flexible but to a degree, spontaneous. Nonetheless, preparation for mediation is essential. All participants in the process, including the mediator, the parties and their representatives and, in some cases, constituents[1] of those at the table, must prepare for the session. The duration of the preparatory stage varies considerably. As the use of mediation increases, greater attention will be devoted to preliminary matters.

A. THE MEDIATOR

The mediator's preparation is frequently determined by the nature of the case and the method of its referral. In many cases, particularly where mediators serve on a pro bono basis, such as during a settlement week,[2] the mediator usually receives information about the case immediately before sitting down with the parties. In such instances, the mediator has little time to prepare for the specific case. Such fast track preparation also occurs at community based programs and dispute resolution centers. In both of the foregoing instances, the cases, regardless of their origin, are assigned to a specific mediator only when that mediator arrives at the center. Likewise, during settlement week or even in an ongoing court-annexed program, where the lawyers serve as volunteer, unpaid mediators, they usually know only the nature of the

---

1. In large cases such as those involving public policy, not all affected individuals will be present at the mediation.

2. Settlement week is a program, sometimes mandated by statute, in which a high volume of pending lawsuits are strongly urged to settle by use of ADR. The ADR method is usually mediation. The courthouse is dedicated to this endeavor during a one week period, such as a "dead week"

where the courthouse would otherwise be shut down. For elaboration on settlement weeks, see Harold Paddock, *Settlement Week: A Practical Manual for Resoluting Civil Cases Through Mediation* (1990) and James G. Woodward, *Settlement Week: Measuring the Promise*, 11 N. Ill. U.L.R. 1 (1990).

case prior to their arrival. These programs handle all pre-mediation details through a central administrative staff. Information is sent to, and received from, the parties without regard to the identity of the mediator. In some programs, the case is assigned to a specific mediator for the primary purpose of scheduling and completing a conflicts check.[3] Other information is rarely exchanged. The mediator is handed a case file or a summary of the case just minutes before beginning the mediation. In these instances, the preparation on the part of the mediator, of course, is minimal with regard to the specific case and facts. However, the mediator can prepare herself in a more global way in terms of being ready to listen carefully, analyze the case, remain neutral and provide an environment for creative problem solving.

When the mediator is engaged in private practice, the nature of the preparation can be dictated solely by the mediator. In essence, the mediator's preparation should consist of asking and answering two basic questions:

1. What do you, as the mediator, want the participants to know prior to sitting down at the mediation table?

2. What do you want to know about the case and the participants prior to beginning the mediation session?

An outlined response to these two questions provides the mediator the necessary steps she must follow in the preliminary stages.

Preparation is viewed as both mechanical and mental. Mechanical preparation involves logistics, housekeeping and administrative details. First and foremost, the mediator should arrange to have the session held in a neutral location. A neutral site is not the office of one of the parties or their counsel. In most cases, the neutral location will be the mediator's office. In some instances, because of the number of parties or because the mediator is not serving in her jurisdiction, the location will be a hotel room or other type of conference center. The mediator should be certain that there is sufficient room for the number of participants who will be attending, including additional rooms for break-out or separate caucuses.

Room decor is also an important part of the mediation session. Since many mediators already have private offices, this is pre-determined. However, as the mediation profession grows and individuals select offices with a primary focus on conducting mediations, additional attention will be given to the mediation environment. The way the room is arranged will affect the communication and behavior of the parties. For instance, most communication is directed across a table, rather than around it. Moreover, seats at an end of a table often indicate a leadership and task orientation, while a center position leads to a more participatory role. Therefore, the mediator should give

---

3. Issues surrounding potential conflicts of interest, particularly for the attorney me-   diator, are examined in Chapter 14, infra.

particular attention to the seating arrangements, especially in multi-party cases. Arrangements for items such as access to telephones as well as the necessities of food and beverages should also be handled by the mediator.[4]

Once the location is identified, the time for the mediation should be determined. Where courts are active in the referral process, the date is sometimes specifically set forth in the court's order. In most cases, however, these arrangements are left to the agreement of all participants and the mediator. Of course, if any of the participants is reluctant to attend, the entire scheduling process may require a mediation effort. Far more often, the mediator, by conference call herself or with the assistance of a coordinator, secretary, or administrative assistant, can work with the parties in hammering out these details.

One emerging problem for mediators in private practice is the cancellation or postponement of scheduled sessions. Most mediators, except those handling family cases, block out an entire day for a mediation. When cancellations occur, the mediator is left with down time and no income. When the session is postponed the income eventually is received, but the previously scheduled day remains open. A few mediators have responded by requiring a non-refundable deposit at the time the mediation is scheduled, while others have attempted to charge a cancellation fee. The policy with regard to cancellations should be addressed by the mediator at the time the mediation is arranged.

The amount of the mediator's fee should also be determined in advance. Private mediators' fees may vary significantly and are not currently subject to regulation. Most mediators charge either an hourly rate or a flat, per day fee.[5] The hourly rate is advocated by those who traditionally use this format, such as lawyers, accountants, and therapists. Such approach is quite simple and straightforward, although it should be clarified in advance whether pre-mediation preparation is included. Others believe that the participants will constantly think about the mediator being "on the clock"; in order to avoid additional cost, they will rush to a settlement that they may not be satisfied with. The effect of each alternative has not been researched, but so far there does not appear to be a clear preference for one over the other. Fee structure is a matter of personal choice for the mediator. Imperative is that the format, estimated amount, and billing practice[6] is clearly conveyed to all participants in advance. Most often the mediator or her coordinator or administrator will include administrative information in a letter to the participants.

This pre-mediation correspondence should also provide information about the mediation process as well as the mediator, herself. In many

4. For more detail about an appropriate mediation environment, see Eric R. Galton, Representing Clients in Mediation (1994).

5. A very limited number of mediators charge on a contingency fee basis. Most

codes of ethics are viewing this as a clear conflict of interest, and hence unethical.

6. That is, whether payment is expected in advance of the session or whether the bill will be sent subsequent to the mediation.

cases, where the participants or their representatives select the mediator in advance, relevant information in terms of education and training is already known. In cases of court appointment, participants may have been informed about the mediator by the court or other appointing entity. Even so, it may be helpful to include a brief curriculum vitae in the materials provided to the parties although a complete dissertation on one's life history is not necessary.

Just how much information the parties should receive and assimilate prior to the mediation is subject to debate. At one end of the scale are those who propose that very little education be provided. In other words, the less the parties know about what will happen at mediation, the better. Although not often articulated, these mediators presume that if the parties are completely familiar with the techniques and strategies that the mediator may utilize during the session, they may attempt to undermine her work. The theory is that the mediator is in control of the process and only she should know the intricacies of the process. It is presumed that most individuals go to a mediator because of her expertise and do not themselves want or expect to know everything about mediation. On the other hand, some believe that the more the participants know about the process in advance, the better. These mediators send the parties a very complete and detailed outline of the process including the component stages, along with possible modifications. Most mediators fall within the center of these two extremes. They want the participants to know something about the process and what will take place, but believe that a detailed study of it by the participants is not necessary or appropriate.

Mediation is the facilitation of negotiation; the participants will be negotiating, while the mediator facilitates. Therefore, most mediators conclude that it is important that the participants focus primarily on the negotiation process and prepare accordingly. Some mediators will briefly describe negotiation as they see it; others will send each side either a loaner or complimentary copy of *Getting to Yes* [7] prior to the mediation session. In many instances, a two to three page outline of the negotiation or mediation process is sent out by the mediator. This generally accompanies the letter which includes the administrative details. All other items that the mediator wants the participants to review should also be included in this packet of information. Examples include: a statement of disclosure of possible conflicts of interests; an agreement or contract to mediate; forms disclaiming mediator representation; waiver of potential mediator liability; confidentiality agreements; and evaluation forms.

In the correspondence that is sent to the participants, the mediator should include a request for the information that she wants prior to the mediation session. Therefore it is important that the mediator determine how much information she thinks is necessary to have in advance

7. Roger Fisher & William Ury, Getting to Yes (1981).

of the actual session. In making this determination, the mediator must keep in mind that she is not making a decision about either the facts or the law of the case. Consequently, it is not necessary to know and memorize in advance, each factor or legal argument that the parties might propose at the mediation. It is imperative, however, where a lawsuit is pending, that the mediator know the status of the case along with any pending motions or deadlines. In some instances, these case variables effect how the mediation is approached. The mediator must be sure the parties consider these factors when looking at settlement options. Moreover, any resolution reached at mediation should not be in conflict with a court order.

Much of the theory and philosophy of mediation is to move away from legalities, and identify the underlying issues and interests of the parties. Cases will be resolved by finding ways to satisfy those interests. When individuals set forth a legal position or written analysis of a problem, these underlying issues and interests are not stated. Parties usually first state their positions at an intake center [8] or by the filing of a lawsuit in a court. In either case, these statements are made in terms of the expected audience at that time. This is not the mediation audience. Therefore the mediator should be careful in reading this material. For similar reasons it is rarely advocated that the mediator look at all of the pleadings in the case. The goals to be achieved by pleadings differ dramatically from the goals of a mediation. The mediator does not serve as counsel or judge in the case, and therefore, should not review the pleadings from such a viewpoint.

Since it may expedite the session for the mediator to have some familiarity with the case, most mediators will ask the parties to provide a written overview of the case. These may be referred to as a summary memorandum or pre-mediation submission.[9] Most mediators request that the parties submit these documents at least 7 days prior to the session, although in reality if they are received a few days in advance, it is usually sufficient. Many mediators ask that each participant provide a memorandum, under separate cover which is not shared with the other parties. The mediator maintains the confidentiality of the contents. On the other hand, some mediators request that counsel exchange the documents as they would pleadings. In such cases, a provision for any confidential information may be made in a separate document. There is yet a third minority approach. Some mediators feel that the process might be expedited if the lawyers are able to draft a form of joint statement, much like a joint pre-trial order, with stipulations as to

8. Intake is the term utilized to describe the process by which a citizen involved in a dispute can be referred to mediation. Intake takes place at most community dispute resolution centers and court-annexed programs. A citizen meets with an intake specialist in a personal interview and an attempt to find the most appropriate door or avenue to resolve the dispute is made.

9. These are but two terms that have been used to describe these documents. There are numerous other ways to refer to written information that the mediator receives prior to the mediation session.

specific areas of agreement and disagreement. A fourth option is to request a combination of the foregoing documents.

In all cases the mediator should think through what type of information she is looking for and how much time should be spent in preparation for the session. For instance, in some cases the parties have sent the mediator video tapes. These can take hours to review. Since the mediator is not making a decision as to the outcome, elaborate pre-mediation submissions may not be necessary. The extent of detail in the submission may depend on the complexity of the case.

Pre-mediation submissions serve other functions in addition to educating the mediator. Mediation is a relatively new activity for lawyers, particularly litigators. The courthouse is familiar—the mediator's office is not. Preparation for court is common—for mediation it is not. Even in jurisdictions where court annexed mediation is common,[10] it is not uncommon to see lawyers arrive at the mediation session, never having looked at the file or discussed the case with the client. By requiring each party's representative, usually an attorney, to submit a written memorandum in advance of mediation, the case is at least reviewed. In those instances where the submission is exchanged, advance education of the opposing parties can occur. Information about the matter previously not disclosed is revealed which can be beneficial in opening discussions. As lawyers differ in their degree of preparedness for trial, likewise they differ vastly in how they prepare for mediation. It is up to the mediator to do what she can to encourage the participants to be prepared for the mediation and assist her in preparation as well.

The mediator must also identify who will be participating and, if at all possible, assure that everyone who is necessary for a binding decision be present at the mediation table.[11] How the mediator will deal with lawyers and their clients is also something that should be considered by the mediator in this preliminary stage. It is important that the lawyers and their clients know in advance what role each will play in the mediation. Some mediators allow the lawyers to basically control the process and dictate what role the client will have. Most mediators, however, know that it is important that the client participate, and in fact, subscribe to the belief that the case belongs to the parties and not the lawyers. Therefore, decision making with regard to settlement options should be left with the client.[12] Most clients know more about the subject matter of their dispute and are consequently in a much better position to evaluate alternatives. And, in some cases, the attor-

10. For example, both Florida and Texas courts refer thousands of cases a year to mediation.

11. This was discussed in Chapter 4, supra and is a very important element of the process. Getting all participants to the mediation table has been a very difficult part of mediation. Many mediators claim this is one of the primary reasons why mediations do not result in an agreement.

Any effort the mediator can make in this regard prior to the actual mediation hearing is strongly advised.

12. See Robert F. Cochran, *Legal Representation and the Next Steps Toward Client Control: Attorney Malpractice for the Failure to Allow the Client Control Negotiation and Pursue Alternatives to Litigation*, 47 Wash. & Lee L. Rev. 819, 854–862 (1990).

ney's interest is in conflict with that of the client.[13] In order to reach a final resolution it is extremely important for the parties to fully participate in the mediation. Hence, some mediators will request that the lawyers take a back seat (sometimes, literally, in that they move them away from the table). In other cases, however, clients are uneducated and lack negotiating skills. It is important that these individuals are represented at the mediation. The merits of each approach can be argued, and this author will leave each mediator to make her own decision. What is important however, is that these items are considered and determined in advance. And, whatever the decision, it is advised that, where attorneys are involved, the mediator inform them of what is expected at the session. In most court-annexed cases, direct participation in mediation has become a dual role. Mediators look for participation from both client and representative.

The specific nature of how the opening statement will proceed should also be conveyed to the participants. For example, the lawyer may speak first with subsequent comments by the client. In some cases, the client first presents the situation, followed by a legal analysis by the lawyer. In instances where the mediator expects the lawyers to take a very limited role, this information should also be conveyed in advance. In most cases, complete exclusion of the attorney or representative is not advised. However, consider the following.

§ 3182. Authority of mediators; exclusion of counsel; exclusion of domestic violence support person [14]

(a) The mediator has authority to exclude counsel from participation in the mediation proceedings pursuant to this chapter if, in the mediator's discretion, exclusion of counsel is appropriate or necessary.

(b) The mediator has authority to exclude a domestic violence support person from a mediation proceeding as provided in Section 6303.

————

The mediator is a neutral third party to a dispute, before, during and after the mediation. Throughout the mediator's preparation, and particularly while the mediator is reviewing the mediation submissions, she should avoid ex-parte telephone calls with any participant. Any telephonic communication should be done in a conference call format. This is to assure actual, as well as perceived, neutrality in the case.[15] Also, the mediator in her preparation should begin to identify possible areas of mutual concern or interest. As an objective party, these are much easier for the mediator to identify. Because mediation deals with

13. Id. at 854. See also Chapter 14, § B, infra which examines attorney-client conflicts in mediation in ethical terms.

14. West's Ann.Cal.Civ.Code § 3182 (1994).

15. *For details* on neutrality issues, see Chapter 7, infra.

human behavior, these interests are always subject to change. The mediator must maintain an open mind, and be careful to avoid making any prejudgments about the case.

Mediation is termed a dispute resolution alternative; thus, mediation is usually seen as a method to resolve a dispute or conflict. However, the mediation process can provide assistance in the negotiation of transactions. In these instances, the mediator's preparation will differ slightly. In the disputing context, a resolution is usually desired. Determining what it consists of constitutes much of the mediation, and options are wide open. In the transactional context, the parties are more focused. They are aware of the goal they wish to accomplish, e.g., a lease agreement or an employment contract. In these instances, it is helpful for the mediator to be familiar with the business endeavor of the parties. In preparation she will be much more focused on assessing vehicles through which the parties might reach their goal, rather than on what past events occurred.[16]

B. THE PARTIES AND THEIR ADVOCATES

Recognizing that mediation is a very new field and in a state of continuous change, it is not surprising that participants might differ in their approach to mediation or in their mediation strategy. However, in most lawsuits, a great deal of thought and attention is given to preparation for trial or other event which indicates final determination of a case, such as a hearing on summary judgment. Because in a large percentage of mediation cases settlement is reached,[17] this is the final stage of the matter. Therefore, the degree of preparation should be appropriately dedicated to it.

A strategic planning session should take place between the participant or decision-maker at the mediation and any representative who will be attending, including the lawyer. The lawyer should not be picking up the file as he runs to the mediation session, although this has been the case on more than one occasion. In a matter where the representative attending the mediation represents other interests, such as in a large public policy case or where there is a hierarchy of authority, then a meeting with all constituents should take place prior to the mediation. As part of preparation, a review of the factual dispute should be discussed and condensed, the manner of presentation should be outlined and then, of course, certain options or alternatives for settlement might be preliminarily identified. As the attorney[18] and client discuss prepara-

---

16. For more detail on the mediation of transactional matters, see Chapter 16, infra.

17. In pre-litigation as well as pending cases the national average indicates that about 80% of all cases that are mediated are settled at the time of the mediation.

18. In the majority of the cases, if participants have representation at a mediation, it is usually in the context of an attorney-advocate. That is not to say that other representatives, such as a financial consultants or supportive friends or relatives would not attend. However, for purposes of simplicity, the words representative and attorney will be used interchangeably.

tion for the mediation, goals and objectives, along with how to achieve them, should be included.

With regard to a presentation of the history of the dispute, participants should remember that no one is making a factual determination of right or wrong. One of the most important factors to remember from a participant's view is the difference between mediation and the courthouse. Unlike a trial where a determination based on the past is made, mediation is primarily future oriented. The focus is on how the matter will be resolved. This resolution will entail some action by the parties which will take place in the future. However, that is not to say that some attention to the past is not given, particularly in the first part of the mediation. This usually occurs in each side's opening statements.

Another difference which participants should be keenly aware of is the identity of the decision-maker. Unlike trial or arbitration where the decision-maker is the neutral party, in mediation it is not the mediator who is the decision-maker, but rather the other side. If persuasion or advocacy is to take place, it should take place across the table. It is important therefore that all decision-makers be present and listen to each other as each side presents an opening statement. Another significant part of planning or preparation is to decide who will make the opening statement: the party him or herself, the advocate representative or a combination. It is important to remember that it is the parties who own the dispute. It does not belong to the attorneys and certainly not the mediator; therefore, the parties must participate in the process. Much of the philosophical basis of mediation surrounds the concepts of self-determination and empowerment. Even in the event of active representation, the party to the dispute must be given an opportunity to be heard.

Most mediations provide time for an uninterrupted opening statement by each side, and this should be prepared by the participants in advance. While not scripted in detail, it should at least be outlined and its duration kept reasonable. Most mediators do not put time limits on the opening statements, but less than an hour seems appropriate in most instances. This can be modified, of course, where there are a large number of parties or in very complex cases.

The use of any other documentation such as charts, graphs, or video tapes should be considered in advance. A determination should be made as to whether these are to be used in the session as part of the opening statement or in a later segment. The mediator should be advised so that proper equipment such as an overhead projector or VCR and monitor are available.

As part of preparation for the mediation, the parties may also want to determine what, in fact, are their underlying interests and issues. What are the ultimate goals of the case? Is it money or perhaps are there non-monetary needs, interests and wants here? How might these goals and objectives be specifically achieved? It is important to be cautious here. From the mediator's standpoint she does not want to encourage the participants to come into a mediation with their minds made up—even within a range of settlement. This would severely limit the possibilities for alternatives. On the other hand, the mediator would like some thought to be given to options so that the participants have some idea of the direction in which the mediation might go. The participants should be encouraged to engage in a preliminary discussion of options. However, since mediation is premised on flexibility, listening to the other side, and options generated during the session, it would be helpful to remind parties to maintain an open mind.

Moreover, another overlooked, but important part of preparation for the participants is to consider the goals, objectives and interests of the other side. While most disputing parties hope to go to mediation and obtain the best they can for themselves, the process is premised upon give and take; and without that exchange, no progress will be made. Any time there is a give and take situation, that is, a negotiation, both sides must be motivated. Therefore, in the preparatory stages some thought should be given to the possible interests and objectives of the opposing side. The party and advocate on one side should be at least thinking about what the other side may really desire while avoiding a hard and fast decision prior to the mediation session. If possible, areas of mutual interest should also be identified. Likewise, in cases where the primary focus is on a monetary settlement, it is important to have a basic idea of a range of settlement, keeping in mind that all of the information has not been exchanged.

This leads to probably the most important aspect of mediation preparation from the standpoint of the parties and their advocates or representatives: to be prepared to listen. While it is inherent in the process that participants attend a mediation to express their views, it is also important that they listen to other views expressed at the table. It is only by the exchange of information that all parties are able to determine exactly what the main issues and interests are. Information exchange will also assist a great deal in identifying areas of mutual interest. Assuming the parties, their representatives and the mediator show up at the previously designated time and place, they are ready to begin the mediation session.[19]

QUESTIONS FOR DISCUSSION

5–1. You are preparing to mediate a dispute over a sales contract between parties who have been doing business together for over four years. One individual is the manager of a restaurant, and the other the owner of a small, but highly reputable fresh fruit and vegetable wholesale supply company. The dispute centers around alleged inaccurate deliveries, in terms of time and content. Although suit has not been filed, the attorneys for both parties will be attending the mediation. You

19. For a more detailed approach to the attorney-advocate, and to client preparation for mediation, see Galton, supra note 4.

have arranged your conference room so that the clients are closest to you. It is part of your strategy to engage them in a dialogue. As the parties enter, before you can direct them to the seats, the attorneys take over, sit at the head of the table closest to you and direct their clients to take a back seat. What do you do?

5–2. West's Ann.Cal.Civ.Code § 3182 clearly allows exclusion of the lawyer from the mediation. How might this impact the attorney-client relationship? In the case where the mediator excludes an attorney during the session, what effect will this have on the mediation?

5–3. Some mediators arrange the chairs around a conference table and allow all participants to pick their own place at the table, feeling that parties will sit where they are most comfortable. Comment on this approach.

5–4. You are the mediator in a medical negligence case. One participant, the Hospital Administrator (Defendant) arrives at the mediation with her attorney. Both appear to be fully prepared for the mediation. In fact, you received a twenty page bound mediation notebook as a pre-mediation submission from the attorney's office three days ago. The notebook contained both a summary of discovery as well as cites and copies of the alleged controlling cases. The plaintiff, a relatively uneducated dock worker, arrives at the mediation with a lawyer he just hired two days ago. You are told by the new lawyer that the previous lawyer withdrew from the case due to a change of employment. It appears that plaintiff's counsel is completely unfamiliar with the case. This was confirmed when, on the way into the mediation, plaintiff's counsel, within hearing of plaintiff, states in a joking manner that he hopes you will let him know what the case is about. The matter was referred to mediation and scheduled on the specific date by the court. What are your options? Which course of action would you choose, and why?

5–5. An agreement to mediate is essentially a mediation contract. What should be included in the contract? By whom should it be signed?

5–6. The Bargaining Bank

On January 2, 1992, the Bank of Alpha, located in Alphaberg, Pennsylvania, loaned the Harris Company, a Pennsylvania Partnership, $8 million. The loan was secured by a Deed of Trust on 100 acres of raw land owned free and clear by the limited partnership. The personal guaranty of two of the limited partners, Theodore Deltak and Catherine Zeff also secured the loan. Each spouse, Georgette Deltak and Harvy Zeff were also required to sign the guaranty.

On or about June 1, 1993, the required principal and interest payments, of approximately $65,000.00/month were in default. The Bank sent a notice of default to the Harris Company along with notices to each of the four guarantors. Notice of acceleration in accordance with the loan provisions was included.

Simultaneously, in June 1993, the Bank entered into discussions with the Deltaks and the Zeffs regarding a potential restructure of the loan. After several weeks of negotiation, the bank obtained approval from its loan committee to extend an additional $1.5 million loan, and take as additional collateral, deed of trust notes on the residences of the Deltaks and the Zeffs.

The restructured loan included scheduled draws over a two year period for construction of a residential development. During negotiations, the Harris Company submitted a budget to the bank. Loan documents evidencing the restructure agreement were prepared and included a provision which required the borrowers to comply with the budget and schedule as a condition of the loan.

After five months the borrowers cease to comply with the budget. The bank subsequently filed a lawsuit seeking, among other things, foreclosure on the residences. The borrowers responded with a counter claim of "lender liability" alleging "bad faith" on the part of the Bank. The borrowers claim that during the period of the restructuring negotiations, they passed up an opportunity to obtain financing from another bank, because an executive at Alpha Bank represented that the budget was only a "formality", and that the bank would be flexible and work with the borrowers to prevent default. The borrowers further maintain that since their spouses, Georgette and Harvy, had no involvement in the Harris company, the bank violated federal regulations in seeking and requiring the spouses' guarantees.

Two weeks after the suits are filed, lawyers for Alpha Bank and the Deltaks and Zeffs request that you mediate this dispute. In preparation for the mediation, which is scheduled in 10 days, decide the following:

(a) What information do you want, and how will you obtain it?

(b) Who should be present at the mediation?

(c) What will you ask the parties to supply you with?

(d) What information, if any, will you provide to the parties?

Chapter Six

BEGINNING THE MEDIATION

The mediation session may be the first time that all participants in a dispute, including decision-makers, their attorneys and representatives are gathered together at the same time and place. This is particularly true in matters involving a pending lawsuit. The mediator's handling of this initial meeting can greatly impact the remainder of the session. In most instances, the parties, after being greeted in the reception area, will be brought together in a joint meeting room where the mediator will begin his introductory remarks. There may, however, be situations which require deviation. Like most aspects of the mediation process, there are exceptions to the general rule.

For example, if the mediator has any advance information which indicates a potential volatile situation should the parties come into direct contact with one another, he may alter the structure of the session. In this case the mediator should make certain that the receptionist or individual responsible for greeting everyone is aware of the problem, and that the parties are initially kept separate. While this may occur in a very small number of cases, if handled incorrectly, the mediation can be doomed before it begins.

A. THE MEDIATOR'S INTRODUCTION

The mediator's introduction establishes the tone and tenor of the entire mediation session. The introduction is the primary vehicle through which the mediator begins to build trust with the participants. Trust must be established if the participants are to share information, remain open to discussion and allow the mediator to facilitate the negotiation. Although the use of mediation has increased dramatically, the mediator can still safely assume that in the majority of cases, mediation will be a new experience for the participants. This is particularly true for the parties, often involved in their first lawsuit. Therefore, while the introduction may become "old hat" for an experienced mediator, he should still give some thought and preparation to it in each case. The introductory remarks should be very familiar to the mediator; yet, they should not be so over rehearsed that the delivery results in a speech-like monotone. In fact, experienced mediators must be careful not to become so bored with the introduction that it becomes rushed and adequate time is not given to it.

The specific style of the mediator's introduction may vary a great deal. In family or other types of cases where emotional issues are paramount, an emphasis on relaxing and building trust with the parties is appropriate. In other cases, such as a construction matter, a more direct, businesslike tone may be used. Where conflict is overt, the mediator must exert control over the session and will establish it during his introductory remarks. However, the mediator's introduction should more closely resemble a conversation than a legal proceeding. The mediator can set the stage for the session by exhibiting an enthusiastic, positive, and encouraging attitude. The mediator's introduction serves a number of purposes. Likewise, the introduction should include specific items, although it can be modified in content, depending on a number of case variables.

1. PURPOSE

In general, the purpose of the mediator's introduction is to inform the participants about what is going to happen. Many people, having arrived at the mediation table for the first time, are nervous, apprehensive, and unsure of what to expect. Even though the mediator may have sent detailed information to the parties and their representatives in advance of the mediation, there is no guarantee that it has been read. Even in those cases where the information is reviewed, it may not be fully understood. Upon arrival at the place of the mediation, a sense of trepidation may come over the parties. The mediator can use this introductory time to provide the parties time to relax and feel more at ease with the surroundings, the mediator and the process.

This is also the time during which the mediator can set the tone, and let the participants know that he is in control of the mediation process. The mediator also begins to build trust with all the participants. The mediator simultaneously establishes his credibility and demonstrates knowledge of the process. In terms of credibility, the mediator may provide the participants some information about his background, training, and previous experience. This is not the time, of course, for the mediator to go into great detail about the heritage of his great-grandparents; however, the mediator should at least let the parties know that he knows a little bit about the process.[1]

The mediator's introduction informs the participants about why they are at mediation, and how, in general, the session will proceed. This provides them at least some idea of what to expect. The mediator should not be too specific, so that room for flexibility and modification

1. Of course, background and experience may be a difficult subject for the novice mediator. The novice mediator might want to discuss any particular expertise that he may have with regard to either the content matter of the case or experience in another area that may add to his credibility. In cases where none exists, then the mediator may merely say that he is a trained mediator.

remains. The mediator's introduction also serves as the vehicle through which rules of the procedure are introduced. These include how the parties will proceed to discuss their case. Any ground rules should be established during the introduction. Providing general introductory remarks also allows the mediator time to size up the participants. It is anticipated that during this introduction all parties at the table will begin to feel more comfortable with one another. As the mediator describes the process and its purposes, a positive atmosphere may be created, where, ideally, all participants acknowledge the benefits of a collaborative approach to problem solving.

2. CONTENT

The very first item that should be included in the mediator's introduction is a complete introduction of all the parties sitting around the table, including the mediator himself. In most instances, the mediator will ask the parties and representatives to introduce themselves, identify with whom they are affiliated and confirm that they have the adequate authority to settle the matter. Any potential conflicts [2] which have been identified and disclosed should be restated, along with everyone's agreement to participate. Any documents, such as agreements to mediate, disclaimers of legal representation, or confidentiality agreements should be finalized at this time, if not before.

The mediator should then spend some time discussing the mediation process. Even though some background information may have been given to the participants by the mediator, court or administrative agency, the mediator cannot be sure that it was completely read or understood. Therefore, discussion of the mediation process, and in particular its purpose, should be included so that the parties have a better understanding of the nature of the proceeding. Also a general discussion of the benefits of the mediation process should be included in the introductory remarks. While this is not the ideal time to "sell" the process, some individuals may still be reluctant to participate. The mediator's role, in part, is to motivate the parties in the direction of a satisfactory resolution. During the introduction, the mediator can begin to positively reinforce their attendance at the mediation, and ideally their open-mindedness and determination to proceed with the process. Obtaining an affirmative commitment from the parties to listen to each other, and explore a variety of options for settlement, can be of great assistance in establishing a positive tone which will further the mediation. In this manner the mediator can also begin to elicit cooperation of all of the parties.

Once the mediator describes the process, he should move into a discussion of his role in it. This will clarify for the parties exactly what he will do. Some mediators choose to do this in terms of what the mediator is not, such as a judge, jury or fact finder. Others choose to describe the role in terms of the mediator's action in the session, such as

2. See Chapter 14, infra for a discussion of potential conflicts of interest.

assisting in communication, facilitating negotiation, pointing out areas of agreement, and searching for settlement alternatives.

Next the mediator should set forth a brief procedural outline. This includes how the opening statements will proceed; whether the parties will immediately move into separate sessions or remain together for a period of time to exchange information; and whether any documents or outside individuals will be brought in. Thereafter, specific ground rules should be explained. These might include rules against interruptions, time limits, time commitments and confidentiality. The confidential nature of the session should be explained including any statutory, common law, case law, or contractual basis of confidentiality. The nature of the private session or caucus should also be explained. There is a great variation as to the use of the private session. Some mediators premise the structure of the mediation on the constant use of private meetings. A small minority of mediators almost never use them. The majority of mediators take a wait-and-see posture, which results in intermittent use of private meetings. However, rather than waiting until the time a caucus is needed, the parties should be told in advance what can be expected from a caucus, including any confidential provisions which surround its use.[3] The primary portion of the mediator's introduction should conclude with a request for a commitment of a good faith effort at settlement.[4]

While some mediators wait until the introduction for the discussion and collection of fees, it is strongly advised that this is done as part of preliminary arrangements and is not made part of the session once everyone is seated. The mediator's introduction should also include housekeeping details such as provisions for lunch, breaks, parking, telephones, and faxes. Lastly, before moving into the opening statements, the mediator should inquire as to whether there are any questions regarding the process. He is then ready to proceed to the content of the dispute. A few mediators begin by summarizing their understanding of the case. One advantage to this approach is an expedited process. However, unless there are strict time limits, this approach is not advised, since the participants should be given sufficient time to discuss the matter in their own words.

B. OPENING STATEMENTS

Once the mediator completes his introduction, it is time to hear from the participants. In most cases, the focus will be on the nature of

---

3. While most caucuses are considered to be confidential, private meetings, some mediators begin with the premise that they plan to share the information learned in private session with the other side. Whatever the method, it should be specifically clear to the parties in advance. The mediator should discuss this, both during the introduction as well as at the time of entering or moving into the caucus. This also will be further examined later in Chapter 10, infra.

4. Although it is acknowledged that good-faith usually cannot be mandated, see Chapter 4, § B, supra, nevertheless getting a personal commitment from the parties is often helpful.

the dispute that brings everyone to the mediation table. However, this dispute may not be what the mediator assumes it is. The mediator must be careful not to have made any presumptions about the case based on the information previously received. He may also want to stress this to the parties as a method of encouraging each person to listen to the others. The mediator may mention something to the effect that opening statements offer all participants around the table the opportunity to take part in an information gathering process.

Where there is a pending lawsuit, most mediators will follow normal litigation procedure and ask the plaintiff, (attorney or client) to first present an opening statement. Exceptions to this general rule exist, such as when the defendant's claim, whether in terms of a counter-claim, cross-claim, or affirmative defense is the primary focus of the mediation. In these instances it is appropriate to allow the defense to begin. In either instance, the rationale should be briefly explained to all participants so that the choice of who begins does not appear to be based upon partiality of the mediator. In the pre-litigation context, often one party is the primary claimant, the one who is making a complaint and requesting a resolution to the dispute. It is appropriate to begin the opening statements with this individual. It is also likely that one of the participants, (and this is often the claimant) is responsible for getting the matter to the mediation table. In these instances, the mediator should explain that since this party is responsible for bringing the matter to mediation, it is proper and normal that the opening statements begin with this party.

The discussions in most mediation sessions are not limited to the nature of the case as previously described, but rather are open to all areas of controversy between the parties. These include the primary and underlying causes of the conflict, as well as tangential issues and interests. Therefore, most mediators begin with a broad request for information by making a statement such as, "Tell us what brings us here today." [5]

1. IMPORTANCE OF OPENING STATEMENTS

In the majority of cases, the opening statement segment of a mediation is the first time that the parties have sat and actually listened to an uninterrupted statement of the views of the case from the other side. In most instances, this is also the first time that the parties and their representatives have had an opportunity to provide a complete, uninterrupted statement of their perceptions of the case. The mediation is often the first opportunity that the disputing parties have to "get off their chest" what the problem is, as they see it. Many times this is what the parties have been waiting for, and what they expected to get in court. Therefore, it is important for the mediator to be patient and model good

---

5. However, some cases, for a variety of reasons may need to be more focused. Examples include victim-offender matters, which focus on restitution only, or complex cases with multiple parties, where specific matters may be discussed at specific times. In directing the opening statements, the mediator will usually control the content.

listening skills, which can encourage the other parties to listen as well. The mediator will gather information, not only about the case, but also about how the other, non-speaking participants view what is being said. This is done by paying close attention to the non-verbal communication of the non-speaking parties.[6]

Neither the mediator nor the other parties should interrupt the speaker during the period of time reserved for the opening statement. The opening statement provides each individual, whether the disputing party or representative, an opportunity to present the case in the manner and fashion desired. Each participant should be permitted to do so. But if the presentation is very confusing, or if another party begins to interrupt, or if the session begins to disintegrate into a negative exchange, then it is appropriate for the mediator to intercede and take control of the situation. To do so he might remind the participants of the ground rules and procedures. Other than those exceptions, an opening statement should proceed in an uninterrupted fashion.

During the opening statements the mediator will probably take notes, while listening very carefully to what is said.[7] This will be the portion of the mediation for which the participants are most prepared, and many important aspects of the case will be highlighted. The mediator should look for areas of agreement as well as note matters of perceived disagreement. It is important to emphasize perceptions at this point. Many times what is first perceived as a matter in conflict, after information is exchanged, becomes one of shared interests.

Disagreement between the parties sitting across the table from one another is expected. However, it is quite possible that discord exists for those ostensibly on the same side of the case. Inconsistent goals can surface between a lawyer and his client or other parties on the same side of a table. While the mediator should refrain from calling attention to these potential conflicts in the joint session, he should be mindful of them and perhaps address them during a private session.

It is important for each party or entity who is represented at the table to have an opportunity to make an opening statement. There is some debate about this in those instances of a personal injury or products liability case, where there is one plaintiff with counsel, and four, five or six defendants, each with counsel. However, because of the variety of issues, claims, cross-claims, counter-claims, etc., it is recommended that each defendant be given at least an opportunity to make an opening statement. Only through a complete exchange of information can the mediator acquire a thorough understanding of the case.

2. PARTIES

In most instances the mediation is the individual's day in court and it should be treated as such. This is the time for the parties to explain,

---

6. While it takes an effort to maintain eye contact with the speaker, take notes and simultaneously keep an eye on the other parties, doing so can often provide important information.

7. The skill of combining note taking and listening was previously discussed in Chapter 3, § B, supra.

in their own words, just how they feel and how they think they have been wronged; not only in a factual sense, but also in an emotional sense. In some cases, this can become a time of accusations and finger pointing. A few individuals will detail what they expect to get out of the proceeding. If the individual is well prepared by his representative or attorney, the statements may be structured and limited to the parameters of the lawsuit. Additional concerns or underlying interests may not be disclosed. However, if the mediator is listening attentively, the parties' true feelings and interests will often become apparent.

Ventilation, the expression of anger, frustration and other emotions, is a part of the mediation process and should be encouraged. Nonetheless, the mediator should be careful not to allow venting to become a direct attack on the other side. Where venting becomes destructive, the mediator must take control of the situation.[8]

The mediator should also keep in mind that the mediation is often the parties' first. They are unfamiliar with the situation, which can itself can evoke emotion, particularly if they are nervous. Unlike most mediators, educators, and legal professionals, many people are uncomfortable speaking publicly, particularly about something uniquely personal to them. Consequently, opening statements may be disorganized, repetitious, or quite brief. Rather than interrupt and clarify during the opening, the better practice is to allow the party to complete the opening statement. It is likely that the party's representative will provide clarification later. Alternatively, in an additional information gathering segment, the mediator can go back and fill in any information that is missing or confusing. Supplemental information will also be provided by the opening statements of others at the table.

3. ATTORNEYS

In most instances when an attorney attends a mediation, there is a lawsuit pending. It is important that the mediator determine the status or stage of the lawsuit in advance. Although a detailed analysis of the lawyer-client relationship is beyond this work, some consideration is appropriate.[9] The initial perception is that the lawyer attends the mediation representing the best interest of the client. However, it should not be overlooked that the lawyer has interests too, not only in representation of his client, but also in other terms which may conflict with those of the client. Possible conflicts include a financial interest and an interest in establishing a trial record. The mediator should be

8. A mediator's ability to deal with anger, and other emotions is discussed in Chapter 3, supra.

9. For detail about the lawyer-client relationship in terms of legal representation, see David A. Binder & Susan C. Price, Legal Interviewing and Counseling: A Client–Centered Approach (1977); James E. Moliterno & John M. Levy, Ethics of the Lawyer's Work, Chapter 3 (1993). For an in

depth examination of the role of the attorney in terms of settlement and ADR use, see Robert F. Cochran, Jr., *Legal Representation and the Next Steps Toward Client Control: Attorney Malpractice For the Failure to Allow the Client to Control Negotiation and Pursue Alternatives to Litigation* 47 Wash. and Lee L. Rev. 819 (1990).

cognizant of this possibility.[10] Exactly what the mediator's role is in the event of direct conflict between a party and her representative is unclear.[11]

The lawyer-advocate is attending the mediation on behalf of the client, and it is important that she be provided an opportunity to present the case as she sees it. While this may be in terms of an advocate for the client, it may not be helpful in terms of assisting settlement. In fact, very aggressive presentations by advocates tend to obstruct settlement. However, as more lawyers become educated about and familiar with the mediation process, they realize that advocacy in mediation is not the same as advocacy in a trial or in arbitration. Where the neutral third party is a decision-maker, the advocate's role is adversarial. Mediation is a non-adversarial approach to conflict resolution. However, some lawyers still choose to utilize a competitive or adversarial approach in opening statements at mediation.[12] If possible, the mediator should attempt to constrain some of this prior to the presentation. For example, initial education about the appropriate structure of the opening statements can be included in the preliminary materials. The mediator can also reinforce the non-adversarial nature of the attorney's role at the end of his introduction. The mediator might first acknowledge the competence of the lawyers, and point out that while a very aggressive, adversarial presentation is appropriate in the courtroom setting, mediation is different. Many lawyers feel compelled to present the case in an adversarial manner because they assume that is what the client expects. And, in fact, many clients probably do expect this, not realizing the considerable difference between a trial and mediation. Part of the mediator's role, then, in making the transition to the lawyers' opening statements, will be to constrain some of the very aggressive, adversarial presentations by convincing the lawyers and clients that such an approach is not necessary.

The mediation session is likely the first time that the participants, particularly the parties, have heard the case presented by the opposing lawyer. Prior to mediation, there may have been meetings, depositions or motion hearings; but the client was probably not present. Moreover, there has likely not been a detailed presentation of the entire case. Therefore, not only should the mediator be attentive during the opening statements, but should encourage the other participants to listen as well. It is by listening that the other side may see the matter in a different light, or at least understand the other side, which may open up discussion and movement at subsequent stages of the process.

10. These are examined more closely in Chapter 14, infra.

11. In cases of overt conflict some mediators will attempt to mediate between the lawyer and client, particularly where this is the only impediment to settlement. Others will ignore the matter. And a few mediators will ask the lawyer and client to privately resolve the matter before coming back to the mediation table.

12. For a more complete examination at the role of lawyer advocacy in mediation, see Eric R. Galton, Representing Clients In Mediation (1994).

The lawyers should be careful to not use the opening statement at mediation as they would an opening or closing argument at trial, but should use the time to set forth the specifics of the case. The mediator should refrain from requesting specific offers from the lawyers. Likewise, lawyers should not further aggravate the conflict by making unrealistic demands at this early stage of the case. However, general statements about goals and outcomes of the session can be encouraged by the mediator.

4. OTHER REPRESENTATIVES

In some instances, there may be non-lawyer representatives attending with the parties. This may be a friend or relative who perhaps, has more expertise in the substantive matter. This individual may be more familiar with the court system or mediation process. Some representatives may be accountants or financial planners. Although uncommon, it is also possible for an individual's therapist or counselor to attend a mediation, particularly in family disputes. Some non-legal representatives attend in merely a supportive role, while others attend in an active representative capacity. The mediator should determine in advance the nature of the representative's role.

Representatives attending a mediation in a primarily supportive role usually do not take a direct or active role in the session. If, however, representatives are present to assist in the process, then they should be provided an opportunity to present opening statements. In these situations, the mediator should also learn how much decision-making authority the representative may have.

A particular problem arises where a representative is in the role of translator. Unfortunately, mediation has not grown to the extent that all mediators are bi or tri-lingual, and many times translators are necessary. While the ideal situation would be for the translator to be a neutral party, not brought by either side, at the current time, this is unrealistic. Therefore, on many occasions, the non-English speaking party brings his or her own translator. How the translator interprets what is said can impact the mediation. The mediator should be aware of this, and request that an accurate and direct translation be provided. And while the mediator may not understand the content of the statements of the non-English speaking party, he should still be attentive to paralinguistics and body language. These are not part of the translation, but are part of the communication.

5. USE OF DOCUMENTS, WITNESSES, AND EXPERTS

In complex cases, parties and their representatives may use documents, even witnesses and experts, to clarify certain points. In most instances, however, these are adjuncts to the process and should be kept to a minimum, particularly witnesses and experts. Mediation is not a fact finding or decision-making process. However, in complex, highly technical cases, some assistance may be necessary so that everyone has an adequate understanding of the case, and the issues in controversy.

Depending on the affiliation of the witness or expert, the timing and method of the presentation may vary. The specifics should be determined by the mediator in advance of the session, if possible.

In most instances, each side in the case should be given an opportunity to first complete their presentation. Additional information from "outsiders" should be avoided at this initial stage. Once all participants have been afforded the opportunity to present opening statements, additional parties may be introduced to the mediation. These witnesses or experts may provide a statement either prior to, or as part of, the mediator's follow-up information gathering. During the questioning stage of the session, these experts can assist in clarification. The use of charts, graphs, or drawings for explanations is also encouraged during the follow-up stage, rather than as part of the opening statements, unless they are essential to the opening.

C. FOLLOW-UP INFORMATION GATHERING

It is the rare mediation where, after the opening statements of each participant, everyone at the table is sufficiently knowledgeable about the matter and can not only identify the issues, but move into option generation. However, this is usually the first thing that a novice mediator wants to do; find an immediate solution. Therefore, it is imperative that the mediator keep in mind, and actually remind the participants, that not all of the information about the matter has been shared. Certainly, where there is a pending lawsuit, the lawyers and clients may desire to withhold certain information.[13] While complete disclosure of every item is not necessary and should not be demanded by the mediator, after the opening statements there is still information that the mediator needs to assist the parties in generating their own ideas and options for settlement.

Information gathering is a significant stage of mediation and should not be overlooked or hurried through. Once parties begin to focus on issues and options for settlement, they become reluctant to share information, are closed to listening, and become entrenched in positions. Therefore, it is imperative that the information exchange occur early in the session. Information gathering in terms of questioning and clarification can be done by the mediator as well as each of the participants.

1. EFFECTIVE QUESTIONING BY THE MEDIATOR

The mediator, rather than rushing to identify specific issues, should continue to gather more information from the participants. There are a number of reasons for this. The first, of course, is to clarify and understand any confusing factors or issues. It is acceptable, in many instances, for the mediator to act a bit uncertain about some of the matters in dispute in order to encourage the parties to disclose informa-

---

13. This has been stated in terms of not showing the *entire hand,* and is a strategy, the use of which will depend largely on the nature of each case and the individual lawyers.

tion. However, he should try to avoid appearing completely bewildered lest credibility be lost. The mediator should let the participants know that additional information or clarification is needed for a complete understanding of the dispute. After all, this is usually the mediator's primary introduction to the case. This is probably also true for at least some of the parties, but for a variety of reasons, they may not want to openly admit it. The mediator's role will be to continue to gather information, not only on his behalf, but also on behalf of the other parties.

The mediator must not narrow the focus of the dispute too soon. In most instances, the first approach that the mediator should take after each participant provides an opening statement, is to focus on the main areas of contention. He should request general information, primarily by the use of open-ended questions. A helpful rule of thumb for obtaining general information is for the mediator to begin to gather information by asking at least three open-ended questions. New mediators, especially those with a legal background, will attempt to use pointed, leading questions aimed at specific facts and figures. Certainly this is appropriate and necessary where there is confusion. However, completion of the opening statements is still very early in the mediation session; it would be premature at this time to determine the primary issues and interests. Instead, this is an appropriate time to continue to obtain a broad picture of the dispute.

Most people are comfortable in providing a narrative response to questions. More often than not, what is most important to an individual will become clear during such a response. Therefore, general, open-ended questions that search for areas of mutual agreement are appropriate at this stage of the process. Seeking background and historical information about the dispute can also be helpful in detecting areas of mutual concern and overlapping interests. For example, in a lease dispute, the mediator may ask general questions about the duration of the landlord-tenant relationship. When describing the relationship, a party may mention that, for the most part, it has been a good experience, and that this dispute is the first time that real problems have occurred. The mediator can easily determine that the parties have a mutual interest in maintaining the lease. On the other hand, if the relationship is recounted as one wrought with conflict, the mediator will realize that termination of the relationship is probably a shared interest.

The information gathering phase should include summarizing and reframing by the mediator. He should begin to use neutral language at this stage, in an attempt to rephrase areas of agreement and point out areas of mutual interest.

After an open-ended request for general information, the mediator may begin to use a variety of other types of questions. The specific combination of types of questions cannot usually be planned for in advance. However, the skilled mediator, like any skilled interviewer, becomes a master of asking the right question at the right time. A closer look at some of the forms of questions and their appropriate use follow.[14]

a. Open-Ended Questions

Open-ended questions allow for the broadest possible answer. They can be completely unfocused, such as, "What do you think?" or more focused on a specific topic. Examples include questions or requests for information that begin with:

"Tell me more about ...",

"Could you explain ...",

"Please explain further about ...",

"How did you feel when ...",

"What happened?",

"Is there anything else that you believe is pertinent to ...",

b. Open-Focused Questions

The open, but focused, question consists of requests for information similar to the general open question, but it is more directive. Examples include:

"Between the time the cast was put on and the time it was taken off, did anything else happen that is related to this situation?"

"How did you feel when you first learned that ... ?"

"Why do you want to continue a business relationship with X?",

"What happened after you first noticed ...",

"Describe the kind of streets that are at the intersection.",

c. Requests for Clarification

Requests for clarification are open to a degree but even more focused than the two preceding types of questions. Examples include:

"Could you explain to me how your product is not similar to product Y?",

"Help me understand why the lawnmower is not worth x",

"What specifically about your health is your main concern?"

d. Leading Questions

Leading questions suggest the answer, often in terms of one or two words. Example:

"You've had back trouble in the past, haven't you?"

---

14. These are examples of the most commonly used questioning techniques. For additional information on questioning in general, see David A. Binder & Susan C. Price, Legal Interviewing and Counseling: A Client–Centered Approach, (Chapter Four) (1974).

"What type of traumatic experience has the accident caused your family?"

e. Either/or, Yes/No Questions

These questions are close-ended and ask for very short, specific answers. Examples include:

"When you left the house was it one o'clock or two o'clock?",

"Were the headlights either too bright or too dim?",

"Tell me, yes or no, do you want to be friends with Steve?"

f. Compound Questions

Compound questions consist of more than one request for information at once, and should be avoided. Example:

"What type of party was it; social, professional or was it just people from the neighborhood, and how did everyone know each other?"

Some trainers and authors have tried to identify particular times which are better than others to utilize some of these questioning techniques. For instance, open-ended questions are good in the early part of the session, and can be followed by a narrowing of the questions. Close-ended and leading questions are used for later focus. Yes/no or either/or questions should be limited, but are useful when very specific information is needed. This will occur during the negotiation and review of agreement stages. A more focused open question can be used in the middle of the information gathering process.[15]

It is important that the mediator remain neutral in his information gathering. This includes the question and how it is asked. In some instances, a party might say something that is somewhat unbelievable; the mediator must remember that he is impartial,[16] and is not in a role to make a judgment, including one on the credibility of the information. Questions should be as neutral as possible. Nevertheless, it is likely that some questions will elicit certain judgmental, value-laden information from the parties.

Judgmental language can be categorized into five primary areas. First, the "should or have to" language aimed either at the other side or at a party himself; second, limiting language, in which the party immediately closes himself to certain options or ideas; third, blame language where one person is blaming another for an event; fourth, value judgments where an activity has a value, such as, right or wrong; and finally, assumptions based on inferences.[17]

It is very important that the mediator, particularly, remember that these judgments are not necessarily valid. Rather, these statements

---

15. Jay Folberg & Alison Taylor, Mediation: A Comprehensive Guide To Resolving Conflicts Without Litigation 113 (1984).

16. Although this can be debated. See Chapter 7, infra.

17. Lawrence J. Smith & Lorraine A. Mandro, Courtroom Communications, Strategies, Supp. 24–25 (January 1988).

embrace the conclusions or opinions of the party; but as such, they are valid to that party. The mediator should refrain from commenting on judgmental responses. The mediator may begin a summarization and in doing so may, to some degree, neutralize this language. This is often done by the restatement or reframing of the issues.[18] Neutralization can also be accomplished by the way a question is asked. The mediator's job here is to uncover the underlying basis for these statements by asking more specific questions. However, the mediator, particularly in highly emotionally charged situations, should tread lightly. The participants can be very defensive. These matters are often better dealt with in a private session or caucus.

As the mediator asks questions or clarifies, he may also begin to reframe some of the issues. Ideally, the mediator wants to reframe or restate in as general a way as possible, yet retain accuracy. Accusatory language should be limited, but the accusing party needs to know that the mediator has heard what was said. The mediator can neutralize and acknowledge this information by highlighting the main issues and re-phrasing the statement in terms of the party's interests and needs.

2. ADDITIONAL INFORMATION GATHERING BY PARTICI-PANTS

In many mediations the parties are also present to gather information about the other side's view of the case. With this additional information, parties can better assess their cases for purposes of settlement. In most cases, the mediator should permit questioning to take place between parties across the table. A participant, whether it be the party or a representative, should feel free to ask the other side specific questions. However, the mediator must stay in control of this, so that it does not disintegrate into a deposition-like question and answer session or an open discovery process. In a few cases there have been reports of one side requesting that a mediation be scheduled for the primary purpose of gathering information about the other side's case. The mediator's role, if this intent is made clear, is to first remind the party of the purposes of the mediation process. If the party persists, the mediator will have to follow his instinct as to where to draw the line. If the session results in such an abuse of questioning and the other party becomes uncomfortable, a last resort is to terminate the session.

However, in most instances, assuming all parties are present in good faith, an exchange of information can be very helpful. In fact, the mediator can point out to the parties the benefit of exchanging information so that each side can begin to see the matter from a different perspective, and consequently be more open to a variety of settlement options. Therefore the mediator can assist the process by encouraging questioning by each side, but must, simultaneously, maintain control over the process.

18. This will be discussed further in Chapters 7 and 8, infra.

DISCUSSION QUESTIONS

6–1. In her opening statement, the attorney for the defendant, insurance carrier in a wrongful death case refers to the deceased as a low-life alcoholic. She is referring to the fact that at the time of his death, the 26 year old defendant was working odd jobs. He was at a construction site, when an electrical explosion occurred, killing him instantly. Although the autopsy revealed a small amount of alcohol in the bloodstream, there has been no evidence submitted that this contributed in any way to the accident. Present during the opening statement are the deceased's mother and sister. What, if anything, should the mediator do?

6–2. Parties or lawyers unfamiliar with the mediation process sometimes refer to the mediator as "Judge" or "Your Honor". When this is done in the opening statement, what is the proper response of the mediator?

6–3. As part of an opening statement, the lawyer says "We're here only because we were ordered; we do have all the appropriate authority, but we do not intend to negotiate." What should be the mediator's response?

6–4. You are the mediator in a dispute over a car repair. During the opening statements made by the car owner and the manager of the repair shop, you learn the following:

The car owner had taken her automobile, a 1987 Nissan, to The Repair Shop because of trouble with the transmission. The repairs took 5 days rather than the 3 that had been estimated. The estimated charge was $900.00. Upon pick up of the car, the owner of the car refused to pay an additional $480.00 charge. Consequently, The Repair Shop claimed a lien on the car, and did not permit the owner to take possession of her car.

Both parties contacted their attorneys, who agreed that mediation should be tried before any formal legal action is taken. Both attorneys advised their clients to attend without them, in an attempt to not only limit costs, but also to try to reach an amicable resolution.

(a) As the mediator, what are at least three appropriate follow-up questions?

(b) To whom will they be addressed?

6–5. A Case of Suite Sheets

You learn the following information in the general session:

Plaintiff is the manager at a small hotel, named the STATELY SUITES. The hotel prides itself for offering suite and large hotel services, in a friendly, personal, almost Bed and Breakfast manner. Defendant is Lum's Laundry which for the past several years was the primary launderer for the hotel.

Mr./Ms. Lum is the owner of the laundry. A few weeks ago on a Monday, the hotel, in anticipation of a large business meeting took a majority of its linens to Lum's. Included were sheets, towels and table cloths. Plaintiff claims that it was made very clear that the laundry MUST be done no later than Thursday morning, as all guests were to arrive that evening.

When the laundry was not delivered on time Thursday morning, Plaintiff called Defendant. Lum stated that there must have been a mistake; that the laundry was on the truck and scheduled for early morning delivery.

When early afternoon arrived, still without laundry, Plaintiff stormed into Lum's irate. After some discussion, it was discovered that the laundry was "misplaced", and Plaintiff ran to the local department store to purchase the required laundry. The cost was over $2,500.00, as all 30 rooms were booked for the conference. At approximately 5:30 p.m., on its last delivery, the truck stopped and delivered the laundry to the hotel.

Plaintiff refused to pay its bill of $747.59, and has sued Lum's in small claims court for reimbursement of the other expenditures. Lum's alleges that the laundry was in fact on time and has countered for the charges.

(a) As the mediator, will you continue a general meeting, or meet separately with each party?

(b) What are the questions you would ask the hotel? The laundry?

6–6. The Termination

This dispute involves a recent termination of employment at a general practice clinic located within the local medical complex. The claimant, Terry Totten, was employed as a bookkeeper at a ten physician general practice clinic, Daytime Doctors. Totten worked for about eight months, and was terminated by Dr. Greer, the managing partner. All employment related communication, including this termination was by and through the managing partner, Dr. Greer. Reasons voluntarily provided for the employment termination included alleged continuous tardiness and carelessness on the job. Totten contends that s/he has not been late any more than most of the other employees, and that great care has been taken in all work performed. In fact, the only evaluation which was completed about three months ago was exceptionally high. The termination occurred almost four weeks ago, and the claimant has not yet been able to find employment.

The management committee of Daytime Doctors wants to end this silly matter, and wants nothing more to do with Totten; yet, it does not want to be sued. Totten wants the job back, the missed month's salary, and a written acknowledgement of the wrongful actions which are alleged. While suit has not been filed, a demand letter has been sent by Totten's attorney; however, no attorneys are present at the mediation.

6–7. Complaint of Threats

A neighborhood dispute which has existed for about two months has resulted in the complainant, Steven Joyce, attempting to file charges of threats against the respondent, Nancy Johns. The case has been referred to mediation and no charges have yet been filed.

The final incident happened last Sunday afternoon; both parties are single parents, and were inside when a fight ensued between their children. (Joyce has 2 children, ages 9 and 7, while Johns has 1 child age 8.) Johns felt the two were ganging up on her child, and ran out to break up the fight. Joyce claims that when she appeared, Johns shouted angry threats in front of all of the children, using some rather colorful language.

Each wants the other to leave the neighborhood. In the past few months the children have not been allowed to play with one another although they attend the same grade school.

Chapter Seven

NEUTRALITY

A. OVERVIEW

Neutrality is a central concept of mediation. As an intervenor in a dispute, the mediator is often referred to as the third party neutral, as are many of the other ADR providers.[1] In other ADR processes, such as arbitration and case evaluation, it is clear that the neutral will develop an opinion of the case during the process. On the other hand, in mediation, the mediator is expected to remain neutral throughout the process: before, during and even after the mediation session.

However, attempts to examine just what neutrality means have proven to be quite difficult. Neutrality as a concept has been recognized as central to the theory and practice of mediation.[2] Neutrality is included in many contexts of mediation practice, such as in the professional standards of a number of mediator organizations. Yet as central as neutrality is, specific guidelines for its practice do not exist. Neutrality remains primarily unresearched in the scholarly literature.[3] In fact, it is suggested that due to this lack of research, neutrality functions more like a folk concept. Neutrality is discussed and even practiced rhetorically; yet, there is an absence of data demonstrating specifically what neutrality means.[4] Nonetheless, neutrality will be examined here because it is considered crucial to the role of the mediator and because of the divergence of opinions concerning the specific effect of neutrality upon the mediation process. Clearly very different results may occur depending upon how the mediator approaches neutrality.

Neutrality is often used interchangeably with a variety of other words and phrases, including: impartiality; free from prejudice or bias; not having a stake in the outcome; and free from conflict of interest. Other synonyms include unbiased, indifferent, and independent. While the latter are from a lay or generic standpoint, all are similar words.

---

1. See Chapter 1, supra for a description of the various roles of the third-party neutral.

2. Sara Cobb & Janet Rifkin, *Practice and Paradox: Deconstructing Neutrality in Mediation*, 16 L. and Soc. Inquiry 35 (1991).

3. Id. at 36.

4. Id. at 37

However, there is dissention within the mediation community about whether all of these terms define neutrality, and, moreover, whether all, or any, are appropriate characteristics for the mediator.

While in the mediation community the term neutrality is often used interchangeably with impartiality,[5] some mediators claim that impartiality is a very different concept and should not be confused with neutrality. A code developed by family mediators states that mediators shall at all times remain impartial. Yet the Code also implies that impartiality is not the same as neutrality, if neutrality means refraining from making any decision with regard to fairness of the outcome. For example:

> "While the mediator must be impartial as between the mediation participants, the mediator should be concerned with fairness. The mediator has an obligation to avoid an unreasonable result."[6]

Similarly, the Academy of Family Mediators also distinguishes between impartiality and neutrality, stating that:

> The mediator is obligated to maintain impartiality toward all participants. Impartiality means freedom from favoritism or bias, either in word or action. Impartiality implies a commitment to aid all participants, as opposed to a single individual, in reaching a mutually satisfactory agreement. Impartiality means that a mediator will not play an adversarial role.

> The mediator has a responsibility to maintain impartiality while raising questions for the parties to consider as to the fairness, equity, and feasibility of proposed options for settlement.

> Neutrality refers to the relationship that the mediator has with the disputing parties. If the mediator feels, or any one of the parties states, that the mediator's background or personal experiences would prejudice the mediator's performance, the mediator should withdraw from mediation unless all agree to proceed.[7]

However these distinguishing characteristics have been suggested in the context of family law mediation. It might be argued that in family cases the mediator's role differs from that expected in a business context. In divorce and child custody mediation, an underlying continuing relationship is present. Moreover, the mediation can affect third parties who are unable to represent themselves, such as children. Even so, family mediators debate the specifics of the mediator's role with regard to impartiality.

Another Code of Conduct, directed at all mediators, provides separate sections for neutrality and impartiality, although a close examination reveals clear overlap.

---

5. Id. at 42.

6. Family Mediation Council Western Pennsylvania, Ethical Principles and Code of Professional Conduct for Mediators, (1984).

7. Academy of Family Mediators, Standards of Practice for Family and Divorce Mediation.

Neutrality. A mediator should determine and reveal all monetary, psychological, emotional, associational, or authoritative affiliations that he or she has with any of the parties to a dispute that might cause a conflict of interest or affect the perceived or actual neutrality of the professional in the performance of duties. If the mediator or any one of the major parties feels that the mediator's background will have or has had a potential to bias his or her performance, the mediator should disqualify himself or herself from performing the mediation service.

Impartiality. The mediator is obligated during the performance of professional services to maintain a posture of impartiality toward all involved parties. *Impartiality* is freedom from bias or favoritism either in word or action. Impartiality implies a commitment to aid all parties, as opposed to a single party, in reaching a mutually satisfactory agreement. Impartiality means that a mediator will not play an adversarial role in the process of dispute resolution.[8]

There has also been exploration of neutrality with regard to environmental disputes. Specifically, there is debate about whether the mediator has a duty or responsibility to assure a just and stable outcome. It is pointed out that in the environmental context, if the parties do not achieve all the benefits possible, then environmental quality and natural resources will be lost. Moreover, public health and safety could be jeopardized.[9] Consequently, the mediator should accept responsibility for ensuring that interests of all stakeholders are met; and that agreements are fair and indicated for the entire community.[10]

A very different view is that of the mediator who must be neutral with regard to outcome.[11] If a mediator is to be responsible for a particular outcome, it follows that he is not neutral, and in essence becomes an advocate or moral judge.[12] In order to determine possible benefits, the mediator must take a position. Impartiality may be lost.

Obviously, a considerable amount of controversy surrounds the duties and responsibilities of the mediator with regard to neutrality, impartiality and fairness. Authors Rogers and Salem capture the essence of this controversy in their discussion of the tension between fairness and neutrality.[13] While mediators are generally viewed as neutral, there may be an underlying duty to be fair. In an attempt to be fair, neutrality may be lost.

Others contend that impartiality and neutrality signify merely that the mediator separates her opinion of the outcome of the dispute from the desires of the disputants. Thus, the mediator focuses on ways to

---

8. Christopher W. Moore, CDR Associates, Code Of Professional Conduct for Mediators, 1982. The entire code is Appendix B, infra.

9. See Lawrence Susskind, *Environmental Mediation and the Accountability Problem*, 6 Vt. L. Rev. 1, 8 (1981).

10. Id. at 18.

11. Joseph B. Stulberg, *The Theory and Practice of Mediation: A Reply to Professor Susskind*, 6 Vt. L. Rev. 85, 96 (1981).

12. Id. at 116.

13. Nancy H. Rogers & Richard A. Salem, A Student's Guide to Mediation and the Law (Chapter Six) (1989).

help the parties make their own decisions. Specifically, the mediator is impartial and only helps the parties make their own choices, whatever they may be.[14] However, fairness is not mentioned. Other standards demand that mediators balance power by assuring that all interests are represented. This mandate directly collides with that of impartiality.[15]

The view of neutrality and impartiality as similar, if not synonymous, terms is reflected in a number of training and mediation texts. Others observe however, that there is also tendency to see them as different concepts.[16] This debate over the meaning of neutrality, impartiality, and fairness has only begun. Close examination of the issues is necessary, but easy answers to these issues do not currently exist.

Some of the early writers in this area looked to the overall theory of the mediation process, which was seen as the opportunity for individuals to come to their own decisions and determine the outcome of a matter. In a courtroom or litigation situation, decisions are made within the safeguards of procedural rules. Results are theoretically fair, based on social norms. This, by design, is not the case in mediation. In fact, it is clear that the mediation process is not concerned with achieving conformity to broader societal norms, but rather to creating individual norms for the parties themselves.[17] If this view of the mediation process is taken, then how should fairness be determined?

Before looking more specifically at this debate about the mediator's duty or role, a closer examination of the meaning of neutrality is necessary. Each individual has certain values. These are established, developed and shaped by the larger culture in which an individual is born and raised. In most instances, if a person remains within the same culture and subcultures (including location and family), these values or judgments are continually reinforced. Biases then develop based upon strongly held values. The fact is often ignored, if not forgotten, that not everyone we encounter holds the same or similar values. People look at things differently, and are motivated to make decisions for a number of reasons. The mediator's values may differ from those held by the parties. The difference may be slight or great. Herein lies the concern. In making judgments about fairness, whose values are to be considered? Those of the parties, the mediator or some objective entity?

Much of the concern about the mediator's impartiality and neutrality can be discussed in terms of power imbalances; that is, the mediator's duty to balance the dialogue or the negotiation process. Power can be determined by a number of factors. Power is often seen in terms of wealth or money. Often, wealth and power go hand in hand. In mediation, wealth and power are most often apparent where the parties attempt to gain an advantage by hiring counsel or other experts. Some

14. See Christopher W. Moore, The Mediation Process: Practical Strategies for Resolving Conflict 15 (1986).

15. Sara Cobb & Janet Rifkin, Neutrality As a *Discursive* Practice, 11 Law, Pol. & Soc'y 69, 70 (1991).

16. Cobb & Rifkin, supra note 2, at 42.

17. Lon L. Fuller, *Mediation: Its Forms and Functions*, 44 S. Cal. L. Rev. 305, 308 (1971).

mediators feel a duty to provide the less financially able person with information or advice to equalize the balance.

Related is the power provided by knowledge. In many cases one party will have greater or more sophisticated knowledge about the subject matter of the dispute or the potential alternatives for its resolution. If one party is clearly more knowledgeable, should the mediator intervene and provide the requisite knowledge to the other party? In the alternative, should the mediator at least acknowledge this disparate knowledge and allow the less informed party the opportunity to obtain that information. Should the mediator, on the other hand, merely encourage the party to gather that information? Another source of power is that of community or numbers. One side of the table might be perceived, or in actuality may be, more powerful because of the number of parties on one side of the table. Does the mediator have any duty in these instances to compensate by limiting the amount of time for discussion to equalize the imbalance or perceived imbalance?

These questions have been answered in a number of different ways in the variety of programs throughout the mediation community. At this point, this is something that still remains a personal choice for most individual mediators, but should be thought through and determined prior to the mediation.

B. DEBATING THE DUTY OF THE MEDIATOR

When moving from theory to practice, most of the literature assumes that the mediator has a duty to be neutral and impartial. And, even if these two terms mean something different, there remains the difficulty in determining specifically what those meanings are.

Missing in much of the literature is a differentiation between the process and the content of the mediation. Looking at the issue of neutrality from these two different perspectives will provide a more complete examination of the controversy. For instance, does the mediator always remain neutral in the process and allow whatever occurs, to occur? Or, should the mediator inject and modify her neutrality to assure a "neutral" result? Conversely, should the mediator be concerned only with issues of fairness in the process, or should she abandon process neutrality for fairness of the result?[18] These are the primary questions which, when answered differently, dictate a completely different role and action on the part of the mediator. Hence, establishing guidelines for the mediator is quite troublesome.

The mediator must concern herself with neutrality and impartiality in two distinct, and yet related, aspects of the mediation: one, the balance and the conduct of the negotiations which she facilitates throughout the mediation; and two, the ultimate result or outcome of the mediation.

18. This is also examined in Rogers & Salem, supra note 13, at 140.

1. PROCESS

What specifically constitutes fairness in the mediation process? Fairness in the negotiation process has been identified as having four components: structural fairness, process fairness, procedural fairness and outcome fairness.[19] Issues of structural, process and procedural fairness will be examined in terms of the mediator's conduct in the process, while outcome fairness will be looked at separately. Often there is overlap in these categories. The mediator should consider what action is appropriate, if any, in each case.

Structural fairness relates to the overall structure of the dispute and the relations between the parties. The mediator has little control over these variables. Yet some allege that the mediator should influence the structural fairness of the dispute. This would include for example, providing advice to one of the parties. Others advise mediators to "take the parties as you find them". Instead, it is argued that fairness in the process and procedure is where the mediator should focus. This includes focus on how the parties treat each other, the dynamics of the negotiation process, and the procedures used in arriving at an agreement.[20] If the mediator approaches the mediation by following an outline of the structure of the process, these variables will not be neglected. It is likely that procedural or process fairness can be achieved. On the other hand, consideration and assurance of process factors alone does not assure fairness in the result.

2. THE RESULT

Should the mediator be concerned at all with the result of a mediation? Does the mediator have a duty to determine fairness in the outcome of a mediation? In some instances, an imbalance of power at the table may lead to what the mediator perceives as an imbalanced result. In other instances, even though there is a perceived or real balance at the mediation table, the parties may reach a result or outcome that the mediator believes is unfair or imbalanced. Does the mediator have any duty to intervene in either instance?[21]

The issue of empowerment is also related. Mediation is often described as a process which empowers the parties to make their own decisions. If this is so, why then should a mediator intervene in the decision-making? However, it is urged that a lawyer-mediator specifically guarantees that the agreement reached is not one which a court would refuse to enforce, due to the presence of fraud, duress, overreaching, imbalance in bargaining leverage or basic unconscionability.[22] Since

19. Cecilia Albin, *The Role of Fairness in Negotiation*, 9 Negotiation J. 223, 225 (1993).

20. Id. at 230.

21. Clearly, if the result is something which is illegal or which the mediator, for reasons of moral choice, does not want to

participate in, the mediator should make that known and excuse herself from the case. These are not the instances discussed here.

22. Leonard L. Riskin, *Toward New Standards for the Neutral Lawyer in Mediation*, 26 Ariz. L. Rev. 329, 354 (1984).

judges and juries differ, how could a mediator properly make this call? If such standards are established, will inaccurate predictions lead to an increase in claims of mediator malpractice.[23]

If the mediation process is, in fact, one of self-determination, then the parties ought to, within the realm of reality, be able to make their own decisions. There are a number of factors which motivate people to make certain decisions. To ask the mediator to intervene and make judgments for those parties is to require conduct arguably outside of the mediator's role. However, in the absence of strict guidelines, the individual mediator must make the choice. Basically, if the parties are satisfied, then absent illegality, the agreement should be executed.

Lastly, if there are instances where the mediator feels so strongly about an issue that she may attempt to influence the outcome, there is little doubt that she should not take the case. Likewise, where the parties *perceive* the mediator as biased, most mediators voluntarily withdraw from the matter.

A number of other issues such as ethics, real or perceived conflicts of interest, and standards of conduct overlap with neutrality, and will be examined in more detail in subsequent chapters.[24]

PROBLEMS FOR DISCUSSION

7–1. Can the payment of a fee affect the mediator's neutrality?

(a) Most mediators split their fee for services, whether an hourly rate or a per diem charge, evenly between the parties. In a commercial landlord-tenant case, the tenant is a small start-up company, with very little cash. Both parties want to participate in mediation and have agreed on James Lewis, a known businessman, as the mediator. The landlord agrees to pay 80% of the $2,000 per day fee. Might the mediator's actions with regard to treatment of the parties differ?

(b) Would the circumstances change if the fee were to be divided equally and billed at $280.00/per hour? How can the hourly rate affect the less wealthy party?

(c) Can the fact that the landlord may have a large number of other cases to refer to the mediator affect neutrality?

7–2. If a party conveys, in confidence, to you as the mediator, specific information, which, if known to the other side would negate an agreement, what is your duty? For instance, in a case over a sale of damaged goods, the Defendant has offered to convey to Plaintiff real estate in satisfaction for the debt. Just as the agreement is being finalized, the Defendant in caucus discloses to you, the mediator, that there are substantial tax liens on the property.

(a) Can you, should you, or must you disclose this new information to the Plaintiff?

---

23. See Chapter 15, § F, infra for an examination of mediator liability.

24. See Chapters 14 and 15, infra.

(b) What are the potential consequences if you draft and finalize the agreement?

Chapter Eight

IDENTIFICATION OF ISSUES AND INTERESTS

Once the mediator is certain that he has gathered sufficient information about the dispute or case, he should begin to identify the primary issues. Some trainers and writers refer to this stage as problem identification; however, the word "problem" has a negative connotation which can contribute to polarization of the parties. Issue identification or issue determination are more neutral ways of describing this stage of the process. During this phase, the mediator should simultaneously attempt to identify the underlying interests of each party. These may or may not be the same as the issues which have been publicly stated.

Issues are those items which both sides are willing to openly discuss as the predominant points of contention, and about which the negotiation has been initiated. In most cases, each party also has certain underlying issues or interests. These matters may not have been disclosed or identified at this stage of the process. Therefore, the mediator should initially focus on the identification and restatement of the main, or apparent issues. He should keep in mind, however, that there may be other matters which should be discussed before a final resolution can be reached.

It is recommended that at this stage of the process, absent overt hostility, the mediator have the parties together. When identifying the issues, there should be mutual agreement on what they are, or at a minimum, an acknowledged agreement to disagree. If the mediator is gathering information in private meetings or caucuses, and in the process, identifies issues with each party separately, there is a significant risk that there will be misunderstanding or disagreement on specifically what the issues are. In some instances, particularly where the parties are not forthcoming with certain information, the mediator must meet privately with each party early on in the process. In these instances, specification of the issues in separate caucuses is necessary. However, the problem with this approach is that what may be an issue for one party is not an issue for the other. Of course, this may occur even when the parties are together. However, in that situation, each party is likely to at least hear the other's issue expressed. They then will be in a position to better understand that different issues exist for each side.

If it is necessary to conduct this stage of the process in private sessions, the mediator's job becomes much more difficult. He will have to go back and forth to confirm exactly what issues need to be resolved. Explaining the issues from each perspective may also be necessary. Because caucuses are commonly confidential, another dilemma is presented for the mediator. A party may disclose an issue to the mediator, but not authorize the mediator to share it with the other party. Of course, unless it is openly discussed, it cannot be resolved. In these instances, the mediator must then encourage, but not pressure, the party to allow disclosure of this information. In addition, when this issue is one of which the other parties were unaware, the mediator must confront questions such as "and why hasn't he told us that before?"

Once identified, the mediator should then restate and reframe these issues in such a manner that will leave the parties open to a variety of potential solutions. The mediator should utilize his listening skills to determine any issue and interest overlap or areas of potential agreement. Skill in the reframing and restating of these matters will assist in moving the mediation forward.

Once the mediator has obtained the parties' agreement on the specific issues, he should, particularly in complex cases, determine an agenda for the mediation. This will dictate the order of discussion of issues for the remainder of the session. In simple cases, an elaborate agenda is not necessary. In others, the way the mediator approaches the agenda will determine how the negotiation proceeds. Restatement and ordering of the issues for discussion moves the mediation from information gathering to the problem solving phase.

A. IDENTIFY, REFRAME AND RESTATE: THE USE OF LANGUAGE

Restatement of what one party has said, or reframing the way a party has related a problem, is one of the most effective tools the mediator uses. There are several purposes behind restating and reframing. Not only does this let the party know that she has been heard and understood by the mediator, it may also assist the others at the table in hearing another point of view. Reframing can also cause the author of the statement to look at the problem or concern in a different light. By using more neutral language, the mediator urges the parties to approach the dispute in a more neutral and positive manner, which can attempt to de-polarize the parties. By restating, the mediator also begins to refocus the language used by the participants. After they hear statements made a different way, the parties may subsequently choose different words to explain themselves. Reframing is also used to identify the main issues and points, and make a transition to the problem solving stage of the process. By hearing neutral language, and a broad view of the issues, the parties may become open to a more creative problem solving approach.

Restatements may be used by the mediator at a number of times during the process. Some mediators have been trained to restate almost every thought or point that a party makes. To convey empathetic understanding and engage in other techniques such as separating the people from the problem,[1] restating can be an effective tool. However, continuous restatements, not only will become monotonous, but also cause the mediation session to take twice as long. Therefore, in most situations, the mediator should wait until the parties have completed their opening statements and then restate the primary points in neutral, general terms. Where there are complex, or lengthy, opening statements, the mediator may need to restate the issues after each party provides an opening statement. In those situations where the case is not complex or lengthy, and the opening statements are brief, the mediator should wait to make primary restatements until each person has delivered an opening, and he has gathered some additional information about the issues. That is not to say, however, that from time to time, particularly in volatile situations, that a single restatement is not necessary. However, the mediator must be careful not to engage in a constant parroting of the problem.

Exactly how much time is spent in this stage will depend on the nature and complexity of the dispute, and the parties' need for understanding and clarification of issues. There can be overlap between identifying the issues and setting the agenda. In some cases, these tasks can be performed simultaneously. In others they occur sequentially. And in still other cases, it is possible to identify an issue and completely resolve that issue before identifying others. While the single issue approach is not recommended in most instances, it can be effective, particularly if there is only one issue that the parties are initially willing to discuss. In most cases, however, the mediator will at least make an attempt to reach consensus on all issues as they are put on the table. By first identifying most of the issues before initiating negotiation, there usually results a number of items for discussion. Give and take is then possible, leading to a more integrative bargaining approach.[2]

Positive reinforcement is a powerful motivator for most individuals. The mediator should not overlook the use of pointing out the positive aspects which he sees in the dispute. Because the mediator sits in an objective chair, he is much more likely than any of the parties to see some middle ground; to observe that there is not as much disagreement as each side may initially perceive; and to identify areas of overlapping interests. Where these are directly stated, and obvious, the mediator should begin the issue identification with these matters. A common

---

1. This is the first step of "Principled Negotiation", a concept first put forth by Roger Fisher & William Ury of the Harvard Negotiation Project in their book, Getting to Yes (1981).

2. Negotiation theory and styles are discussed in Chapter 9, infra.

example is the mutual benefit a landlord and tenant or supplier and purchaser can gain by continuing their relationship. Once this is pointed out and acknowledged, renegotiating the terms of the contract is much easier. In a family case the mutual concern is often the best interests of the children. In personal injury litigation, parties want to conclude the lawsuit and get on with their lives. Where these areas of common interest are more discreet and not obvious, the mediator may not be as specific in his restatements, but should keep these in mind (and in his notes) for later discussion.

Some mediators will also ask the parties themselves to do some restating and reframing. The theory behind this approach is that the parties will better understand the other side, and begin to acknowledge another view of the situation if they are required to restate it. Use of this method will depend primarily on the nature of the relationship between the parties and how comfortable they are with the idea. In some cases, after the mediator has restated some of the issues, he may ask each of the parties to restate what they think the other party has said. Other mediators may request that the participants do all of the restating. This may be done by asking each party to restate the opposing view before they put forth their response, position or statement. Caution is advised in using this approach. Many individuals may be uncomfortable with this process. The mediator may lose the trust and cooperation of the parties.

Some new mediators, as well as more experienced ones, wonder how many issues there are in a case. Some mediators will go to great lengths to avoid the single issue case, which most likely leads to positional, distributive negotiation.[3] The mediator will attempt to fractionalize the issue, that is, break it into smaller components to create more items for discussion and bargaining.[4] An example is a dispute over the payment of a sum of money. While most negotiators (and some mediators) will discuss only the amount to be paid in an offer/counter-offer format, most mediators will look to find at least one other item for discussion. One example is the time of payment. This, at a minimum, provides another issue for negotiation.

Related to the strategy of numbering or fractionalizing issues are the concepts of linkage and non-linkage. More specifically, this means that in some cases there are a number of issues which are linked, or contingent upon each other. If there is a direct nexus, the resolution of one issue will be contingent upon the others. The linkage may be indirect where issues are related, but resolution is not necessarily co-dependent.

In the case of unconnected issues, the items are not related, and one may be resolved while the other is not. There is no dependency. In

3. For further detail on the types of negotiation, see Chapter 9, infra, and Roger Fisher & William Ury, Getting to Yes (1981).

4. For a discussion of reducing conflict by fractionalization, or breaking down the primary issue into sub-issues, see Joyce L. Hocker and William W. Wilmot, Interpersonal Conflict 194 (1991).

these instances, it is possible to conclude the mediation with partial agreements.

The mediator, in gathering information and identifying the issues, will be able to determine, in most instances, which issues are linked and which are not. It is, of course, possible to have some of each in the same case. The more difficult task for the mediator is to decide whether he will attempt to link otherwise unlinked issues, or in the converse, unlink linked issues.[5] The specific technique the mediator uses here will depend upon the information he has regarding the interests of the parties.

The identification of issues is only the beginning of the problem solving process. As the parties begin to discuss the issues and generate options and alternatives, not only will the mediator be gathering supplemental information, but additional issues and interests may come to light. Therefore, the mediator must be careful to not make a premature assessment that he has reached the conclusion of information gathering. Likewise, an early determination of the issues can be limiting. Since these items are subject to change, the mediator must never close his mind to additional issues as the process continues.

B. SETTING THE AGENDA

Setting the agenda can be a strategic move for the mediator. When and how each of the issues are approached for discussion and resolution will influence the progression of the mediation. Conflicts can be defined to magnify or minimize the dispute. The mediator should approach agenda setting and the discussion of issues in a way which can minimize the dispute. Controlling what is perceived to be at stake is a method of preventing destructive conflict.[6] In some cases, the matter is not complex. There may be only a couple of issues, which are related. In this instance, it is not necessary for the mediator to spend time considering the variety of agenda options. However, many times, particularly where there are a number of agenda items or issues to be discussed, the method of approach can set the tone for the negotiation. For instance, if the easiest matters are considered and resolved, a positive tone will be established, which may assist in resolving the remaining matters. Because the mediator is in control of the process, he should give some thought to which issues or items previously identified should be discussed first.

There are a number of approaches to agenda setting, each with its benefits and drawbacks. These differ, and the mediator should weigh each in light of the specific situation. Of course, agenda setting is always subject to modification. If the mediator initiates discussion in a

---

5. For further discussion of the linkage concept, see Christopher W. Moore & CDR Associates, Effective Mediation (1989).

6. Morton Deutsch, The Resolution of Conflict; Constructive and Destructive Processes 370 (1973).

certain manner and finds that it is not working, it is appropriate to stop, rethink and take a different approach.

A number of different approaches to agenda setting follow. The mediator should give thought to the use of these and not fear testing each to determine which work best.

The variety of approaches to the agenda which have been identified include: 1) ad hoc; 2) simple agenda; 3) alternating choices by the parties; 4) principled; 5) less difficult first; 6) most difficult first; 7) order of importance; 8) building-block or contingent agenda; and 9) tradeoff or packaging.[7] Each will be briefly described. The mediator should remain cognizant that if one approach does not seem to work, it is acceptable to change the strategy.

In an ad hoc approach, the mediator proposes examination of an issue as it is discussed. It will be analyzed thoroughly until a resolution is reached. The mediator moves through all issues in this manner, taking them in the order in which they were placed on the table. This may allow the more vocal party to exert control over the agenda and can be confusing. In less complex cases, however, it works quite well. The ad hoc approach calls for less direction from the mediator.

The simple agenda is very similar. In this approach, there is one main issue taken for discussion. Even if there has been some division of issues, or smaller issues arise, the primary item is dealt with and settled before discussion of others is commenced. This process works well in simple disputes where there is very little overt conflict. It is not applicable where there are a number of issues with varying importance. It is also inappropriate where issues are contingent upon one another. Neither the ad hoc nor simple agenda approach encourages compromise by exchange.

In some instances, the mediator may allow the parties to alternate choosing the topic of discussion. This method provides the parties more control of the process. However, choosing who goes first can be problematic. The non-choosing party may refuse to participate. Moreover, in many cases the mediator may lose control of the process. This approach works mainly where the parties are experienced negotiators and the level of conflict is at a minimum.

In a principled agenda, the mediator, with the assistance of the parties, establishes general principles that form the framework for settlement. The specific details of how these principles will be applied to specific issues then follows. This procedure works well where the parties are willing and able to negotiate at a fairly high level of generalization or abstraction. It is also appropriate where there is a strong desire for settlement by all parties. The parties are then willing to defer decision making on minor issues until later in the bargaining

7. Most of these were first identified by Christopher W. Moore, The Mediation Pro-   cess 182 (1986).

process. One example is in the business context where the agreement in principle is the renegotiation of a contract. Once this is agreed to in principle, the specific contents are then addressed. Another situation where an agreement in principle has been effective is in multi-defendant personal injury litigation. An agreement in principle is reached on the total amount to be paid to the plaintiff. The remainder of the mediation is devoted to how the defendants will allocate this amount.

In taking the less difficult items first, the mediator identifies those issues where probability of agreement is high. Reaching the agreement should not take a long time. Issues which appear to be less difficult are often less important matters, and the parties move quickly to resolution. These easy items constitute the beginning of the agenda. This will assure agreement on some matters early in negotiations, and promote an atmosphere of agreement. Once these agreements exist, the parties will be reluctant to forfeit them as the result of an impasse later on in the process. On the other hand, there may be drawbacks. Time and money in terms of mediator and attorneys' fees, will be spent dealing with the less important matters, and if no final agreement is reached, the parties will feel as if the mediation has resulted in a waste of time and money.

In other cases, the mediator may want to tackle the most difficult issues first. This is very closely related to the following approach of order of importance, particularly where there is agreement on the most important item. If agreement is reached on the most difficult, then it is likely the other issues will fall into place. On the other hand, beginning with the most difficult can result in an early termination of the session if agreement is not attained.

In the order of importance approach, the parties, with the mediator's assistance, choose the most important item for each of them and place them first on the agenda. The assumption is that if these items can be agreed upon, the remainder of the less important items will follow suit. This procedure depends upon the parties being able to agree on the most important issues and the order in which they will be handled. Of course, if both pick one item as most important, it is the source of the primary conflict and, consequently is the most difficult.

In a building block agenda, the mediator identifies issues which must be dealt with first because they provide the groundwork or foundation for later decisions. In essence, the remainder of any agreement will be contingent upon the answer to the primary question. This approach can become fairly complicated. The parties must clearly express the contingent nature of the issues. However, in cases where the issues are interrelated, this approach can prevent deadlocks due to incorrect sequencing of issues. An example is in the business arena where the foundation issue may be termination versus continuation of the joint venture. Another example in the employment sphere is the initial issue of whether the employee will continue to be employed.

Another approach to agenda formation is issue trading or packaging. Parties unwilling to move on a single issue will use combinations of issues. Offers will be made in return for concessions. The mediator orchestrates this exchange. Issues may be traded one for another in a way that mutual bargaining results. Trading can also be conducted on an issue-by-issue basis so that all issues are eventually resolved. In essence, this is the basis of integrative negotiating. Packaging of proposals which contain multiple-issue solutions can be particularly effective where the issues are linked. The parties can see that mutual gain is possible. Because of the packaging, which is often done by the mediator, some of the reluctance involved in presenting alternatives for settlement is eliminated. The give and take does not appear so great since the proposal comes all in one package presented by the neutral mediator. However, the mediator must be careful in this approach to not control the outcome.

Regardless of the way the mediator sets the agenda, if, as the mediator proceeds, problems should arise, movement to another issue or topic is appropriate.

EXERCISES

The ability to hear a statement expressed in value-laden terms and restate it in more neutral language takes practice. There are a number of ways by which these statements can be restated. Use the following statements as examples. First restate the sentence with intent to let the maker know she has been heard, yet without offending the other party. Secondly, try to reframe the issue in a manner which will move the parties to the option generation phase.

Original Statement : "I want $4,780 for the damage to my car that this stupid, inconsiderate, irresponsible, teenager caused."

Becomes :

Becomes :

Original Statement : "My hippie, punk neighbor had better stop having loud barbecue parties every weekend. Stereos play trash until the early morning hours."

Becomes :

Becomes :

Original Statement : "You arrogant, selfish, pin-striped bankers want to use the Taj Mahal for collateral on this loan when a merry-go-round from the local playground would do."

Becomes :

Becomes :

Original Statement : "John is a materialistic, spoiled new age 'professional' who just wants me out of the way. He has no respect for the people who have done the 'real work' around here, and only uses people to satisfy his selfish motives."

Becomes :

Becomes :

Chapter Nine

THE NEGOTIATION PROCESS

A. GENERAL OVERVIEW

It has been observed that negotiation is much like sex. It is something most of us do to a degree at various points in our lives—yet no one has taught us anything, nor is there much open discussion about it. But as the use of ADR has increased, so has awareness of the negotiation process. In fact, it is now looked at as a process, with its own stages and dynamics. The mediator's role is essentially to facilitate negotiation. Therefore, it is imperative that the mediator be intimately familiar with the negotiation process.

Negotiation is at the heart of all settlement; in fact, it is a part of everyday life. Although negotiation is often included as one of the dispute resolution procedures, ADR processes differ from negotiation because of the intervention of one or more third parties. Traditional negotiation, on the other hand, involves only the parties to the dispute and if represented, their lawyers or other advocates. Nonetheless, negotiation is a process, and like most processes, a variety of types and styles exist.

Negotiations take place informally all of the time, as we go about our everyday routines. Purchasing items on sale is, in essence, a negotiation. So is deciding which television program to watch on Tuesday evenings, or where to order pizza. When there is a successful negotiation, there is no longer a dispute. Unsuccessful negotiations result in continued disputes. Negotiations also take place on a daily basis in more formal or structured settings. Obtaining employment involves negotiation, as does the selection of a place to live.

In the legal context, negotiation is the essence of transactional law. In the litigation arena negotiations may take place informally on an ad hoc basis, as the lawyers discuss other aspects of the case. More structured or formal negotiations occur when there is a stimulus to settle the matter, such as a trial date.

Like other processes, negotiation is composed of various stages. How the parties in a negotiation pass through these may differ. In informal situations, the stages are often blurred. In more formal negotiations, the phases can be observed more easily. There are a variety of ways to label the stages of negotiation. One example is the six stage model. The phases can be described as:

(1) planning and preparation;

(2) establishing initial relationships between negotiators;

(3) opening offers or initial proposals;

(4) information exchange;

(5) narrowing of differences; and

(6) closure.[1]

While these have been depicted in the context of legal negotiations, they are applicable in all types of negotiations. Like any flexible process, there is overlap in the phases of a negotiation as well as movement back and forth between the stages.

B. NEGOTIATION THEORY

Negotiation is examined and studied primarily in the context of dispute resolution. It is viewed as a method for resolving a dispute or problem. However, the use of negotiation in the context of a transactional matter should not be ignored. Negotiation takes place each time two or more individuals put together a deal, contract or lease. The theoretical basis of the negotiation process in ordinary business transactions is very similar to that observed in dispute resolution. A primary difference in negotiation in these two contexts is that in the dispute resolution arena, feelings and emotions may be involved and are often negative. There is also a personal or professional history between the parties. On the other hand, in transactional cases there may or may not be a prior relationship between the parties to the negotiation. However, in transactional matters the goal of the negotiation is to establish a relationship, whether it be shortlived such as in the purchase of a car, or more lasting such as in the creation of a business organization.[2] Despite these differences, in both the dispute resolution and transactional arenas, the underlying theories of the negotiation process are nearly parallel.

There are a number of basic theories which have been used to describe the negotiation process. The term theory is used in this manner to refer to the underlying method of how the procedure or process of negotiation works. This is not to be confused with style or stylistic differences, which is an individual matter of choice that the

1. Donald G. Gifford, Legal Negotiation 8 (1989).

2. In many cultures, such as the Japanese, this focus on the future relationship is a primary, if not the main, point of the negotiation process, without which the remaining part of the negotiation would not take place. For further information on cul-tural factors which influence negotiation and hence mediation, see Chapter 16, § K; Dean A. Foster, Bargaining Across Borders: How to Negotiate Business Successfully Anywhere in the World (1992), and Center for the Study of Foreign Affairs, National Negotiating Styles (Hans Binnerdijk, ed. 1987).

negotiator makes. Theory should also be distinguished from negotiation strategy, which has been identified as a specific set of negotiating behaviors.[3] This is not to say, however, that there is not overlap between the theoretical basis, types and styles of negotiation. For instance, a certain style of negotiator may prefer to use a particular type or strategy. On the other hand, when involved in a particular type of negotiation with a distinct theoretical basis, one might find certain styles more effective than others. Expert negotiators are able to change their styles depending upon the styles and strategies of the other parties, as well as the type of process. Not so simple, however, is a change of the type of negotiation that is taking place.

The mediator must be aware of all of these variables in negotiation. Her main task may be to change the type of negotiation or theory under which the parties negotiate. Far more difficult for the mediator, if not impossible and outside of her role, is to change or influence the specific stylistic approaches of the negotiators. Yet, in reality there is often overlap between the theoretical basis, the style and strategy used.

In negotiation theory, some distinct types of negotiation have been identified. Most experts have identified these types by comparing and contrasting two methods of negotiation. Two primary theories of negotiation have been explored in detail: one is the negotiation process as either distributive or integrative; the other is the negotiation process as either positional or principled.

Negotiations can be described as either distributive or integrative. In a distributive or linear negotiation, there is a fixed pie. There is only so much (usually money) with, or about which, to negotiate. More for one necessarily means less for the other. This has also been described as a zero sum game. It is assumed, and likely true, that there is a fixed quantity of resources, and one person's gain is necessarily the other's loss. In a distributive bargaining situation, there is a direct conflict of interest between the parties; hence an adversarial, competitive style is most often observed.[4]

On the other hand, integrative negotiations involve the exploration of a number of options, many of which are not in direct conflict with one another. There is an "expanded pie", which provides an opportunity for mutual gain in the negotiation. The interests of the parties are not necessarily in direct conflict, and therefore there is not an inverse level of satisfaction inherent in the process. There is room for creativity, and a collaborative problem solving approach is usually observed in this type of negotiation. While some see these approaches as two completely discernable ways or methods of negotiating, others have viewed them as part of the same negotiation. In the latter view, the negotiation process

---

3. Gifford, supra note 1, at 18.

4. In fact, at least one author has identified the distributive phase of negotiation as the same as the competitive phase. See Charles B. Craver, Effective Legal Negotiation and Settlement 107 (1993).

proceeds from a distributive phase into an integrative one, unless, of course, the matter is completely settled while in the distributive phase.[5]

The negotiation process has also been described as either positional or principled.[6] In positional bargaining, the parties align themselves to a position and spend effort defending it against attack. It is similar to the distributive approach, or the "more for me, less for you vs. less for me, more for you" mode. However, in positional bargaining, the parties sometimes do not focus on what they really want. Rather, they remain stuck on their position, or the cause and support for the positions they take. The specific styles identified with positional bargaining are hard and soft. Hard style negotiators are adversarial and confrontational. A soft style in positional bargaining is a friendly, cooperative manner. But soft negotiators yield and concede to avoid confrontation.[7]

Principled negotiators, on the other hand, attempt to identify underlying interests and come up with a number of alternatives for settlement. Rather than a single answer solution, the principled negotiator looks for possible solutions which might satisfy everyone's interest, with the objective being a final resolution with which everyone is satisfied. Specific styles are not as relevant. This looks very much like the approach in the integrative negotiation.

Negotiation can also be looked at as either interests-based or rights-based. These characterizations are similar to the principled versus positional approach previously discussed. Interests-based negotiators look to the underlying interests of the parties which is essentially the same approach taken in principled negotiation. Examination of interests is a focus of an integrative approach as well. When underlying interests are considered, it is often possible for the negotiation to result in gains or satisfaction for all participants. Hence, interests-based negotiation is also known as mutual gains bargaining or MGB.[8] In a rights-based approach to a problem, the negotiators look to the entitlement of rights between the parties in an attempt to determine a solution based on those rights. This is similar to the positional bargaining approach. Distributive negotiators often look to rights to slice the pie.

Another way the negotiation process can be described is in a simple win-lose vs. win-win approach. The win-lose approach is similar to the distributive or positional method where one party will win and get more, while the other party necessarily gets less. When approaching negotiation as an integrative, principled or interests-based process, joint gain and mutual satisfaction is probable, resulting in a win-win or "all gain" situation.

5. Id. at 156.

6. These terms were first used by the Harvard Negotiation Project. See Roger Fisher and William Ury, Getting to Yes (1981).

7. Id. at 8.

8. Deborah G. Ancona, et al., *The Group and What Happens on the Way to "Yes,"* Negotiation J. 155, 156 (1991); see also Lawrence Susskind and Jeffrey Cruikshank, Breaking the Impasse: Consensual Approaches to Resolving Public Disputes (1987).

The preference for a specific type of negotiation in the mediation has often been discussed. Some educators and trainers,[9] strongly urge the integrative, principled approach. And, in fact, these proponents of integrative bargaining train mediators to constantly search for integrative potential when gathering information in the mediation. The theory is that not only will it be easier to achieve an agreement when engaged in an integrative negotiation, but moreover, the result will be one with which the parties are more satisfied; consequently the parties will comply with the terms of the agreement. One study has produced empirical data which strongly supports this theory.[10]

C. COMMON STYLES AND TACTICS

Within each of these types, the negotiator may vary his or her style. Negotiators' styles have often been described as competitive, adversarial, cooperative, problem solving or collaborative. Studies have been conducted to gauge effectiveness of some of these styles, particularly within the legal community.[11] Attempts were made to identify certain factors which indicate that one negotiation style is more effective than another. Williams studied the traits of attorney negotiators and found that while there are distinct differences in approach between the competitive and cooperative negotiators, both types are rated as highly effective negotiators.[12] Common traits of both such as preparation, ethical guidelines, trustworthiness and honesty were the factors which were indicia of effectiveness. Likewise, there were ineffective negotiators in both groups.

Some scholars have stated that both the cooperative and competitive styles are integral to the negotiation process [13], and are to be used at different times and under different circumstances. Yet most individuals have not been educated in negotiation theory and hence lack these specific skills. Most rely on intuition and the legal process. An effective negotiator studies the various styles and strategies in order to choose that which is most effective in a given case. The mediator should recognize when the negotiators are unaware of strategy as opposed to the case where there is a specific, predetermined use of a style. In these two situations, the mediator's resulting intervention will differ. In fact, in some cases the mediation results in an education for the negotiating parties.

In discussing negotiation, a number of individuals have identified certain tactics or strategies that negotiators use. These do not fall directly within one specific type or style of negotiation, but rather

---

9. And I am one.

10. Raymond A. Whiting, The Use of Mediation as a Dispute Settlement Tool: A Historical Review and Scientific Examination of the Role and Process of Mediation (Dissertation)(1988).

11. For details of the study, see Gerald S. Williams, Legal Negotiation and Settlement (1983).

12. Id. at 25.

13. John S. Murray, *Understanding Competing Theories of Negotiation*, 2 Negotiation J. 179 (1986).

constitute a certain behavior which is demonstrated in a given situation. While initially seen by many negotiators as advantageous, in reality many of these tactics backfire. Once recognized, the tactical negotiator is seen as no longer trustworthy. Hence, the negotiator should weigh carefully both the pros and cons of the use of these tactics. Some of the more common strategies are as follows: [14]

1. Use of additional individuals on the negotiating team;
2. Initial large demand or low offer;
3. Limited authority;
4. Real or feigned anger/intimidation;
5. False demands;
6. Take it or leave it;
7. Create/induce guilt;
8. Mutt and Jeff;
9. Alleged expertise/snow job; and
10. Brer Rabbit.

The mediator must be able to recognize the theory, the styles and the tactics, to deal effectively with them. However, she must also be careful to not get into the process, that is, begin negotiating herself or position herself as the negotiating opponent. Each negotiator must stand on his or her own. However, the mediator can, as pointed out in the next section, control the climate and tenor of the process and provide a situation that increases the likelihood of an effective negotiation.

D. COMMON PROBLEMS IN NEGOTIATION

One of the primary problems for the negotiator is the lack of knowledge or skill about the process. Most negotiations in the business community, and even more in the legal arena, take a "seat of the pants" approach. Often in the legal arena, negotiation and settlement take place on the courthouse steps. In fact, legal negotiations are often like dice throwing, not thought through at all. In a similar vein, if one is uneducated about the process, then the preparation is non-existent for the negotiation. The lack of preparation and planning for negotiation contributes to a very haphazard approach to the process. The mediator must encourage the participants to prepare in advance of the mediation.

Another very common problem in the negotiation process is the parties' lack of specific focus or ability to keep on track. Many times the stages get muddled; people become disagreeable and are not able to stay focused on the main issues. This is less a problem in negotiation in the transactional arena, since all negotiators are present, and theoretically, have a common goal: putting the deal together. In the area of dispute resolution, however, the focus often gets lost once parties become preoc-

14. For elaboration see Craver, supra note 4, Chapter 10.

cupied with a positional approach. Finding a workable solution is often sacrificed in order to be "right." The mediator can help the negotiators maintain focus on interests.

Parties in a negotiation may have failed or refused to exchange information. Without information, informed decisions cannot be made. An intermediary may assist in this exchange. Furthermore, many negotiators are very reluctant to make the first offer. A longstanding myth has been that making the first offer is a sign of weakness. Such misperception persists even though much has been written to the contrary. For instance, many believe that putting forth the first credible offer is a sign of strength in a position or a case. Moreover, it has been established that the opening party can control the negotiations. Nonetheless, many still hold tight to the idea that making an unsolicited offer may appear, particularly in the legal context, as an admission of a weak position or case.

Another problem in the negotiation process is the inability of some parties to take responsibility for finding a solution. There exists a misconception that there is a single "right" answer to any dispute or problem. Hence the parties are not compelled to negotiate. Also in the dispute resolution context, because there is a dispute, the parties lack the requisite trust of each other. They remain closed to proposals presented by the other side. The mediator can help the parties "own" the dispute, share responsibility and therefore determine its resolution.

There probably are as many problems in negotiation as there are negotiators. The mediator must be aware of some of the more common situations if she is to effectively facilitate the negotiation process. Specifically how the mediator will enter a failed negotiation as a neutral third party and assist the parties in moving toward settlement will depend on the problems encountered.

E. THE MEDIATOR AS CONDUCTOR FOR A NEGOTIATION DANCE

Negotiation can be seen as a dance. It takes two to tango, and to negotiate; and in both instances some individuals go more willingly than others. Like two dancers, negotiators may proceed very quickly and deliberately, certain of their direction and steps. In other instances, they may hesitate or step on each other's toes.

The negotiation process itself may parallel a dance. The preparation stage is when one dancer is looking for a partner. The request and acceptance to enter the dance floor is the establishment of an initial relationship. The first steps, over which many dancers stumble, may be seen as the opening offers or initial proposals. Primarily, dancing is the information exchange; and as the differences narrow, the dancers are more synchronized. The length of the dance will often vary, depending on the energy of the dancers. Likewise, the speed at which the dance, or negotiation takes place, may vary as well.

The mediator has a role in this dance; namely, to keep it going. She can first be seen as a conductor of the music, and where necessary, the choreographer. This role is more crucial where the parties need assistance in their direction due to inexperience. The mediator may have to introduce the music as well as explain the steps to novice dancers. In this way, the mediator facilitates the negotiation process.

A mediator must also keep in mind that negotiation is a ritual for many participants. Certain elements of the ritual must be experienced. And, the ritual unfolds over time. While the mediator cannot and should not completely change the ritual, by her intervention she can modify some of the stages, and in particular, the timing.

Parties often begin negotiating in good faith, but for some reason do not continue on this path. Sometimes the music changes, and they are unaware of how to react. Or perhaps they are tired and lack motivation. The parties may be uncertain how to keep the process going. A mediator can help the parties continue with the negotiation or dance. Other neutral third parties are also used in negotiations in a number of different ways.[15]

In the transactional area, the negotiators are often motivated to deal with each other. They have a common goal, a transaction. However, in dispute resolution negotiations, the parties are frequently initially unwilling to dance because of the conflict itself, or the negotiating environment has been inappropriate, or the right music has not been played. A mediator may change the music. The environment may be modified to set a tone that provides a safe and more workable atmosphere for the parties. Moreover, in the dispute resolution area lack of trust between the parties is often a problem. The disputants are at odds with one another. In essence, they hear completely different music and have no appreciation for another view. The parties fail to see the other's offers in an objective light. And, in doing so, the disputants may pass over options to which they otherwise would agree. The mediator may assist the actual communication process by restating the offers or counter-offers to the parties. They may open their ears to the neutral.

The specific tactics the mediator uses to assist negotiation will vary, depending upon the variables of the dance in progress, if any. In many instances, the role of the mediator may be only to bring the dance partners together and begin playing the appropriate music. Thereafter, the disputants may be able to progress on their own until the process is completed. Such an approach is effective when the parties have an ongoing relationship or are sophisticated in the negotiation process; i.e., two business partners. In these instances they have danced together in the past. In other instances, the mediator will virtually have to lead each party, step by step, through the entire dance, selecting the type of music to be played and choreographing the steps the parties take. In this instance, the mediator has a very active and directive role in facilitating the negotiations. She must keep the process going or the

15. These were examined in Chapter 1, supra.

negotiations will fail. Most mediators usually find themselves between such extremes. Many times the mediator will not know exactly what her role will be until she opens the mediation session, asks questions and listens, and learns just where the parties are in their dance. The mediator will figure this out by observing the dancers. Sometimes she will even directly ask each party, in confidence, what music is playing and further what their preference is.

In instances in which the parties have not made any movement, the mediator's first task will be to facilitate an information exchange. The mediation in and of itself can assist the parties in exchanging and gathering information about the case—their own as well as the other side. The mediator, in the initial stages of the mediation session, further encourages an exchange. The negotiations will not proceed unless and until such information has been exchanged.

The mediation also provides an environment in which an offer is not only acceptable, but expected. This will remove the negative stigma that has, unfortunately, been attached to making the first move. The mediator's role in this regard is to not only encourage movement by the parties, but to also to encourage the parties to negotiate more reasonably. The tempo of the music, or timing of the offers, can also be directed by the mediator.

In a neutral, objective role, the mediator is more able to recognize alternatives or options as possible solutions which might be likely to satisfy all the parties at the table. Often, the parties may reject these ideas and refuse to continue dancing. The mediator may point out the similarity in the music and dance steps and help the parties continue. If the negotiators grow tired, the mediator can assist in moving them. She keeps the music playing.

Chapter Ten

FINDING A RESOLUTION

Once the mediator has identified the primary issues of the case and obtained confirmation from the parties, he should begin to guide the parties toward identifying and generating a variety of options and alternatives which may lead to a final resolution. The mediator at this juncture should also keep in mind the parties' underlying interests. A number of alternative solutions should be considered, rather than a focus on finding a specific answer. However, generating options or solutions is not a process with which most individuals are familiar. Many people do not see problem solving as a process. Therefore, the mediator should provide guidance.

The majority of mediation models have a separate stage or segment which deals specifically with the attempt to identify, create or generate a variety of options and alternatives for settlement. This stage of the mediation process is key to the goal of finding and agreeing on a solution with which all parties will be able to live, and feel at least somewhat satisfied. Many times the negotiation process, as previously pointed out, is seen as a win-lose situation; one party obtains what he or she has identified as a goal, and the other party has been "beaten". Alternatively, in some negotiations there is compromise on both ends and a midpoint is reached. However, in both instances the focus is narrow, and in many cases in which a midpoint is reached, both individuals are dissatisfied. Throughout the process, each party has remained stuck on a position or single solution; thus, once movement was made, they will feel as if they have "given up" something. In fact, some courts and judges have been known to say that a good settlement is where everyone walks away unhappy or dissatisfied. Unfortunately, this is often a lose-lose negotiation.

One of the benefits of the mediation process is to find alternative solutions and resolutions which will be agreeable to, and at least partially satisfy, the disputants. Therefore, it is necessary that there be an actual stage or a time in the process devoted to searching for these alternatives or options. However, many people do not know how to invent options, and, hence, are not familiar or comfortable with such a process. The mediator may, in fact, encounter some parties who are reluctant to generate ideas and alternatives. Therefore, the mediator's first task in this segment of the process is to assist the parties in overcoming their reluctance to participate in the search for alternatives.

A. OVERCOMING RELUCTANCE WITH PROBLEM SOLVING

Most individuals do not think of the problem solving as a distinct process. Rather, it is approached as ongoing; when one encounters a problem, a dispute or a situation, the instinctive response is to try to find an answer. Many times this immediate reaction is necessary. For example, if, as an individual is crossing the street, a car runs a red light, the individual's immediate, and proper response is to jump out of the way. This problem necessitates a quick response. Likewise, if each situation we encountered necessitated a lengthy, mechanical problem solving process, advancement might be obstructed. However, the expectation of an immediate solution has become so automatic that we approach all situations in the same manner. In instances involving a more complex dispute, one that should require a more intricate problem solving process, we fail to allocate time for such an analysis. Rather, we assume automatically that there is a single solution which can be found. Our focus is narrow and restrictive. Disputes exist because two or more people have different feelings, views, perspectives, and needs. And, when each individual looks at the problem, each has a single option or idea for its solution. Collaboration in developing options does not come naturally to most people, particularly those involved in a conflict. The mediator's task is to move disputing parties from their search for a single answer and to broaden their perspective.[1] He begins the transition by restating the issues in dispute in broad terms.

An additional impediment to problem solving is the reluctance of the parties to share responsibility for a dispute, let alone its resolution. The most common reaction is an attempt to allocate blame. The mediator must get the parties to recognize that mediation is a problem solving process which uses collaboration, and that each person must share the responsibility for the process.

While it is important that in the first few stages of the process the parties have been able to fully express their frustration and talk about the dispute, the mediator must then focus them on the future. One technique that is helpful in this endeavor is for the mediator to explain the differences between trial and mediation. It can be pointed out that in an adjudicative process the past is examined and a determination about it is made, whereas in the mediative processes, the focus is future oriented. Therefore, once the parties have been able to fully express their concerns about the past, the mediator can simply state that it is now time to look forward. He should recognize in a restatement that an

---

1. This search for a single answer is one of several obstacles to invention of options that is pointed out in Roger Fisher & William Ury, Getting to Yes 61 (1981).

activity or event has occurred, and then solicit options from the parties regarding possible solutions. Focus is on the future. The mediator may elect to be specific, asking the parties how they plan to deal with each other during the next six months or year. Such a technique is especially effective in situations in which the parties have an ongoing relationship or where it may be mutually beneficial for a relationship to be established. Once focus is placed on the future, the parties usually begin working with one another to resolve the dispute.

B. THE CAUCUS

The caucus describes that portion of the mediation session where the mediator meets privately with each party, or combination of parties. A mediation often relies on candor of the parties. Yet, individuals involved in a dispute do not typically feel comfortable with candor, and in particular complete candor. Hence, in order to gather additional information or to explore alternatives, the mediator may need to meet separately with the parties.

Some mediators suggest caution in the use of caucus, particularly in community settings or when the disputing parties have an on-going relationship. In these cases it is important that the parties engage in joint problem-solving. Joint problem-solving occurs between the disputants, as opposed to the caucus where the mediator and each party engages in separate problem-solving.[2] However, studies indicate that problem-solving occurs more frequently in caucus.[3] More information is disclosed in a private session and the parties feel more comfortable in offering a number of alternatives. The mediator also takes a more active role in prompting options. It appears that where disputants are hostile and unable to generate options the caucus is quite effective in overcoming these barriers.[4]

In most cases, each caucus is confidential, and the mediator shares only that information which he has been given permission to divulge. It is therefore crucial that the mediator, in each private meeting, determine with accuracy, that information which he is authorized to disclose to the other side, and that which he is not. Note taking is imperative, and many mediators have devised a system to distinguish between information that is permissible to disclose and that which is not. One example is to place an asterisk beside only those items which may be revealed. Another approach is to circle the matters for general discussion.

Private sessions with the parties are also used by mediators as times where certain conduct of the mediator, seen as inappropriate in a joint session, is proper. This conduct includes certain strategies such as assisting the parties in evaluation of the case; urging the participants to

---

2. Neil B. McGillicuddy, et al., *Factors Affecting the Outcome of Mediation: Third-Party and Disputant Behavior* in Community Mediation 142 (Karen Grover Duffy et al., Eds., 1991).

3. *Id.* at 143.

4. *Id.* at 144.

take a realistic look at their objectives; and educating the parties about the negotiation process. In essence, when the parties are together, they fear "losing face" in front of their perceived opponent. A private, confidential setting enables the parties and the mediator to be more direct.

C. IMPASSE, AND THE WAYS BEYOND

The impasse, or stalemate, is not encountered in each mediation; yet when it occurs, it can be an extremely frustrating situation for the mediator. As with most elements in this process, an impasse is defined in a number of ways. Authors and educators in the field have discussed the causes and solutions of impasse ad nauseam. Although impasses often occur, the mediator should not project the potential of impasse into every case he mediates. The mediator should not assume that just because the parties have declared their "bottom line", that they are unwilling to move. Often these types of statements are part of negotiation strategy. However, the mediator should be open to the alternative of declaring an impasse for the purpose of terminating the mediation. The impasse in mediation is a situation best described by "you'll know it when you experience it!"

There are some methods that the mediator may employ when it appears the mediation is "stuck". Some of these strategies are to be used alone; others in combination. And many times, if one doesn't work, try, try another. Some examples include:

- Change the focus or topic. If the negotiation gets stalemated on one issue or interest, move to another. Remember the mediator controls the process and the agenda.

- Divide the issues, if in a distributive mode. Remember integrative bargaining is usually easier than distributive.

- Take a break. Often after a relaxing break or private time to reconsider, parties see things a little differently.

- Be silent. People are somewhat uncomfortable sitting silently. Complete silence in the mediation often "motivates" a party to say something new.

- Discover or remind parties of their BATNA (Best Alternative to a Negotiated Agreement) or WATNA (Worst Alternative to a Negotiated Agreement).[5]

- Use words of encouragement. If any progress at all has been made, acknowledge and positively reinforce it. This can go a long way in motivating further movement.

- Call a caucus. If meeting together is not productive, a separate meeting can provide the mediator information which moves the negotiation.

5. First described in Fisher & Ury, supra, note 1.

- Come back together. If in a caucus, or involved in a shuttle negotiation, bringing the parties back together can often initiate productive discussions.

- Bring in snacks. If parties have been kept separate, this is a good way to reconvene the group.

- See if partial agreement can be reached. Emphasize this area of agreement.

- Humor the participants. While the dispute should not be made light of, appropriate humor can often ease tension.

- Call it quits. Sometimes if the parties are told that the mediation is being terminated, they move off of their positions. The mediator must, however, be prepared to end the session if neither party budges.

D. PROBLEMS IN GENERATING ALTERNATIVES

When involved in disputing, most individuals hesitate to advance ideas for resolution. Part of this apprehension stems from a fear of rejection of the offered ideas. It is feared that ideas will be criticized and not accepted. Individuals refuse to make suggestions and worry that they may be exploited. Moreover, when people are involved in a dispute or conflict with each other, the emotional aspects of the conflict often impairs their willingness to hear or trust the content of any option or alternative suggested by the other party. The mediator's task, then, is to create an environment where the parties are no longer reluctant to generate, identify, or create a variety of options and alternatives for settlement. The mediator will also encourage them to be willing to look at those ideas suggested by the other parties at the negotiation table.

The mediator can accomplish this task in a number of ways. The first is to explain that an essential part of the mediation process is to identify and consider all options; otherwise, a mutually satisfactory resolution may not be reached. The mediator must emphasize that this is a condition precedent to the selection of solutions or decision-making segment of the mediation process. The evaluation and selection of alternatives for settlement must be separated from the stage of generating and creating those options.

By this point in the mediation, the parties will likely feel comfortable enough with the process and the mediator to share information. The mediator should nurture this atmosphere and continue to build trust so that the parties feel at ease in coming up with ideas that they otherwise may not have suggested. Therefore, this critical stage should not be rushed. The parties must be provided sufficient time during the process to overcome their frustration and to develop a collaborative working environment, not only with the mediator, but in many situations, with each other.

E. THE IMPORTANCE OF A NUMBER OF OPTIONS

When approaching a problem solving process, most people, including lawyers, will immediately gravitate to one idea or option and disagree or argue over the validity of that option. For example, the payment of money is often viewed as the only solution to a problem. However, in most instances, regardless of the type of problem or dispute, there are a variety of alternatives that might be suitable. This is particularly true in situations in which the parties have a number of interests to be met. Therefore, the parties, before rushing to finalize a solution, should explore a number of options and alternatives. The mediator will facilitate this process, and stress that in examining these options, the parties should understand that any alternative, whole or part, may provide a workable solution to the problem. The mediator should suggest that to find a single solution or to negotiate over a single item, may obscure other more creative and satisfying options. Therefore, it is important that the parties be open minded to the broad range of possible solutions.

Because the parties should consider a number of solutions, the mediator must be cautious to not ask for specific solutions or options early in the negotiations. Even though the parties may want to complete their opening statement with a demand, inasmuch as is possible, the mediator should explain to the parties that there will be a time later in the process where a number of options will be examined. This will minimize the likelihood that a party establishes a specific solution or resolution, and then becomes entrenched and unwilling to move away from it. Parties should not commit to a resolution until all options have been placed on the table. This maximizes the number of options for consideration, which increases the likelihood of agreement.

Mediation may be looked at as a creative problem solving process. As such, the parties are free to be creative in fashioning or designing their own solution. A phase of the mediation process should be devoted to allowing this exploration and creative thinking to occur. By generating creative alternatives during the negotiation, the parties are better able to fashion a resolution which they are truly satisfied with because they have had a direct hand in creating it. Such process increases the likelihood that disputants will find solutions that will meet the needs of everyone at the table simultaneously. Experienced mediators have reported that a bright light may flash at the moment of such a convergence of ideas.

When moving into this stage the mediator should emphasize to the parties that the creation or identification of options and alternatives is separate from the actual selection process. The parties, directed by the mediator, engage in a brainstorming session, after which they will begin to select the alternatives which are most likely to resolve the issue. The mediator will find, within certain limits, a direct relationship between the number of options available and the likelihood of attaining a final resolution.

F. USE OF LATERAL THINKING

Understanding the creative process is helpful for the mediator who is assisting disputing parties in finding innovative solutions to their conflict. Most individuals take thinking for granted and assume that it is automatic. Like walking and breathing, thinking is an instinctive act, and there is nothing one can do about it. However, according to some scholars, thinking is a skill. And like a number of other skills, some people are better at it than others. Yet, everyone may acquire a reasonable amount of proficiency in the skill of thinking. Such proficiency requires desire as well as practice. Edward de Bono has written and lectured extensively regarding thinking skills.[6] As de Bono points out, we often think far too quickly. Thinking slowly and deliberately can increase effectiveness of the thought process. Deliberation permits more focus on the subject matter about which we think.[7] This is particularly true in a problem solving process.

Certainly much of our thinking must be automatic or we would not get through the day. We cannot carefully consider and deliberate every piece of information which enters our thought process. Instead, a pattern of information has become pre-recorded in our brains. This pattern permits us to almost effortlessly drive a car, cross a street, etc. In these situations, the actions that we take are no longer contemplated; but rather, have become involuntary within our individual information systems. However, in many other instances, particularly problem solving, our thinking should be slowed down. Immediate, automatic responses do not often produce creative options and solutions. Recognizing and emphasizing these principles, de Bono has identified a concept which he has labeled *lateral thinking*.[8] While the concept of lateral thinking is similar to that of creativity, de Bono felt it important that the terms be distinguished because of value judgments already associated with the term creativity. Lateral thinking is now recognized and included in the Oxford English Dictionary, defined as "pattern switching within a patterning system".[9]

Lateral thinking can be described as an attitude as well as a number of defined methods or skills.[10] At the very least, mediators must possess this attitude. Lateral thinking involves a way of looking at things, but also can be practiced as a re-patterning of the way the mind works. Specifically, lateral thinking will call on other processes that take place including insight, creativity and humor. Lateral thinking is used for the

6. See, for example, Edward de Bono, Teaching Thinking (1976); De Bono's Thinking Course (1982); Lateral Thinking (1970).

7. Edward de Bono, de Bono's Thinking Course 10 (1982).

8. See Edward de Bono, Lateral Thinking (1970).

9. See de Bono, supra note 7, at 58.

10. Id. at 59.

generation of new ideas or invention. It is related to creativity, but perhaps is more deliberate. Lateral thinking may also be used to re-pattern or reprogram prejudices and similar patterns that we have established.

Lateral thinking is explained as a process which differs in a number of ways from vertical thinking.[11] Vertical, or traditional, thinking is described as the step-by-step logical thought process. Vertical thinking is utilized in analyzing any situation. In this analysis, sequential steps are used and only relevant data is considered. A conclusion is reached by a series of organized steps.[12] In lateral thinking, one may include irrelevant data. The lateral thought process may not proceed in a logical direction. In lateral thinking, one can be wrong at stages or explore various tangents and still achieve a correct, valid, and usable solution. On the other hand, in vertical thinking, most often used in logic or math, irrelevant or tangential steps are impossible.

Lateral thinking is provocative, whereas the vertical thought process is more analytical.[13] Additionally, in a lateral thought process, nothing need be sequential; that is, jumps in different directions may be made. A vertical thought process is not only sequential, but it is a step-by-step process. In vertical thinking, part of the analytical ability consists of using negative thoughts to block off or make decisions. Alternatively, in lateral thinking, there is no negative thought; nothing should be exclud-ed from consideration. In essence then, when employing a vertical thought process, the most logical or predictable result usually comes about. On the other hand, with the use of lateral thinking, the result is unpredictable at the beginning of the process.[14] Hence, particularly in those cases where there is a need for creative solutions, it is very important that the mediator encourage the parties to employ lateral thinking.

Only in a rare case would the mediator actually tell the participants about lateral thinking. Rather, as the time approaches in the mediation session to search for alternatives, he will explain in general terms the concept of inventing options before making decisions. He may even use the term brainstorming. Since the normal tendency is to make a judgment immediately after hearing an idea, the mediator may need to intervene during the option generation phase to strongly discourage decision-making.

It is recognized that both vertical and lateral thinking are necessary processes; in fact, they are complementary. By the use of lateral thinking, a number of ideas and options are generated. When followed by a vertical thought process, the ideas or information which are most appropriate are then selected and put to their best use. The use of these two complimentary processes is very important to the problem solving segment of the mediation process. The mediator can help the parties

11. de Bono, supra note 8 at 12.   13. Id. at 40.

12. Id.   14. Id.

think in a lateral manner by both identifying and creating a variety of options; thereafter, through the vertical thought process, an analysis can take place. The selection of the appropriate or workable alternatives will be made.

However, because it is difficult for most individuals to purposely engage in lateral thinking or in a process where lateral thinking is used, the mediator must first understand it. In fact, often the mediator is anxious to think logically about the problem and its solution, and rush to a conclusion. The mediator will, out of habit, employ vertical thinking. The first step in the process, as the mediator, therefore, is to remember that there is room for creative solutions. In fact, most disputes require them. The mediator must create an environment which encourages lateral or creative thinking. He therefore must be careful to avoid statements which favor or focus on specific solutions prematurely. Rather, it should be made clear that the mediator's role is to assist the parties in creating their own solutions.

It is not inappropriate for the mediator to be thinking of options. As stated previously, the mediator should first encourage the parties to develop their own options and solutions since they own, and consequently know more about the dispute. However, as a last or final resort, if the parties have been unsuccessful, the mediator may indirectly suggest options and alternatives. The mediator should always come up with several ideas. If the mediator makes only one suggestion, it is likely that the parties, particularly where unrepresented, will see this suggestion as "the answer". The mediator will have then become an adjudicator. When suggesting alternatives, the mediator should not suggest them as correct solutions to the dispute, but only in terms of ideas. The mediator, in the event he assists the parties in option generation, must also clear the vertical or logical step-by-step process in order to be open to new and creative solutions. When the mediator suggests options, phrases such as "what about ..." or "some people have ..." are appropriate. It should be made clear that these options do not belong to the mediator. To do otherwise may result in the mediator inadvertently becoming an arbitrator in the case. Ideally, the parties will consider the options as if they suggested them, thereby developing ownership in the ideas.

The most basic principle identified in the lateral thinking process is that any particular way of looking at things is only one of any number of possible alternatives.[15] The option generation stage, rather than a search for the best approach, is the search for many different approaches. When lateral thinking is used in a creative process, for instance, in inventing, designing, and marketing, it is appropriate to invent the maximum number of alternatives. In a mediation, however, it is not always practical to spend an inordinate amount of time generating an extensive number of alternatives. In most cases, the parties do not expect to have a hundred alternatives to consider. The specific

---

15. Id. at 63.

number of options will depend on the case and its appropriateness for creative solutions. The mediator may also need to point out to the parties that the options or alternatives that are first suggested do not need to be perceived as realistic. In brainstorming, one idea leads to more. It is during the subsequent evaluation and selection processes that these decisions are made. It is important that the parties understand this so they refrain from making judgments while ideas are generated.

While employing lateral thinking, or brainstorming, to identify solutions to a problem or dispute, the parties must suspend judgment. This is also true in the mediation setting. In this way, the process itself encourages cross-stimulation; that is, the suggestion of one idea (which is not judged) may stimulate another. Parties are hesitant to express an idea because they are fearful of what the others will think or say; likewise, their own decision making process may reject the idea as being inappropriate or even silly. By requesting that everyone suspend or postpone judgment, the mediator ensures that the parties become more comfortable with the process of suggesting options.

The mediator should also emphasize that because one individual puts forth an idea, that person does not "own" it. That is, just because an idea is suggested by a party does not mean that the individual agrees with it. In other words, during the brainstorming process, it is acceptable to suggest alternatives, which later the suggesting party can reject. If judgment is suspended, the mediator will be better able to assist the parties in maximizing the available options. The mediator must also be careful not to indicate his feelings or judgment about any of the suggestions but rather to remain focused on the process.

Some mediators contend that to expect parties to act without judgment is fairy-tale like. Perhaps it is. Nonetheless, even if the parties do not completely "buy into" the process, a request from the mediator to postpone decision making may at least result in consideration of options previously or otherwise dismissed.

When discussing options in a joint session, many mediators will sit and take notes of all suggestions in sequential order. Thereafter the mediator will request a discussion of each, one at a time. An alternative is the use of a flip chart or chalkboard on which the ideas are written out as they are proposed. Another option is to ask each party to comment on those options she suggested. All of these are acceptable techniques for moving into the decision-making segment of the mediation.

When the mediator is conducting the entire session in a separate caucus format, option generation will not resemble traditional brainstorming where all parties work together. A disadvantage is that it is very difficult to cross-stimulate the thinking; therefore, creativity may be more limited. Another downside is that a collaborative working relationship between the parties will not be fostered. Cultivation of a cooperative working relationship between the parties is one by-product of mediation, which is particularly significant in cases where the parties will continue either a personal or professional relationship. Additionally, a separate meetings approach will take longer since the mediator will have to shuttle proposals back and forth.

However, there is a benefit to using the separate caucus to generate settlement options. The parties may be more likely to disclose their true interests, and thereby bring out options which are workable and acceptable. They may also suggest options which they would not state if the other party were present.

The selection of ideas and alternatives for discussion and evaluation is also part of the mediator's role. The amount of input he will have in that process will be influenced, in part, by the degree of directiveness that the parties need from the mediator. Once there are a number of ideas to explore, the mediator should then turn the participants to decision making. The mediator will have to use his discretion in determining when to move into the evaluation phase of the process. A realistic evaluation of the alternatives and the selection process will then follow.

G. SELECTIONS OF ALTERNATIVES

"You can't always get what you want ... But if you try, sometimes, you just might find, you get what you need."

Keith Richards and Mick Jagger

In this phase of the mediation, the parties undertake to examine all of the options and alternatives that have been previously put forth and make selections. In many instances, this phase of mediation is not clear cut. Additional information often comes to light during the evaluative process. Such additional information results in modification of an alternative or an additional option. In some instances, it is possible that, as the parties look at their options and alternatives realistically, new information and even new issues are advanced.

The role of the mediator in the selection phase is to assist the parties in examining each of the proposed alternatives. There is no specific format for this process; it can be accomplished in a number of ways. For example, the mediator, with the input of the parties, could immediately eliminate some of the options that have been suggested because they are unrealistic or unworkable. An example of this could involve a neighborhood dispute where two parties live next door to one another. Neighbor A has suggested that Neighbor B sell his house and move from the neighborhood. The economy is bad, houses are not selling and neither wants to leave the neighborhood. The mediator will assist both parties to realize that this does not appear to be a realistic alternative.

Once the unrealistic alternatives are discarded, others remain which merit further exploration. Some of these may be immediately accepted by the parties and will be items of agreement. Others can be modified for acceptance. There may also be partial acceptance of an alternative. A portion of an option can be extrapolated and used. The evaluation, negotiation and selection process can take anywhere from just a few minutes to days, or even weeks. The longer time period is seen primarily in cases in which outside information in terms of comment or ratification is necessary.[16] In most cases, particularly where the mediator has successfully assisted the parties in identifying interests, most decisions will be made during the discussion of the alternatives. The mediator's role consists of directing and orchestrating the activity.

Another way of approaching the selection of options is for the mediator to go down the list and have the parties discuss the pros and cons of each alternative. Although this is more elaborate and may take longer than the process of immediate elimination, a discussion of the pros and cons of each proposal may lead to additional options. This approach is recommended where there have been only a few alternatives elicited. The mediator should use his discretion in deciding whether to examine a number of options at one time, or rather to negotiate to conclusion on one.

In most cases, once the parties have generated a sufficient number of alternatives, the analysis or evaluation part will proceed naturally. What is somewhat more difficult, however, is the completion of details. In many instances, once the alternatives have been evaluated, the parties are very anxious to finalize the case. They accept the alternatives as final. However, many of the details with regard to the decision are not complete. The mediator must ensure that all details are understood by all participants. If an option appears to be accepted by all parties, then the mediator must review it to assure that the details have been clarified and are complete. He must also be certain that everyone has the same understanding about specific components of the agreement. Once the mediator has acquired all the details, he will be ready to finalize the agreement.[17]

EXERCISES

10–1. Robert Roy and Dale Rogers have known each other for the past year. They have formed a partnership, and are interested in opening a drive-through vegetarian restaurant, ToFu ToGo. Robert has had extensive experience in growing fruits, vegetables, and seaweed, while Dale's experience has been as a cook. Neither has sufficient collateral to obtain a large business loan.

16. While most mediations are a one time, one day intervention, some take place over a longer period of time. The consensus building process, used in public policy matters, involves input from a number of persons not at the mediation table. This necessarily involves a longer period to obtain input on the available options. Likewise, in divorce mediation, which generally takes place over weeks, each party is allowed the intervening time to make a decision and obtain advice from other professionals. For additional information on these two processes, see Chapter 16, infra.

17. Details on the agreement phase of the mediation process will be further discussed in Chapter 12, infra.

Last week they met with Cosmic Properties, a commercial landlord, to negotiate space. Both the location and the interior of the space were what Roy and Rogers had in mind. However, the rent is more than they can afford. What are some creative options for these negotiations?

10–2. You are the mediator in the following case. In the joint session, you learn:

Plaintiff, Micky Manor has sued Vera Vend for breach of contract, dissolution of partnership, and for an accounting. The undisputed facts are as follows: Manor and Vend have known each other since high school. They served on the student council together at Copperfield High School. After graduation 20 years ago, they both attended college— Micky at CU and Vera at State. They both went into the real estate business—Micky went into commercial development while Vera primarily sold residential properties. They ran into each other, became reacquainted at their 15–year high school reunion, and decided to form a partnership.

An area about 70 miles from Copperfield was being developed as a resort. They thought that Micky's expertise in the commercial area, combined with Vera's knowledge of residential real estate, would enable them to buy, develop, and market the entire resort. This was to include the commercial buildings for restaurants and hotels, as well as a home and condo development. The resort was located in a mountain area. There could be skiing and other winter sports, and a nearby lake could be stocked with fish during the summer months.

When the partnership was formed, no legal counsel was sought by either party. Consequently, there is very little documentation of the agreement. In fact, at a dinner party they basically agreed to split everything 50–50, shook hands and named the partnership Property Acquisition and Leasing, PAL. In the first year, they found and leased an office building together and went to the bank to secure a loan. Micky, who was in a commercial business, already had a line of credit at First National. Although they both were present at meetings with the bank, Micky's background was not disclosed to Vera. Micky was in debt over $300,000 for previous and current ventures. All of the documents with regard to PAL, specifically, the lease agreement and the loans, were signed by both parties individually.

The development of the resort area proceeded relatively well for about two years. A hotel was built, which the partnership managed, and two restaurants were included on the property. A contract was established with a homebuilder, who began the process of constructing a small subdivision, with two condominium complexes.

During the spring of the third year, there were severe storms which adversely impacted the resort. The mountainous area was partially washed away. The lake became contaminated due to a landfill which neither Micky nor Vera knew about at the time of the initial transaction. In essence, the resort area became unfit for its intended purposes. The individual homeowners who purchased the properties have threatened to sue PAL, stating that they were defrauded in the investment.

Though Micky and Vera both drew a decent salary as partners, neither has enough money to pay back the investors. This has strained the partnership, and, for the past six months, neither Micky nor Vera has spoken to the other. They have tried to concentrate on business but have been unable to do so. Finally, Micky, also fearful that his wife may file for divorce, has sued Vera for a partnership dissolution. The case has been pending for four months. Standard form interrogatories have been exchanged, and depositions for each party, along with environmental experts, are set for next month.

During individual caucuses you learn the following confidential information:

FROM PLAINTIFF'S CAUCUS

Although it appeared that Micky was in debt due to his previous commercial venture, he actually owns properties in other countries. No one knows this. He therefore wants to stay out of litigation, and most particularly, out of bankruptcy court. He is afraid that through discovery other assets that he has hidden will be exposed.

Micky has also concealed his business affairs from his wife. He is fearful that if this case is not resolved, he will end up in divorce court as well. That is the last thing Micky wants, for not only does his wife not know about the other properties, he is afraid that because of his activities, she will be entitled to them. Although settlement is his goal, Micky is also frustrated because he feels that it was Vera's sloppy work that got him into this mess to begin with.

FROM DEFENDANT'S CAUCUS

Vera is ready to file bankruptcy, on a personal as well as partnership basis. The residential real estate business had not been that great, and she feels like there is nothing to lose if a bankruptcy were filed. Nothing to lose, that is—except pride. Furthermore, if pushed to provide anything to Micky, Vera's choice would be to file bankruptcy. It is Vera's position that while there was not a written contract, she had outlined with Micky that the responsibility for the debts would be split 65–35 based on Micky's stated wealth. While they had been friends in school, Micky had always been the more popular, and Vera grew tired of it. Vera feels she did all the work during the partnership, and that her work was a major contribution. Therefore, in the dissolution of any assets, Vera's position is that she should get any remaining funds. She also thinks that Micky, as the primary deal-maker in the partnership, should take responsibility for preventing any further litigation against the partnership.

(a) As the mediator, how do you initiate the option generation stage?

(b) What are the specific questions you would ask?

(c) Would you conduct a search for alternatives in a joint session, or in individual caucuses?

Chapter Eleven

CONFIDENTIALITY

One of the most often expressed benefits, in some instances the primary enumerated benefit, of the use of ADR processes is the confidentiality surrounding them. This is even more pronounced in terms of the mediation process than other ADR procedures. While the summary jury trial and arbitration may be subject to rules of disclosure, since these procedures often take place in a public or open hearing, mediation has always been considered a confidential process. In some instances the words mediation and confidentiality are used almost synonymously. In fact, it has been noted that most people operate under the assumption that the mediation process is confidential, even if it is not.[1]

Yet, attempting to determine specifically what is meant by confidentiality may be very confusing. An initial consideration is whether confidentiality is thought of in lay person or lawyer terms, since there is variation between the common and legal definitions. The parties are likely to see issues of confidentiality differently than the lawyers. And even within the legal definition there are differences, which will be discussed in section B of this chapter. Some parties are very concerned with confidentiality. There are a number of reasons underlying their concern which include a variety of personal and professional issues. In contrast, lawyers' concern with confidentiality is usually predicated on the possible effect it may have in future litigation.

While the use of mediation began with the assumption of a cloak of confidentiality, the validity of that assumption is currently not clear. As time progressed, and perhaps upon further analysis, the issue of confidentiality in mediation has grown confusing. In fact, specific duties for the mediator to disclose certain matters discussed in mediation may be unfolding. Before entering into a detailed analysis of what confidentiality in the mediation process means, consideration should be given to the general policies underlying this element of the process.

---

1. Lawrence Freedman & Michael Prigoff, *Confidentiality in Mediation: The* *Need for Protection*, 2 Ohio St. J. on Disp. Resol. 37, 42 (1986).

A. GENERAL POLICY CONSIDERATIONS

The law surrounding confidentiality in mediation is uncertain and subject to change. Therefore, a survey of the policy considerations which underlie the concept of confidentiality in mediation is appropriate. Policy considerations are often cited by courts confronted with confidentiality issues.

Trust is an element of mediation related to confidentiality. For many proponents of mediation, establishing trust between the participants and the mediator is at the core of the process. Only where trust is established will persons disclose important information and personal needs. Because of the existence of a dispute, participants in a mediation are often distrustful of one another and hence unwilling to share information. Nevertheless, the mediator attempts to establish a trusting and safe environment; assuring participants of confidentiality assists in this task. In many cases the mediator must meet separately with the parties. In a trusting atmosphere (cloaked in confidentiality) the parties share additional information, which often aids the mediator in facilitating a resolution based upon the parties' interests. Many mediators contend that only if the process is confidential and the items discussed therein are protected as secret, will the parties be willing to make disclosures and openly discuss their underlying interests, needs, wants and desires. Without this guarantee, they argue, mediations will not be productive.

The longstanding exclusionary rules surrounding compromise discussions is one of the stronger policy considerations for establishment of confidentiality in mediation. Arguably, the policy considerations for confidentiality in mediation are very similar to those which underlie Federal Rule of Evidence (FRE) 408. Rule 408 and its state counterparts essentially prohibit the use of settlement offers as evidence of liability in a trial of a lawsuit.

Parties may be hesitant to engage in settlement negotiations if something stated could later be used against them in a subsequent trial. With the assurance of confidentiality, parties and lawyers are more willing to openly discuss all matters and propose settlements. Offers to compromise disputed claims, as well as settlement agreements, have traditionally been inadmissible at trial for purposes of proof of liability. Two reasons for this exclusion are the lack of relevancy and the policy of favoring settlements.[2] Arguably, the same treatment, for the same reasons, should be afforded to mediation participants. Historically, and to a lesser degree today, both mediators and mediation advocates rely on these grounds to assure a confidential setting.

Another policy which favors confidentiality of the mediation process comes within the concept of mediator neutrality. The mediator is present to facilitate a negotiation as a neutral third party. If the

---

2. Charles T. McCormick, McCormick on Evidence § 266 (John W. Strong Ed., 4th ed. 1992).

mediator is either able or required to convey information to a decision maker, whether it be an agency or a court, the mediator may need to compromise her neutral role. She will be focused on what should be included in her testimony.[3] Further, if the parties are aware that the mediator may make a report to another entity, the mediator is perceived as affiliated with that entity, and perhaps not completely impartial. As a result, most participants would be reluctant to disclose all information pertaining to the dispute.

While initially confidentiality was seen as a protection afforded to the parties and their statements,[4] confidentiality in the mediation process can also serve to protect the third party neutral, the mediator. Most mediators work to facilitate a resolution or agreement, and beyond that do not wish to be further involved in a case. Once the hour, day, or week of mediation is over, mediators see their role in a case as concluded. As with all facets of mediation, there are exceptions. In some instances the mediator continues to facilitate communication, discussions, and negotiations between the parties as part of implementing an agreement. This kind of continued mediator involvement is observed primarily in complex cases involving public policy issues, but it is the exception rather than the rule.[5] The mediator, however, maintains a neutral, facilitator role throughout. If mediators were regularly called to testify about events which occur during a mediation, they might spend so much time at the courthouse that there would be little time left to mediate.[6] If such testimony were permitted, it is likely that both sides would urge the mediator to testify on their behalf. Neutrality would again be threatened. Establishing confidentiality serves to limit the mediator's involvement in the continuation of the case and to maintain impartiality.

Despite all of the benefits afforded to the mediation process by confidentiality, problems can arise. With the increased use of mediation, occasions for concern over misuse have become more apparent. A few years ago, a review of ADR literature would have revealed nearly universal agreement that confidentiality is necessary to the survival of mediation.[7] Although the policy considerations remain strong, there appears to be an increasing number of situations which provide arguments for exceptions to confidentiality. In fact, abuses of the mediation process due to its confidential nature have been reported.

3. While this was a premise of the court in an early case upholding confidentiality, *N.L.R.B. v. Joseph Macaluso, Inc.,* 618 F.2d 51 (9th Cir.1980), in some states mediators may now provide testimony to the court. See, for example, West's Ann. Cal. Civ. Code § 4607 (1992), infra.

4. The majority of the literature and discussion is focused in this manner.

5. More detail on public policy mediation is provided in Chapters 16, § F and 17 § A 2, infra.

6. While this may be an exaggeration, most practicing mediators do not want further involvement in the case. This is especially true for those who serve in a volunteer capacity.

7. Comment, *Confidentiality in Mediation: Status and Implications,* 1991 J. Disp. Resol. 307, 308 (1991).

For instance, if a mediator is prohibited from disclosing anything that happened at a mediation other than the fact that the parties were in attendance [8] (and some would contend even the fact of attendance is confidential), then parties might misuse the session. One example of misuse is to cause delay by scheduling a mediation for the sole purpose of postponing a trial setting. Another tactic is for a party to attend a mediation and refuse to negotiate. Misrepresentations of fact during the mediation have also been reported. In fact, some attorneys, operating under the assumption that the mediation is completely confidential, have bragged about resolving the case by misrepresentation.[9]

There are additional policy considerations against the enactment by courts or legislatures of an overbroad scope of confidentiality. If everything that transpires in mediation remains absolutely confidential, then most likely there is no check on the mediator's conduct. Some witnesses of only the before and after part of the mediation process have wondered if actions behind the closed door are like a "seance". Others have asserted that to maintain integrity of the process, the public ought to be able to observe the process. If allegations of mediator misconduct are made, what information will be available to confirm or deny such matters? As alluded to, some parties, because they were protected by the confidentiality of the process, have been less than honest in their negotiation. In decision-making, the other side may rely on certain representations. If the mediation remains strictly confidential, remedies may not be available to the aggrieved party. A party would not be able to challenge the agreement by establishing contract defenses such as fraud. There would be no consequence for parties who abused the process and such actions would likely continue. Once injured, a party may choose not to participate in mediation again. The integrity of the process would eventually be eroded.

In addition, in specific cases, it may be against public policy to preserve confidentiality. For instance, in matters adversely affecting the environment, the general public should not be denied pertinent information. Where public agencies are involved, "sunshine" or disclosure laws may take precedence. Many states have Open Records Acts which allow the public access to governmental records. In these cases, mediation may no longer be a private, confidential process.[10]

In other cases, where concerns for confidentiality and needed information are weighed, the balance may be in favor of disclosure. One example is where individuals need to confront or call witnesses in their defense. In some instances, the mediator may have a duty to disclose information such as when someone may be physically harmed. Another

8. See, for example, V.T.C.A., Civ.Prac. & Rem. Code § 154.053 (Supp. 1993).

9. While perhaps unethical, if there is no ability to disclose the information, no action can be brought against the attorney. This was the issue in *Wagshal*, included in § G, 4, infra.

10. See Thomas S. Leatherbury & Mark A. Cover, *Keeping Public Mediations Public: Exploring the Conflict Between Confidential Mediation and Open Government*, 46 SMU L. Rev. 2207 (1993).

relatively established duty is to report child abuse. When these duties confront the need for confidentiality, the courts often apply a balancing test. But how far will the scales tip? Will the confidentiality pendulum swing so far that it reaches the point where the many exceptions to confidentiality become the rule? This will be considered in more detail in the following sections.

B. EXCLUSION OR PRIVILEGE

A survey of case law reveals that where a statute provides for confidentiality in mediation, courts will uphold it.[11] What is somewhat more problematic is a determination of the type, and extent of confidentiality provided by such statutes.

Even though confidentiality in mediation is discussed a great deal, there is still confusion about its precise meaning. From the standpoint of a non-attorney, a statement that the mediation is confidential could be construed in a number of ways. Many people understand "confidential" to mean something secret: not to be disclosed to anyone—ever. Those individuals believe that absolutely no one other than those present in the mediation will know anything about what occurred. This is one extreme view. At the other extreme is the understanding that "confidential" means that the mediation is protected from disclosure to the court, but it can be disclosed to the rest of the world. A middle approach is that only the participants, plus individuals directly related to and affected by the dispute, will know about the case and the details of the mediation.

Lawyers are likely to understand confidentiality to have at least two distinct meanings: exclusion and privilege. Unfortunately, when discussing the confidential nature of a mediation session, many commentators and mediators, as well as many courts, fail to distinguish between the two. Confidentiality is discussed, yet it is not made clear whether the discussion is in the context of an evidentiary exclusion, which will prohibit certain evidence from the mediation from being admitted at trial; or whether, it is a mediation privilege, which would prevent disclosure for other purposes.

1. AN EXCLUSION—SCOPE AND LIMITS

When considering an evidentiary exclusion, the rules of evidence provide guidance. They will determine what can be admitted at a trial of a case. Federal Rule of Evidence 408 provides an evidentiary exclusion for settlement discussions. Most states have similar provisions. However, Rule 408 is silent about whether information disclosed in a compromise discussion could be discussed with other entities, including, for instance, the press. The exclusion pertains only to the courthouse. Because of the similarity between settlement discussions and mediation in situations where there is a pending lawsuit, the policy supporting

---

11. For detailed analysis, see Nancy H. Rogers & Craig A. McEwen, Mediation: Law, Policy and Practice (Chapter 8) (1989 & Supp. 1993).

Rule 408 is relevant to mediation. The mediation process is a settlement device, and as such it would appear that Federal Rule of Evidence 408 applies. Federal Rule of Evidence 408 provides:

Compromise and Offers to Compromise

Evidence of (1) furnishing or offering or promising to furnish, or (2) accepting or offering or promising to accept, a valuable consideration in compromising or attempting to compromise a claim which was disputed as to either validity or amount, is not admissible to prove liability for or in validity of the claim or its amount. Evidence of conduct or statements made in compromise negotiations is likewise not admissible. This rule does not require the exclusion of any evidence otherwise discoverable merely because it is presented in the course of compromise negotiations. This rule also does not require exclusion when the evidence is offered for another purpose, such as proving bias or prejudice of a witness, negativing a contention of undue delay, or proving an effort to obstruct criminal investigation or prosecution.

Yet Rule 408 has limited application; all statements made during the discussions are not covered by the rule.[12] However, a trend to extend the protection to all statements during a compromise has been noted.[13] Expansion of FRE 408 to apply specifically to mediation would be consistent with the general purposes and policies behind the rule. If all comments made during mediation were admissible at a later trial, there would be very little motivation on behalf of the parties and their attorneys to make any disclosures at the session.

It should be noted, however, that reliance on only Rule 408 in mediation is misplaced. Under Rule 408 and similar state rules, statements are excluded only if used to prove validity of the claim or amount. Statements can be admitted if they are offered for another purpose.[14] Additionally, much of what is stated at the mediation, particularly in the nature of options and ideas are not directly contingent upon one another. In mediations which are conducted in a caucus format, the mediator, as the intermediary, structures the exchange between the parties. Since the communication with each side is confidential, the offers are rarely contingent. These cases would not normally be protected by Rule 408. In a rare instance, a broader evidentiary exclusion applying specifically to mediation has been enacted.[15]

An evidentiary exclusion only limits admissibility of information at a trial. Disclosures or testimony in other situations are possible, if not likely. Exclusions, however, do prohibit all parties from testifying. The information is excluded, regardless of whose testimony is sought: the

---

12. For instance, see *Thomas v. Resort Health Related Facility*, 539 F. Supp. 630, 637, 638 (E.D.N.Y.1982), which held that the evidence of an offer for reinstatement during a settlement meeting was deemed outside FRE 408 because it was not contingent upon compromise.

13. McCormick, supra note 2, § 266.

14. Fed. R. Evid. 408.

15. See Me. R. Evid. 408(b) which excludes evidence of mediation discussions for any purpose.

mediator, an attorney or a party. A privilege, on the other hand, may cover a greater number of situations, but is limited to prohibiting a specific individual from disclosure.

2. PRIVILEGE

A privilege provides a broader scope of confidentiality. Although privilege is a legal concept operating generally to exclude evidence from trial or discovery, there may be protection against other disclosures as well.[16] Privileges involve parties in a relationship and generally prohibit the disclosure by one party of information revealed by the other. A privilege may prevent disclosure for any purpose, and in the mediation context this may even include the files and records of a mediation program.[17] Privileges are created by law in recognition of the sanctity of certain relationships which are built upon trust and the need for protected disclosure. While initially created by common law, most are now statutorily mandated.[18]

The law has established privileged relationships between doctor and patient and lawyer and client. In determining a claim of privilege against disclosure, courts have employed a four-part test, commonly known as the Wigmore test. In the case of the mediation, if a mediator claims a disputant-mediator privilege, it is possible that the court would employ the Wigmore test. The Wigmore test requires that:

(1) The communications must originate in confidence that they will not be disclosed.

(2) This element of confidentiality must be essential to the full and satisfactory maintenance of the relations between the parties.

(3) The relation must be one which in the opinion of the community ought to be sedulously fostered.

(4) The injury that would enure to the relation by the disclosure of the communications must be greater than the benefit thereby gained for the correct disposal of litigation.[19]

It is worthwhile to examine these elements to determine whether the mediator-disputant relationship would satisfy the Wigmore test. In most instances, the mediator describes the mediation as confidential; the first part of the test is arguably met. Most mediation proponents would contend that the second and third elements of the test are clearly established by the nature of the mediation process.[20] Therefore, debate and discussion in the courts will likely be countered around the fourth element of the test. In essence, the fourth element requires a balancing between the need for certain information versus protection of confidenc-

16. McCormick, supra note 2, § 72.1.

17. Rogers & McEwen, supra note 11, at 115.

18. Id.

19. John H. Wigmore, Evidence § 2285 (McNaughton rev. 1961).

20. See, for example, Lawrence Freedman and Michael Prigoff, *Confidentiality in Mediation: The Need for Protection*, 2 Ohio St. J. on Disp. Resol. 37, 42 (1986), and *NLRB v. Joseph Macaluso, Inc.*, 618 F.2d 51 (9th Cir.1980).

es and hence the mediation process. This type of balancing has been performed by courts in the majority of the reported cases dealing with the issue of confidentiality in mediation.[21] Most likely this approach will continue.

In the cases where the courts have upheld the confidentiality of mediation, they have done so by enforcing a statute or agency rule. However, these cases do not indicate a trend toward a generic common law mediation privilege that courts would create and protect. Rather these cases have generally involved labor negotiations, and seem to evidence the courts' recognition of legislative intent to encourage settlements through mediation.[22]

If courts and legislatures establish a mediation privilege, many questions should first be answered. Should there be an absolute privilege, which would prohibit any disclosure whatsoever? Or should a mediation privilege be qualified so that there is room for a balancing test? While courts generally have displayed a trend towards qualified privileges, based upon an utilitarian analysis,[23] at least half of the mediation privilege statutes appear to be absolute. It appears that legislature enacting these statutes fail to indicate an awareness of a need for a more balanced approach.[24]

In a detailed examination of the concept of privilege in mediation another factor which must be determined is the holder of the privilege. In other relationships which enjoy privileged communications, such as the doctor-patient or lawyer-client, there are only two parties. There is an implication and rule that the holder of the privilege is the patient or the client, and only that person can waive the privilege. In the situation of mediation, there are always more than two individuals. Can the privilege be held by the mediator, without regard to the parties? Or are the parties able to waive it?[25] In order to waive the privilege, must all parties agree? Another concern surrounding a liberal mediation privilege is the definition of mediation. In instances of established privilege such as that held by a penitent, patient or client, a relationship exists with a licensed or regulated professional. Mediation has not yet reached the stage where it is a licensed or regulated profession. Therefore, a party could assert a privilege to preserve the confidential nature of information by claiming that any third party present when the statement was disclosed is a mediator. These are just a few concerns surrounding the creation and use of privilege in the mediation setting.

---

21. Some of these are discussed infra, § G.

22. Rogers & McEwen, supra note 11, at 119.

23. *Developments in the Law—Privilege Communication*, 98 Harv. L. Rev. 1450, 1593 (1985).

24. Rogers & McEwen, supra note 11, at 124.

25. Some of these questions have been at least preliminarily answered. See G, infra.

C. CONFIDENTIALITY AGREEMENTS

Another means to acquire confidentiality in mediation is through a confidentiality agreement. While most matters going before a court should not be secretive or confidential, arguably when in mediation, there should be an exception. In pre-litigation matters, it is likely that courts would enforce a confidentiality agreement unless other laws mandating disclosure would take precedence. Because of the current confusion and difficulty surrounding issues of confidentiality in mediation, parties who wish to assure themselves and the mediator of protection, should execute an agreement which provides for confidentiality. In fact, the American Bar Association's Standards of Practice for Lawyer Mediators in Family Disputes indicate that a mediator should ask the parties for such an agreement. However, these standards place a duty upon the lawyer to inform the parties of the limited effectiveness of the agreement as to third parties.[26] Nevertheless, if the subject matter to be protected is not a matter about which testimony is compelled, it is likely that a court will uphold and enforce a confidentiality agreement.[27]

There are several other issues for consideration when contemplating contractual confidentiality as an avenue for protection. In the context of a judicial proceeding, courts generally weigh the issues of established public policy disfavoring confidentiality agreements against the potential harm resulting from disclosure. In most instances, it is likely that courts would enforce confidentiality agreements against those who sign the agreement.[28] If challenged, the circumstances surrounding the signing as well as the nature of the information protected will be considered by the court in a balancing test. If the disclosure is made outside of the courtroom forum, there is little likelihood that the court can enforce the agreement. In the alternative, a new cause of action will lie for a breach of the agreement.[29]

Herein lies the problem with an agreement to not disclose. There may be disclosure before a court can intervene. Even though the agreement is valid, there is no guarantee of protection. A cause of action for breach of the agreement may lie, but often the harm is already done. In response to this problem some confidentiality agreements provide for liquidated damages.

Nevertheless, even in instances where enforcement by a court is questionable, there may be benefit in executing a nondisclosure agreement. The written agreement may serve as a deterrent. Individuals may maintain confidentiality because they have agreed to, not because they are legally bound to. With regard, however, to individuals not a party to the mediation, the effect of a nondisclosure agreement is very limited. In most instances, such an agreement will be viewed as

26. *American Bar Association's Standards of Practice for Lawyer Mediators in Family Disputes* (1984).

27. See *Simrin v. Simrin*, 233 Cal. App.2d 90, 43 Cal.Rptr. 376 (5th Dist.1965), which enforced an agreement not to sub-poena a rabbi who acted as marriage counselor.

28. Rogers & McEwen, supra note 11 at 136.

29. Id. at 137.

suppressing evidence, against public policy and therefore unenforceable.[30] Yet it may also deter third parties from seeking information.

D. COURT ORDERS

Courts can order the parties to maintain confidentiality, specifically through a protective order. Some courts routinely include in their order of referral to mediation a provision that the process is confidential. Of course this protection appears to be limited to the litigation process. In cases of a challenge, the courts will again apply a balancing test. Courts will place a greater burden to show compelling need for the confidential information on those who stipulated to the protective order than outside parties. To increase the likelihood of enforcement of the order, it should include an acceptable, reasonable justification.[31]

E. DISCOVERY CONSIDERATIONS

The majority of the situations in which issues of confidentiality and the subsequent need for information arise occur in the discovery process. While the balancing test previously discussed may be employed where no other indicator is provided, many confidentiality statutes include exceptions allowing for discovery. This is similar to Rule 408 which allows subsequent discovery of matters disclosed in compromise discussions.[32] For example, many statutes which provide evidentiary exclusions and privileges for communications in mediation include a clarification provision exempting from protection matters "otherwise discoverable". These statutes provide that if a matter is otherwise discoverable, then the fact that it is discussed in a mediation does not protect it from discovery. This is consistent with the general rules of evidence with regard to compromise discussions, and Rule 408 specifically. The intent of the exception is to keep parties from discussing information during the mediation process in order to later exclude that information from the discovery or trial process by invoking the rule of confidentiality. However, the result is an extremely confusing, mixed bag of protection.[33]

F. DUTIES TO DISCLOSE

Assuming that confidentiality is established as either an exclusion or privilege, are there instances where the law establishes a duty on the part of the mediator to make disclosures? Some claim that the mediator's duty to preserve confidentiality is paramount. In fact, it is stated that "there is no duty of the mediator greater than the duty to preserve the confidentiality of everything revealed to him or her during the

30. Id. at 136.

31. Id. at 133.

32. *Note, The Discoverability of Settlement of ADR Communications: Federal* *Rule of Evidence 408 and Beyond*, 12 Rev. Litig. 665 (1993).

33. Id.

hearing." [34] In fact, mediation is likened to the Roman Catholic confessional.[35] Yet some claim that as in most other schemes to protect confidences, there are, or should be, duties of disclosure in certain cases.

Under the evidentiary exclusion, there should be very few instances, other than a statutorily imposed one, where the mediator must disclose, that is, testify in a court. The California Trial Custody Program is one such exception. In this program (which some may claim is not true mediation), if an agreement is not reached between the parties, the mediator may make a specific recommendation concerning custody to the court.[36]

Likewise, where a criminal defendant needs the testimony of a mediator as a defense, the court may require the information from the mediator.[37]

In some cases, statutes mandate the disclosure of certain information. The most common is a duty to report child abuse. In some instances, the statutes which establish confidentiality in mediation included a specific provision which excepts from confidentiality matters otherwise required by law to be disclosed.[38] This clarifies potential conflict. In those cases where the confidentiality statute and a duty to report statute are in direct conflict, the mediator must make a personal judgment call. Where a case is pending, it is likely that the court would engage in a balancing test, and first review the matter *in camera.*

More difficult for the mediator are situations in which the mediator suspects wrongdoing, possible criminal action, or injury to one of the disputants or a third party. Is there a duty placed upon the mediator to disclose the information?

When considering the duty to disclose, a number of general issues arise. The first is a determination of to whom the mediator owes a duty. The second is an identification of to whom the disclosure should be made. This may include the other party at the mediation, a third party, or entity, or the administrative staff of a mediation program. The third issue is the determination of what type of disclosure should be made and in what instances.

Defining what duties, if any, the mediator owes to parties not attending the mediation is a difficult task. In the area of family law, it has been alleged that the mediator has an affirmative duty to consider the interests of third parties not present, such as children or grandparents. In other cases, there is an argument that the mediator is only responsible to facilitate the issues and items for discussion that are put forth at the mediation, by the parties. If not advanced by anyone present, then the interests of any third party outside of the mediation

34. Peter Lovenheim, Mediate, Don't Litigate 44 (1989).

35. Id. at 34.

36. West's Ann. Cal. Civ. Code § 4607 (1992).

37. *State v. Castellano*, 460 So.2d 480 (Fla. App. 1984).

38. See V.T.C.A., Civ.Prac. & Rem.Code § 154.073(d) (Supp. 1993) and Utah Code Ann. § 78–31b–7(3) (1992).

should not be considered. Determining whether the mediator owes a duty to persons not present at the mediation is a critical threshold question. If a duty of any type is owed, it follows that information about the mediation must be disclosed to those individuals. The next concern might be the extent of the disclosure. For instance, if a mediator in a divorce action is found to owe a duty to the grandparents, must she disclose the entirety of the mediation session to them or only specific, directly relevant portions.

Once a duty to outside third parties is established, how far does it extend? In instances of environmental concerns, should the mediator be responsible to the entire community? It is likely that in instances where the entire community is affected by the subject matter of the mediation, the mediation can no longer be confidential.

A few specific situations have been excepted from the confidentiality requirement. Such duties to disclose may include a general duty to report crime. There may also be a duty to protect others from potential harm. Where the mediator learns information during the mediation that directly and adversely affects one of the other parties, there is strong argument that she has an affirmative duty to protect that party. The mediator at a minimum, should not continue the mediation, if harm will result. Whether she is under a duty to disclose the specific information to the party may depend on the potential harm and likelihood of its occurrence. The mediator's obligation is even more muddled when the potential harm is directed toward someone not a party to the mediation. Under a line of cases beginning with *Tarasoff*,[39] which established a duty of a psychiatrist to take reasonable steps to protect identifiable persons who are in danger, a mediator could be responsible to third parties. However, since the extension of these cases to other professions is currently unclear, it remains a matter of debate in mediation. Each mediator will have to make an independent judgment call on many of these issues.

G. CURRENT LEGAL PARAMETERS

1. GENERALLY

Confidentiality which is invoked in a mediation may be established by law or by the agreement of the parties. Confidentiality in legal terms might be statutorily created or predicated on common law. In the event that it is important to the parties that confidentiality surround the mediation, the first step is to determine the status of the law in the particular jurisdiction. There currently exist a number of state statutes which provide for confidentiality in the mediation setting.[40] Some pertain only to court-referred or annexed cases. Others protect only those

---

39. *Tarasoff v. Regents of the University of California*, 17 Cal.3d 425, 131 Cal.Rptr. 14, 551 P.2d 334 (1976).

40. For a complete listing, see Rogers & McEwen, supra note 11 at Appendices A, B, & C (1989 & Supp. 1993).

mediations taking place within an established mediation or dispute resolution program. A few are quite general.

The parties may wish to execute a confidentiality agreement. There is some concern, however that certain confidentiality agreements may violate public policy, such as in environmental cases. In many jurisdictions, where the statute or caselaw is unclear, the court, in its order of referral, may include a provision establishing confidentiality in the mediation. This might be drafted rather narrowly as an evidentiary exclusion or may provide a broad protection against any subsequent disclosure of information. The court may also, in its discretion, include exceptions. In essence, a court could dictate the level of confidentiality possible in the mediation.

A few courts have directly faced the issue of confidentiality in mediation, primarily in the labor relations area.

NATIONAL LABOR RELATIONS BOARD v. JOSEPH MACALUSO, INC.

United States Court of Appeals, Ninth Circuit, 1980.
618 F.2d 51.

WALLACE, CIRCUIT JUDGE:

The single issue presented in this National Labor Relations Board (NLRB) enforcement proceeding is whether the NLRB erred in disallowing the testimony of a Federal Mediation and Conciliation Service (FMCS) mediator as to a crucial fact occurring in his presence. The decision and order of the Board are reported at 231 N.L.R.B. 91. We enforce the order.

* * *

In early 1976 Retail Store Employees Union Local 1001 (Union) waged a successful campaign to organize the employees of Joseph Macaluso, Inc. (Company) at its four retail stores in Tacoma and Seattle, Washington. The Union was elected the collective bargaining representative of the Company's employees, was certified as such by the NLRB, and the Company and Union commenced negotiating a collective bargaining agreement. Several months of bargaining between Company and Union negotiators failed to produce an agreement, and the parties decided to enlist the assistance of a mediator from the FMCS.

* * *

Revocation of the subpoena was based upon a long-standing policy that mediators, if they are to maintain the appearance of neutrality essential to successful performance of their task, may not testify about the bargaining sessions they attend. Both the NLRB and the FMCS (as amicus curiae) defend that policy before us. We are thus presented with a question of first impression before our court: can the NLRB revoke the subpoena of a mediator capable of providing information crucial to resolution of a factual dispute solely for the purpose of preserving mediator effectiveness?

* * *

The statute in question does not state that petitions to revoke subpoenas can only be made on the two grounds therein stated, or that the (ALJ) or (NLRB) may revoke only on those grounds. It does provide that a person served with such a subpoena may petition for revocation of the subpoena and the (NLRB) shall revoke it if one of the two specified circumstances exist (sic). Insofar as the statute is concerned, the (NLRB) may also revoke a subpoena on any other ground which is consonant with the overall powers and duties of the (NLRB) under the (NLRA) considered as a whole.

* * *

We must determine, therefore, whether preservation of mediator effectiveness by protection of mediator neutrality is a ground for revocation consistent with the power and duties of the NLRB under the NLRA. Stated differently, we must determine whether the reason for revocation is legally sufficient to justify the loss of Hammond's testimony.

* * *

The NLRB's revocation of Hammond's subpoena conflicts with the fundamental principle of Anglo–American law that the public is entitled to every person's evidence. *Branzburg v. Hayes*, 408 U.S. 665, 688, 92 S.Ct. 2646, 2660, 33 L.Ed.2d 626 (1972); *United States v. Bryan*, 339 U.S. 323, 331, 70 S.Ct. 724, 730, 94 L.Ed. 884 (1950); 8 Wigmore, Evidence § 2192, at 70 (McNaughton Rev. 1961). According to Dean Wigmore this maxim has existed in civil cases for more than three centuries, and the Sixth Amendment guarantee of compulsory process was created "merely to cure the defect of the common law by giving to parties defendant in criminal cases the common right which was already ... possessed ... by parties in civil cases ..." Id. at § 2191, at 68.

* * *

The facts before us present a classic illustration of the need for every person's evidence: the trier of fact is faced with directly conflicting testimony from two adverse sources, and a third objective source is capable of presenting evidence that would, in all probability, resolve the dispute by revealing the truth. Under such circumstances, the NLRB's revocation of Hammond's subpoena can be permitted only if denial of his testimony "has a public good transcending the normally predominant principle of utilizing all rational means for ascertaining truth." *Elkins v. United States*, 364 U.S. 206, 234, 80 S.Ct. 1437, 1454, 4 L.Ed.2d 1669 (1960) (Frankfurter, J., dissenting), quoted in *United States v. Nixon*, 418 U.S. 683, 710 n. 18, 94 S.Ct. 3090, 3108, 41 L.Ed.2d 1039 (1974). The public interest protected by revocation must be substantial if it is to cause us to "concede that the evidence in question has all the probative value that can be required, and yet exclude it because its admission would injure some other cause more than it would help the cause of truth, and because the avoidance of that injury is considered of more consequence than the possible harm to the cause of truth." 1 Wigmore, Evidence § 11, at 296 (1940). We thus are required to balance two important interests, both critical in their own setting.

* * *

We conclude that the public interest in maintaining the perceived and actual impartiality of federal mediators does outweigh the benefits derivable from Hammond's testimony.

* * *

[1][2][3] We conclude, therefore, that the complete exclusion of mediator testimony is necessary to the preservation of an effective system of labor mediation, and that labor mediation is essential to continued industrial stability, a public interest sufficiently great to outweigh the interest in obtaining every person's evidence.[1] No party is required to use the FMCS; once having voluntarily agreed to do so, however, that party must be charged with acceptance of the restriction on the subsequent testimonial use of the mediator. We thus answer the question presented by this case in the affirmative: the NLRB can revoke the subpoena of a mediator capable of providing information crucial; to resolution of a factual dispute solely for the purpose of preserving mediator effectiveness.[2]

2. EVIDENTIARY EXCLUSIONS

Many, if not all, states have a rule regarding compromise discussions similar to FRE 408. The premise has been that rules of procedure and rules of evidence, including 408, will afford some degree of confidentiality in mediation. However, there are limitations which often are not considered. If the court follows a strict interpretation of Rule 408, then the protection is quite limited. Many states have enacted legislation that distinctly applies to the mediation process. Those states which have passed statutes usually include a specific provision which excludes statements from evidence. These include California, Florida, Michigan, North Carolina, Oklahoma Texas, and Utah. Some local mediation programs have specific rules as well. There are currently no reported cases where a court has compelled a mediator to testify in court where such a statute or rule exists.

3. MEDIATION PRIVILEGES

Some statutes purport to provide both an evidentiary exclusion and a privilege of confidentiality.

1. We need not reach the question whether a different result would occur if the FMCS Director granted authority for the mediator to testify pursuant to 29 C.F.R. § 1401.2(b) (1979).

2. The Company argued that revocation of Hammond's subpoena was improper because communications made to him during the course of the bargaining sessions were necessarily made in the presence of the opposing party and were not, therefore, confidential. Such a contention misapprehends the purpose of excluding mediator testimony which is to avoid a breach of impartiality, not a breach of confidentiality.

UNITED STATES v. GULLO

United States District Court, Western District of New York, 1987.
672 F.Supp. 99.

The above named individuals ("the defendants") have been charged in a one-count Indictment with participating in the use of extortionate means to collect, or attempt to collect, an extension of credit in violation of 18 U.S.C. §§ 874 and 2.

* * *

Gullo's motion to dismiss the Indictment arises out of his participation, as a party, in an arbitration hearing. In January 1986 he received from the Community Dispute Resolution Settlement Center ("the CDR Center") a notice indicating that a complaint or grievance had been lodged against him. The subject matter of the complaint was directly related to the events leading to the present Indictment. The complaint or grievance form identified the grievant, the nature of the dispute and the settlement sought, noted that the grievance had been referred to the CDR Center by the Jamestown (N.Y.) Police Department and described the CDR Center as "a project of the Better Business Bureau Foundation of Western New York, Inc., the Unified Courts System of the State of New York and County Youth Services and grants from the Erie County Legislature, and the City of Buffalo."

* * *

The CDR Center operates pursuant to the Community Dispute Resolution Centers Program established July 27, 1981 by sections 849–a to 849–g of New York's Judiciary Law. The statute states in part that there existed a "compelling need for the creation of dispute resolution centers as alternatives to structured judicial settings. Community dispute resolution centers can meet the needs of their community by providing forums in which persons can participate in the resolution of disputes in an informal atmosphere without restraint and intimidation. * * * Community dispute resolution centers can serve the interest of the citizenry and promote quick and voluntary resolution of certain criminal matters."

The program is to be administered and supervised under the direction of the chief administrator of the courts. It provides funds for the establishment and continuance of dispute resolution centers. Grant recipients are defined as non-profit organizations organized for the resolution of disputes or for religious, charitable or educational purposes. To be eligible for funding, the Act provides that the neutral mediators have certain qualifications, that only certain costs be assessable to participants, that agreements or decisions be written, that monetary awards, which may not in any case exceed a certain amount, may be assessed only upon consent of the parties and that the dispute resolution center may not hear certain types of disputes of a more criminal nature.

The centers are selected by the chief administrator of the courts from submitted applications. The state's share of any center's costs may not exceed fifty percent. The statute also imposes certain reporting requirements upon grant recipients. Importantly, the Act creates a privilege of confidentiality for the mediation of arbitration proceedings and decisions. Section 849–b, subdiv. 6.[1]

* * *

As to the first factor, there is a strong policy in favor of full development of facts and admissibility in criminal cases. *United States v. Chiarella*, 588 F.2d 1358, 1372 (2d Cir.1978); *United States v. King*, supra, at 106. As the United States Supreme Court has stated "[t]he need to develop all relevant facts in the adversary system is both fundamental and comprehensive." *United States v. Nixon*, 418 U.S. 683, 709, 94 S.Ct. 3090, 3108, 41 L.Ed.2d 1039 (1974). Suppression here would impinge on such policy.

Secondly, the policy sought to be furthered by the state promulgated privilege is the encouragement of participation in "the resolution of disputes in an informal atmosphere without restraint and intimidation." The confidentiality outlined under subdivision 849–b.6 is core to establishing an atmosphere "without restraint and intimidation." Although it is unclear whether the privilege acts in any primary sense to encourage participation in the program, it directly serves to insure the effectiveness of the program and thereby, secondarily, it serves to promote continued support for and existence of the program. It should be noted that abrogation of the privilege would place funding for the program in jeopardy. Subdivision 849–b.4; *People v. Snyder*, 129 Misc.2d 137, 492 N.Y.S.2d 890, 892 (S.Ct., Erie Co.1985).

With respect to the third factor, the United States has not shown any particularized need for the evidence. In fact, it concedes that, even without the evidence in dispute, the Grand Jury had more than enough evidence upon which to base its finding of probable cause. Government's June 8, 1987 Response to Defendant's Motion dated June 4, 1987, p. 3.

* * *

The final factor for consideration concerns the impact on local policy from not recognizing the privilege in this case. The privilege generally serves to foster participation in the program and serves to promote candor by those participating. Although, this Court grants that few potential parties will likely forego participation in the program because of knowledge that evidence adduced therein would be subject to presen-

---

1. That subdivision provides: "Except as otherwise expressly provided in this article, all memoranda, work products, or case files of a mediator are confidential and not subject to disclosure in any judicial or administrative proceeding. Any communica- tion relating to the subject matter of the resolution made during the resolution process by any participant, mediator, or any other person present at the dispute resolution shall be a confidential communication."

tation in a federal prosecution, the disclosure and its very funding will be called into question.

In balance, this Court finds that the privilege afforded by subdivision 849–b.6 must be recognized in proceedings before this Court. All statements made during the dispute resolution process and all terms and conditions of such settlement shall be suppressed.

* * *

It is likely that courts will continue to uphold privileges where a statute exists, although there are exceptions in rare instances, such as where constitutional rights are at issue.[39] However, most commentators agree that the privilege binds only the mediator. The parties are free to disclose information as they desire.

The exact nature of the privilege, as previously discussed, is unclear. The nature of the relationship between the mediator and the parties is unclear as well. How would specific duties owed to the parties affect confidentiality?[40] Are these privileges so absolute as to prevent any discussions, such as those for teaching purposes? While policy reasons remain strong that matters in mediation should be confidential, there must be limits. An absolute privilege, preventing the mediator from discussing the matter with anyone, is probably what most people expect. However, a survey of the mediation confidentiality statutes along with an interpretation of the cases, does not reveal support for an absolute privilege. Nevertheless, the mediator routinely makes promises and assurances to the parties concerning confidentiality. The mediator must be careful not to create a situation where she may be liable for wrongful disclosure or a breach of contract for disclosures[41] if later required to testify.

In terms of privilege, there is some debate about who holds such a privilege. At least a few courts have allowed the mediator (or mediation center on behalf of the mediator) to claim the privilege, even though the parties waived it, and in fact, requested disclosure.[42] Statutes are beginning to provide clarification regarding the mediation privilege. At least one state has made it clear that the mediator holds the privilege only on behalf of the party, and only that party may effect a waiver.[43] The only clear waiver, though to date not judicially tested, may be in terms of allowing the mediator to testify in his own defense in a malpractice case.[44]

39. Rogers & McEwen, supra note 11, at 126.

40. See Chapter 15, § F, infra.

41. For more on mediator liability, see Chapter 15, § F, infra.

42. See *Fenton v. Howard*, 118 Ariz. 119, 575 P.2d 318 (1978) and West's Colo. Rev. Stat. Ann. §§ 13–22–301–313 (1991).

43. See Wyo. Stat. § 1–43–103 (1993).

44. A few states have provided explicit exceptions to confidentiality for these cases. West's RCWA 5.60.070(1)(g) and (2)(b)

4. CURRENT TRENDS

The trend in mediation until recently was to assure participants of confidentiality. However, as this occurred, there was a slight tendency to misuse the process. Moreover, a broad blanket of confidentiality came into direct conflict with requirements for disclosure. Whether creating exceptions to confidentiality will change the nature of the mediation process is unknown. However, there has been a slight movement by courts and legislatures toward chipping away at the confidentiality of the mediation. In some instances, confidentiality provisions may come into conflict with ethical considerations.[45] For example, attorneys have a duty to report unethical conduct of other attorneys. In a mediation where the mediator is an attorney, is she obligated, to breach a confidentiality agreement, to report an attorney advocate's misconduct?

IN RE WALLER
Court of Appeals, District of Columbia, 1990.
573 A.2d 780.

Attorney disciplinary proceeding was brought....

* * *

In this disciplinary proceeding, the Board on Professional Responsibility found that respondent had engaged in misrepresentation in violation of DR 1–102(A)(4) when, in response to a show cause order issued by the Superior Court, he falsely—and with intent to deceive—told the court that he had previously lied to a court-appointed mediator about his representation of a third-party (a surgeon) and about his reason for that lie....

* * *

On March 29, 1988, before discovery began, the Trial Judge, Henry Greene, ordered the parties to attend a mediation session with Joel Finkelstein, a lawyer in private practice who would serve as mediator.

During the mediation session, it occurred to the mediator that "[t]here was a glaring vacuum in the pleading [i.e., complaint] in that the surgeon was not named as a defendant." At that time, Respondent told the mediator that he "was the surgeon's attorney." The mediator then told Respondent that, in the mediator's opinion, Respondent "had a conflict of interest in this case in that he represented the surgeon who could and probably should have been a named defendant because it was a meritorious malpractice claim." When Respondent disagreed with the mediator's assessment, the mediator told Respondent to bring the matter to Judge Greene's attention.

* * *

(1991); 12 Okla. Stat. Ann. § 1805, F (Supp. 1993).

45. For elaboration on this issue in the legal context, see Comment, *To Disclose or Not To Disclose: The Relationship Between Confidentiality in Mediation and the Model Rules of Professional Conduct,* 95 Dick. L. Rev. 601 (1991).

Receiving no response from Mr. Waller, the mediator then contacted Judge Greene on his own. Judge Greene suggested that the mediator again attempt to reach Respondent in order to have Respondent himself contact the Court. This was attempted, again without success.

Still concerned, the mediator contacted Judge Greene once more and, for the first time, told him about the possible conflict of interest. The mediator felt he could do so despite the non-disclosure provision of the mediation order [1] because "it was a matter that had nothing to do with the negotiations between the parties but might affect the administration of justice in the Superior Court ..." ...

* * *

In response to the Show Cause Order, Respondent filed a document with the Court stating that, notwithstanding what he had said to the mediator, Respondent was not Dr. Jackson's attorney at the time of the mediation. Respondent admitted that the had told the mediator the opposite, but he explained that he had done so only to test whether remarks made during the mediation process would be held in confidence....   Based on the information that has come to my attention in this case, it would appear that Mr. Waller either has violated Disciplinary Rule 5–105(B), which precludes a lawyer from multiple representation where the representation of one client is likely to be adversely affected by his representation of another client, or Disciplinary Rule 1–102(A)(4), which prohibits a lawyer from engaging in conduct involving "dishonesty, fraud, deceit or misrepresentation." Consequently, I bring this matter to your attention for whatever action you deem appropriate.

* * *

On May 20, 1988, Respondent submitted a letter asserting an entirely new explanation by [sic] his actions. Respondent now asserted that he had not intentionally tried to mislead the mediator in order to test confidentiality; instead, he now said that when he had told the mediator that he represented Dr. Jackson, it had merely been a "slip of the tongue." As Respondent put it: What really happened is that I said I represented Dr. Jackson but I really meant that I didn't represent Dr. Jackson. Dr. Jackson wasn't a party so I didn't think it was important.

Respondent's letter of May 20, 1988 went on to justify the nonjoinder of the surgeon in the case in the following terms: The suit was only to compel discovery so we could determine who was at fault. Dr. Jackson fully cooperated so there was no need to bring him in at this time....

* * *

We have pondered why Respondent took the unusual step of admitting to the mediator that the surgeon was his client. Perhaps he failed

1. The order requiring mediation stated: ORDERED that no statements of any party or counsel shall be disclosed to the court or admissible as evidence for any purpose at trial of this case ...

to realize that, by admitting the relationship with Dr. Jackson, he was effectively conceding a conflict of interest. Perhaps he believed, erroneously, that the mediator would not disclose such a startling revelation. For whatever reason, we feel that Respondent did lapse into candor in making the March, 1988 admission. . . .

* * *

Based on all of these factors, we believe that a 60–day suspension would be the appropriate sanction here. . . .

* * *

———

The most recent confidentiality statutes include provisions clearly addressing those specific situations where confidentiality conflicts with other reporting requirements. In most instances, other reporting requirements prevail.

In the majority of cases, uncertainty remains. Moreover, because mediation is in its infancy in the United States, to now lessen its confidential nature may result in distrust of the process. It is likely that a decrease in the use of mediation would follow. The establishment of clear parameters surrounding confidentiality of the mediation process has become a necessity if the use of the process is to continue to increase.

H. CONCLUSION

The most important task for the mediator and the mediation advocate is to determine the status of the law with regard to confidentiality. The law of the jurisdiction where the mediation is being held should be reviewed, as should the law in the jurisdiction where the case is pending. Moreover, the mediator should be very careful to clarify the parameters of confidentiality with all participants. The advocates should ascertain from their clients whether there is a need or desire for confidentiality and its priority.

It is therefore important that not only the mediator and the lawyer representatives have a clear understanding of the law in each jurisdiction, but also, that it is explained in clear and precise terms to the parties. In most cases, it is advisable that the parameters of confidentiality be in writing. This may include an agreement or a court order. Because mediation is such a flexible process, there have yet to be strict rules and regulations concerning mediation and those who practice it. A private mediation between two individuals may be conducted differently than one involving public funds and over one hundred parties. Establishment of specific rules with regard to confidentiality may prove very difficult.

QUESTIONS FOR DISCUSSION

11–1. If "discoverable" information, or even information "leading to discovery", is exempt from protection of confidentiality, what specifically is confidential?

11–2. Many mediation programs, both within university and law schools, as well as general community based programs, have mediators, particularly novices, go through a debriefing session immediately following the mediation. How does confidentiality or a privilege affect those types of discussions?

11–3. In a mediation involving an ongoing landlord-tenant dispute, the landlord informs the mediator, in caucus, that she knows that the tenant has unpaid traffic tickets, and that she has alerted the county sheriff who is scheduled to arrive and arrest the tenant in about 30 minutes. What do you do as the mediator? Does it make a difference if the mediation is being conducted at the courthouse or at your private office?

11–4. Confidences of Colossal Computers

You represent the Colossal Computer Company in a case pending in the superior court of the State of Flax. Colossal Computer was sued by Jim Thomas, individually, and on behalf of his five year old daughter, Michele Thomas, for the alleged wrongful death of Margo Thomas, the wife and mother. Margo Thomas' death occurred when a Colossal truck collided with her automobile. Colossal Computer, from the inception, has taken the position that Margo Thomas was 100% negligent by failing to yield the right of way to the truck.

After the lawsuit was filed, Judge Hardly A. Wake ordered the case to mediation. The court order consisted of a one sentence referral. After four hours of mediation, a capable mediator declared a total impasse with the parties over three million dollars apart. Thereafter, the case went to trial. Two weeks into trial, and during the plaintiff's case, Judge Wake declared a mistrial when a plaintiff's expert mentioned insurance. Judge Wake on his own motion, ordered the parties to mediate a second time. During the hearing on Colossal Computer's opposition to the second mediation, Judge Wake, after ordering the second mediation, commented, "I'll determine when to set the second trial, the extent of jury selection, and the amount of time for final argument based on who exercised the most good faith during the second mediation."

After nine hours, the second mediation reached a total impasse with no progress made from the status of the first mediation. The mediator issued a one page report to the Court which stated only "the parties appeared and the matter did not settle."

Judge Wake, after receiving a telephone call from the Thomas' counsel alleging Colossal Computer's bad faith in the second mediation, has set a hearing to determine who was "in good faith" at the second mediation. The judge has also ordered a bench subpoena for the mediator to appear at the hearing. Plaintiff's counsel also contacted the local press, described what happened at the second mediation; the newspaper wrote an article with the headline, "Colossal Computer Fails to Negotiate at Second Mediation."

Neither the statutes of the State of Flax nor the court's local rules directly address the issue of confidentiality.

You have the following assignments:

(a) Prepare a motion with a supporting brief for the court as to why the mediator should not testify.

(b) Prepare a motion for sanctions with a supporting brief regarding plaintiff's counsel's telephone call to the court and interview with the press.

(c) Prepare a motion to bar the press from the hearing and writing about the mediations. Include a brief in support of your motion.

11–5. You are an attorney-mediator in private practice in California. You were contacted by the attorney for the plaintiff and agreed to mediate the case of Parker v. Secured Parking Systems, Inc. The case was a personal injury suit against Secured Parking for the aggravated sexual assault of Ms. Parker. The attorneys for the plaintiff, Kevin Blair and Gail Reedy of the firm Justice and Reedy, were present at the mediation along with their client.

When the mediation was first discussed, Mr. Blair requested that it be scheduled away from law offices and the courthouse. He stated that in his opinion a more relaxed environment would be better. A Saturday was also requested. As you are a flexible mediator, you complied. The mediation took place about a month ago at the conference center overlooking Malibu beach.

The case essentially involves a claim against a parking garage and its management for the amount of 12 million dollars. Both companies and their insurers were present at the mediation. The case was eventually settled for approximately 3.8 million dollars. During the mediation both parties, for different reasons, stressed the need for confidentiality. Confidentiality was demanded not only for all discussions within the mediation session, but also for the contents of the settlement agreement. The defendants were hoping to avoid publicity and keep the amount paid quiet. Plaintiffs were so concerned with confidentiality that they agreed to dismiss the suit once the terms of the settlement were fully complied with. You thought this was a bit out of the ordinary, having not experienced a plaintiff so willing to maintain confidentiality of the settlement amount. You suspected that there were underlying issues that had not been disclosed. However, despite your expertise in probing, the plaintiffs failed to disclose anything to you other than the need for confidentiality for protection of their client. A confidentiality agreement was executed by all parties, attorneys and the mediator. You facilitated all the other terms of the settlement and closed the mediation late that afternoon.

As they were leaving the mediation, the lawyers requested that you destroy your copy of a brief memorandum outlining the amount in settlement in a week. It also included the time and place of the exchange of the money. The exchange of money and documents was to take place between the counsel for each side within the following two weeks. The following week you were still somewhat puzzled. Nonetheless, you shredded your papers and closed the file.

About a week ago, at a pre-holiday season open house hosted by a local court reporting service, you ran into John Justice, one of the partners in the firm of Justice and Reedy. You did know that attorneys for the plaintiff had a 40% contingency agreement in the case you mediated. Not believing an innocent comment to be within the realm of confidentiality protection, you casually slapped him on the back and said, "I bet you're going to have a wonderful holiday season figuring out how to spend all that money." Mr. Justice looked very puzzled and asked, "What are you talking about?" You responded, "You know, the cash from that big settlement." By the surprised and shocked look on his face, you were at once aware that he had no knowledge of the settlement of the lawsuit, or of the mediation. You quickly mentioned that you needed to talk to someone else, and excused yourself from the conversation. You immediately left the open house.

The following week you received a telephone call from Mr. Justice requesting your voluntary presence at a deposition. You learn during the brief conversation that at the time of the mediation, partner Reedy, as well as associate Blair, were in the process of leaving the firm. They purposefully failed to inform anyone, including support staff of the fact that the mediation took place. In fact, it was their intent to take these files with them and announce the settlement after the dissolution of the firm.

You have been requested by Justice to disclose everything that took place at the mediation as well as the settlement amount. You, having turned white, requested time to think about this, and quickly hung up the phone.

As the mediator, what do you do?

Chapter Twelve

THE MEDIATED AGREEMENT

In the majority of mediations, the parties and the mediator together will eventually arrive at a point where there appears to be agreement on most, if not all, of the issues. It is then time to finalize the elements of the agreement.

A final agreement may not be reached in every mediation. Yet, in many instances the mediation can be termed an achievement. Neither a mediation nor a mediator should be judged solely in terms of whether or not an agreement is reached. There are other factors to consider. For instance, the parties may discuss the case a week later and reach a final agreement. In such a case, the mediation was effective. There may be times where the parties will complete the session by agreeing to disagree. Partial agreements are also possible. Agreements to reschedule the mediation are another option. Each of these results can be termed a mediated agreement. Just as mediation is a flexible process, so are the resulting agreements. Although complete settlement is some indication of the effectiveness of mediation, due to the variety of forms and styles of mediation, the types of cases and pressures to settle,[1] a final settlement should not be the sole determining factor of success.[2]

A. FINALIZING THE MEDIATED AGREEMENT

In instances where the parties themselves engage in negotiation and exchange options directly, there may a tendency on the part of the mediator to take a back seat role. He may allow his listening skills to become less than efficient. Yet, the mediator should be very active at this stage of the process. It is clearly part of the mediator's role and task to continue to guide the parties in concluding their agreement. In many instances, as parties negotiate directly toward a specific agreement, they will include a number of details in their discussions. The parties, however, lacking objectivity and anxious to reach a final resolu-

1. Issues of pressure to settle are discussed in § A(1) herein.

2. This issue is also examined in terms of ethical issues in Chapter 14, infra and quality of practice in Chapter 15, infra.

tion, may inadvertently omit items previously discussed. The mediator, in his neutral role, should have taken notes and identified all of the interests, issues, options and agreements. It is important, then, that he be an active participant in finalizing the agreement and assuring that all of the items previously identified have been included.

After a number of hours at the mediation table, the parties are eager to end the mediation. In cases where relationships have been reconciled or established, participants may be willing to forego details. The mediator's task is to assure that all of the details are covered. A failure to fine tune the agreement could lead to further disputes.[3]

When approaching the finalization of the mediated agreement (actually at all points during the mediation) the mediator should keep in mind that there are three important elements of a satisfactory agreement: procedural, psychological, and substantive satisfaction. While these aspects of satisfaction are sometimes viewed in terms of negotiation, specifically the interest based model,[4] the mediation process itself assists in achieving these results. The mediator, when reaching the stage where the agreement becomes final, should determine from the parties, inasmuch as possible, whether all three elements are achieved, recognizing the overlap between them. For example, if a party is satisfied with the procedure, that satisfaction will contribute directly to her psychological satisfaction. Likewise, when the substance of the agreement is satisfactory, psychological satisfaction is apparent.

Procedural satisfaction is commonly achieved by participation in the mediation. If the mediator has determined that each party has either participated fully in the process, or feels that she has been provided the opportunity to participate without pressure, there is usually subsequent satisfaction with the procedure. In fact, most studies report that the parties are satisfied with the mediation process, even in cases when a final agreement is not reached.[5]

Psychological satisfaction will be present if the parties have not only had an opportunity to be heard, but also have been able to express their anger, frustration, disappointment, sadness, etc. Many times it is important that parties express themselves, that is, ventilate their emotion. This will enable them to thereafter focus on working out a resolution. The mediation process, by design, allows ventilation before cooperation is expected. In many mediation models, the time for expression and ventilation is a separate stage of the process. In many legal and business disputes, parties are required to present their dispute in the form of testimony. It is usually inappropriate to include the feeling or psychological aspect of the dispute in the testimony, although there are exceptions. However, in the mediation process, expression of emotion is

3. This is further discussed in this chapter at § A(2), infra.

4. Christopher W. Moore & CDR Associates, Effective Mediation 5 (1989).

5. Royer F. Cook, et al., Neighborhood Justice Centers Field Test, Executive Summary Final Evaluation Report 15 (1980). Anecdotal reports of this information are very common as well, and includes the author's personal experience.

often encouraged.[6] Moreover, the mediator, by his actions—which include active listening—lets the parties know that they are being heard. This is not always the case in other types of dispute resolution procedures, particularly litigation. Therefore, the mediation process itself contributes to the psychological satisfaction of the parties. When reaching the final stages of the process, the mediator should take a moment to consider whether the psychological needs of the parties, within limits,[7] have been met.

The mediated agreement belongs to the parties, not the mediator.[8] While acknowledging this, the mediator should still take a direct role in determining the substance of the final agreement. This role is not in dictating terms of specific content, but rather in assuring that all items previously discussed and proposed by the parties are included. It is impossible for a mediator, as a neutral facilitator, to completely guarantee that all parties are satisfied with the specific substance of the agreement. However, in most instances if the mediator has identified the interests of each party and those interests are satisfied, the result will be an agreement with substantive satisfaction. Where procedural, psychological, and substantive satisfaction are substantially achieved, it is very likely that the parties will completely comply with the agreement.

1. PRESSURES TO SETTLE

There never was a good war, or a bad peace.

—Benjamin Franklin

Most cases settle, sooner or later. Mediation, necessarily moves later to sooner. In those cases in which the parties are unable to reach a final settlement, there is disagreement about the role of the mediator. This disagreement centers on how subtle or assertive the mediator should be in moving the parties to an agreement. This is also described in terms of mediator directiveness or pressure to settle. There are a variety of specific steps which some view as appropriate for the mediator to take, while others disagree. A push toward settlement may also come from outside sources, which tangentially effect the mediation process.

In the context of mediation in a pending lawsuit, pressures to settle may come from at least three different avenues. One source is from the judge. The court by its mere referral of a pending lawsuit to the mediation process is usually exerting pressure upon the parties to settle. This is also attempted regularly by courts outside of the mediation process, by holding judge facilitated settlement conferences or requiring counsel to "go outside and talk". With regard to mediation referral, a judge sometimes makes obvious comments like, "this case ought to be

---

6. Many mediators focus on asking questions such as "how did that make you feel?" for this reason.

7. By design, mediation is not the same as therapy or therapeutic counseling, and should not be a substitute process. See Chapter 3, § C, supra.

8. See, for example, Lon L. Fuller, *Mediation: Its Forms and Functions*, 44 S. Cal. L. Rev. 305 (1971). Compare however, Lawrence Susskind, *Environmental Mediation and the Accountability Problem*, 6 Vt. L. Rev. 1 (1981).

settled", "can't you settle this?" In other situations, the comment is not as direct, but the message is the same.

Another source of pressure to settle in the mediation process is found in the referral system. Some are not subtle. One method is a requirement that the litigants pay a penalty if they wish to avoid the settlement and go to trial. This is the procedure in "Michigan mediation." While labeled mediation, it is not a mediation process at all. The process is essentially case evaluation, where the parties receive a recommended settlement from a panel of three lawyers.[9] If the parties do not wish to accept the recommendation of the panel, they can go to trial. However, if they do not achieve a result at trial, which is at least 10% better than the panel's recommendation, they must pay the actual costs of the other party.[10] Other programs have imposed sanctions for failure to negotiate in good faith. Some of those methods have passed constitutional challenge, while others have not. When challenged, the methods have been evaluated by courts applying a balancing test: allowing leeway in administrating a program, and yet not placing a financial burden on the parties or denying their constitutional rights.[11]

Another concern is with pressure from the mediator himself. While the mediator's role consists of facilitating an agreement, it is difficult to determine how far he should go in "motivating" the parties. Many mediators, particularly lawyer mediators, discuss this in terms of being an advocate for settlement. The mediator is not an advocate for any party, but rather for the settlement process. In that role, some mediators have been known to engage in tactics which do not meet with universal approval. One such tactic is keeping the parties together until very late, even until the next morning, in hopes of obtaining a settlement. Agreements reached in this manner are more likely to be withdrawn, if possible, by the parties. Many are critical of this tactic. Other mediators stress that the case ought to be settled, and that the court will not be pleased to hear the matter. While some parties see this as pressure to settle, in many instances it can also be seen as the mediator assisting the parties in reality testing. Another approach is to provide the parties with the mediator's proposal for settlement, which, in effect, transforms the mediation into a non-binding arbitration.

In any mediation, the parties will feel pressure to settle if the mediator has the ability to make a report to the court or other third party. The report may consist of the reasons that the case did not settle.[12] It may also be in the form of a recommendation for final adjudication. For example, in California child custody mediation, the courts are permitted to require a recommendation from the mediator if

9. Kimberlee K. Kovach, *Neutral Case Evaluation*, St. Mary's ADR Institute (1989). See Chapter 1, § D, supra.

10. Kathy L. Stuart, et al., *Settling Cases in Detroit: An Examination of Wayne County's Mediation Program*, 8 Just. Sys. J. 307 (1983).

11. For an in depth examination of the issue, see Nancy Rogers & Craig A. McEwen, Mediation: Law, Policy & Practice (Chapter Seven) (1989 & Supp. 1993).

12. This is, for example, in terms of identifying the party, or side, which was uncooperative with the process.

the case does not settle.[13]   On the other hand, to prevent such disclosures, some statutes actually prohibit any report to the court other than whether the case settled.[14]   Conflicting messages are being sent to mediators, although most ethical considerations which address this issue advise against, and even prohibit, reports to the court.   Each mediator must use his best judgment when evaluating the degree of pressure to exert on the parties in "advocating" settlement.   As a general rule, where guidance is limited, the mediator must recall that his role is to assist the parties in arriving at their own settlement.

2.   CONTENTS OF THE AGREEMENT

The content of the agreement, just as the content of the entire mediation, belongs to the parties.   That is not to say, however, that the mediator does not have a distinct role in assuring that all points raised during the mediation are dealt with in some fashion in the actual agreement.   The mediator also plays a role in completing details and fine tuning the mediation agreement.   One of the primary reasons for the failure to comply with a mediated agreement is the lack of clarity in the final agreement.

When finalizing and drafting the mediated agreement, a mediator should ask the following question: **Can it be determined, from reading the agreement alone, who will do what, when, where, how, and how much?**   If this can be answered affirmatively, so that an individual, not present during the mediation and unfamiliar with the facts, will be able to read the agreement and determine specifically what is to happen, the mediator's job is complete.   If any of these questions is not clearly answered by the agreement, then the mediator must continue to clarify issues before drafting the final agreement.

In determining the specific contents of the agreement, the mediator often engages in reality testing.   Another way to look at this is in terms of a discussion of specific implementation of the agreement.[15]   The mediator assists the parties in determining if what they are intending to agree to is really possible, and how exactly it will be carried out.   A simple example is the case of an agreement to make payments for a debt owed.   A party is considering an agreement to pay $500.00 a month. The mediator learned from previous conversations that this individual clears only $1,000.00 a month, with apartment rent of $350.00 and a car payment of $180.00.   Most trainers and educators agree that the mediator has a duty to raise a question of the realistic possibility of compliance with the agreement.   That is, does the party have $500.00 of disposable income per month?   On the other hand, some take the position that the parties should be free to make their own agreement, regardless of the content or ability to fulfill it.   The minority position would suggest that

13. West's Ann. Cal. Civ. Code §§ 4607, 4351.5(f) (1993).

14. V.T.C.A., Civ.Prac. & Rem.Code § 154.053 (Supp. 1992).

15. Implementation is sometimes seen as a separate stage of the process.   Christopher W. Moore, The Mediation Process: Practical Strategies to Resolving Conflict 248 (1986).

in the preceding example the individual may have other means to fulfill the agreement, and the inquiry is beyond the mediator's role. If reality testing involves issues which might be sensitive or personal, such as amounts of money, the mediator should meet with the party privately.

Some propose that the mediator has a duty to assure that the agreement is a fair one.[16] This of course, places the mediator in a difficult role because his perception of fairness may differ from that of the parties. If the agreement is fair from the perspective of the participants, the mediator's job is complete, absent, of course, illegality.[17]

Once the substantive elements of the agreement are determined, the specifics of implementation must also be finalized. This includes how the agreement will be carried out. In the preceding example, the following must be determined: a specific date for each monthly payment; the location where the payment is to be made; how the payment is to be made, e.g. by mail, in person, etc., and whether personal check, cashiers check, credit card debit, etc. is acceptable. Detailed and effective implementation procedures help assure compliance with the agreement.

Although consideration of reality and implementation procedures are discussed as a separate stage of the process, often they are combined in the negotiation phase. This will be particularly true in an integrative negotiation.[18] In that case, as a final agreement is reached, any items which have not been included or determined should be raised by the mediator, in an effort to provide a completely detailed agreement.

In many cases, when confronted with the task of determining specific implementation procedures, parties tend to call on a third party who may not be present to assist with the effort. The mediator must be careful to *not* include in the agreement a provision which requires an action on the part of someone who is not present at the session. In rare cases where no other alternatives exist, the mediator should require that the parties first obtain the consent of the third person before the agreement is finalized. This can be done by telephone.

The mediator's role, insofar as finalizing the contents of the agreement, should also include an examination of contingencies. The mediator, as a neutral party, is more likely to see an indication that the agreement, as specified by the parties, may not be completely workable. In that instance, the mediator should assist the parties in identifying potential problems and finding alternative courses of action. Because the discussion of "what-ifs" could go on forever, the mediator must limit this discussion. This again, is a situation which will vary depending on the type and complexity of the case.

16. Leonard L. Riskin, *Toward New Standards for the Neutral Lawyer in Mediation*, 26 Ariz. L. Rev. 329, 354 (1984).

17. See also, Chapter 7, supra which explored this issue in terms of the mediator's neutrality.

18. See Chapter 9, supra for a discussion of negotiation theory.

An item which should *not* be included in the agreement is a recital of fault. The mediation process is a forward looking process. Inclusion of matters such as blame, liability, or guilt is inappropriate in the mediated agreement. In drafting the agreement, the mediator must refrain from addressing these issues, and avoid using phrases which begin: "because of" ... "due to" ... or "as a result of". Even where an acknowledgement of fault is demanded by one of the parties and agreed to by the other, it should not be included in the written agreement. This, however, raises a question about inclusion of a recital of consideration in the agreement; and the subsequent effect on the enforceability of the agreement.

In most mediations, the agreement which results is not unilateral. The majority contain reciprocal agreements by all parties. Therefore, as a practical matter, the concern with the consideration issue is minimal. Even so, many mediators, particularly lawyers, begin each written agreement with a phrase such as "for good and valuable consideration".[19]

Most agreements naturally contain language describing a course of conduct on the part of each disputant—even if this includes an agreement to no longer pursue the matter. Some mediators attempt to include these in the agreement so that it appears that there is a balance of concessions.[20]

In terms of specific content, a recital or preamble which encourages positive and cooperative behaviors and attitudes may also be appropriate.[21] This may also assist with compliance. Statements reflecting the parties' commitment to the agreement may also be included with the general recitals of consideration.

3. PARTIAL AGREEMENTS

A mediator must keep in mind that the stage of finalizing the agreement, like all other stages of the process, must be flexible. This includes flexibility in the conclusion. In mediation, it is possible that instead of a complete settlement of the case, there will be one or more partial agreements. These may take essentially two different forms. The first is a partial agreement in terms of specific issues or parties to the case. That is, the mediator will carve out certain issues which the parties agree to. These issues can be finalized without reaching conclusion on others. Partial agreement is also possible in multi-party cases where there is complete agreement between certain parties, but not others.

The other type of partial agreement is in terms of an overall intent to agree, or an agreement in principle, which leaves specific details to be worked out at a later date. Many times this occurs where there is a need for additional information. The mediator should be careful to

---

19. While a discourse on general contract law is beyond the scope of this work, because of the potential of these issues being raised, some mediators refuse to draft the agreement. See this chapter §§ B & C, infra.

20. Moore, supra note 15, at 257.

21. Id.

specify exactly what the parties did agree to, and not make any implications.

The mediator should be able to recognize, identify, and clarify a partial agreement. In many instances, he will outline it for the parties. In cases of partial agreements, there is also the possibility that the parties, after a period of time, may obtain additional information, see things differently, and wish to reschedule the mediation. The agreement may even include the specifics of the reschedule date.[22]

4. FORM OF THE AGREEMENT

The mediated agreement can take a number of forms. These range from the least formal, an oral agreement, to the most formal, a formalized legal document. There are many which fall between these two. The form of the agreement will often depend on the nature of the case and whether or not a lawsuit is pending.

It is also possible to have what is termed a self-executing agreement which is carried out completely at the time of agreement.[23] An example is the exchange of goods, or the payment of a sum certain. The item or cash is exchanged during the mediation, and the matter is concluded. Often a written agreement is not necessary.

In many cases, the form of the agreement is related to its enforceability. Issues of enforceability of a mediated agreement often rely on an understanding of general contract law. In some cases, it is specifically provided by statute that there must be a valid contract if the mediation agreement is to be enforceable.[24] In other instances, not only will the form of the agreement need to conform with general contract provisions, but it must include additional elements as well.[25] Therefore, in drafting the agreement it is important to consider the form, not only in terms of the parties and their needs, but also in light of enforceability issues. However, there is lack of consensus on whether it is part of the mediator's role to make determinations about enforceability.[26]

The least formal agreement is the oral agreement. In this instance, the mediator should restate what the terms of the agreement are, and perhaps even have the parties state to each other what they agree to do. Sometimes this is sealed with a handshake or other form of confirmation of the agreement. It is important, in these instances, that all the details are spelled out. Because the agreement is oral, there may a tendency on the part of the mediator, as well as the parties, to ignore or dismiss a need for details. It is assumed that everyone remembers from the negotiation what they have agreed to do, and therefore, no need exists for additional specificity or restatement. Unfortunately, this is usually

22. Rescheduling and following up after mediation are specifically dealt with in Chapter 13, infra.

23. Moore, supra note 15, at 249.

24. See V.T.C.A., Civ.Prac. & Rem.Code § 150.071 (Supp. 1992).

25. For example, Minn.Stat.Ann. § 572.35 (1992). Issues of enforceability are detailed in this chapter § C, infra.

26. See also Section B of this chapter on drafting issues for a discussion of the variety of mediator roles and legal effect.

not the case. The parties have probably not been taking any notes during this segment of the mediation. The mediator should have been taking detailed notes and can rely on these notes to firm up all details. As previously stated, it is part of the mediator's job to review the agreement and assure that everyone is in agreement on the specific details. This is no different in the case where there is an oral agreement.

Another informal type of agreement is an agreement in principle. The parties arrive at a general agreement which includes further details that need to be worked out at a later time. The agreement is usually in general outline form. In many cases, the written agreement is in simple straightforward language, outlining what the parties have agreed to do. The agreement may even include lists. It is important that it is written so that all parties understand the terms. In other cases, the form of the agreement will be more complex, consisting of an original business contract or settlement documents for a lawsuit. In some instances the agreements can consist of a renegotiated contract, which may take days to complete in final form. Finally, legislation, rules, and regulations constitute yet another form, albeit uncommon, of a mediated agreement.[27]

The form of the agreement will differ depending on the circumstances surrounding the mediation. For example, if a lawsuit is pending, different considerations will come into play. The sections that follow detail how the existence of pending litigation may impact the final form of the mediated agreement.

a. Pre-litigation Cases

In pre-litigation matters, no lawsuit has been filed and in the majority of cases, attorneys are not present. Therefore, consideration of court documents is not necessary. These are the cases where it would be possible to utilize an oral agreement, although most mediation centers, programs, and mediators stress the advantages of a written agreement.[28] With a written agreement, the mediator must include all of the factors clearly, so that the parties are certain of what they are to do, including when, where, and how they are to do it.

Issues of enforceability are important here as well. The parties may want to be assured that they have a written contract. Just what a mediator can say and do in this regard is one of those items subject to controversy.[29] If a mediator who is also a lawyer becomes directly involved in making certain the agreement is enforceable, then it is likely that he is providing legal advice. In the case of non-lawyer mediators,

27. This is becoming more common where governmental agencies, along with regulatory and law making bodies, are using the mediation process to achieve consensus. See Chapter 16, infra.

28. These include a permanent record of the specifics of the agreement and the ritualistic nature of the agreement writing and signing. Such procedures may increase chances of complete compliance.

29. This is also discussed in § B, infra this chapter.

many may not know this information, or conversely, may engage in the unauthorized practice of law.

b. *Pending Lawsuits*

In mediations where there is a lawsuit pending, the participants face additional choices with regard to the form of the mediated agreement. Because there is litigation pending, another issue that must be determined prior to finalizing the agreement is the effect of the mediated agreement on the lawsuit. A final settlement via mediation will take one of three primary forms: 1) a dismissal of the lawsuit; 2) a finalization of the lawsuit in terms of an agreed judgment; or 3) a continuation of the lawsuit with certain stipulations. All of these, of course, necessitate different forms for the agreement.

In terms of the dismissal of the lawsuit, the remaining portion of the mediated agreement would most likely be similar to that in a non-litigation case, that is, a valid contract. That assumes, of course, that all elements of the contract are present. In this instance, a dismissal or a non-suit will be filed, and the parties would then rely on the mediated agreement (contract) to indicate the action that will be taken.

In other instances, the parties do not wish to have the lawsuit dismissed, but rather prefer to incorporate the mediated agreement into the final papers or judgment of the case. In some cases the referring court requires that the agreement be submitted. In others, there is a statutory mandate.[30]

Court approval of the mediated agreement can be accomplished in a number of ways. The first is that the mediated agreement is, in fact, the final agreed or stipulated judgment of the court. All elements of the agreement are contained in the judgment proposed to, and signed by, the court. Another option is to incorporate by reference the mediated agreement into the final decree or judgment of the court. Many times in a divorce case, there is too much detail in the mediated agreement to be included in the final decree. Therefore, the agreement is either attached to the decree as an exhibit or incorporated by reference. An additional alternative is to include certain elements of the agreement in the court's order, along with a reference to separate agreement or contract which contains additional items of agreement. All of these options have been used, with no widespread preference yet established. It is important however, that the parties and the mediators are clear, before they enter into the finalization stage, on what form the agreement will take.

B.   DRAFTING ISSUES

There are a number of issues surrounding the drafting of a mediation agreement. These, of course, include the form of the agreement, and its contents, as well as its enforceability. These items, however, are discussed in more detail in other sections. The mediator plays a primary

---

30. See, e.g., West's Colo.Rev.Stat.Ann.
§ 13–22–308 (1993).

role in drafting the document, particularly in the physical production of the agreement. One important topic of discussion for mediators is whether the drafting of a mediated agreement is the practice of law. A related issue surrounds providing advice regarding enforceability of the agreement. Resolution of the issues encompassing this topic turn on whether the mediator is a lawyer.

For the lawyer mediator there is some question as to whether mediation is the practice of law. This issue overlaps with issues of mediator certification, regulation, and ethics.[31] There is no definitive answer, although as a practical matter charges for unauthorized practice of law have not been routinely brought against non-lawyer mediators.[32] If mediating is practicing law, will the mediator be committing legal malpractice for faulty drafting? In most court referred cases where parties are represented, mediators compose only a memorandum of agreement. It is then the lawyer-advocates' responsibility to draft the final documents, whether they be court documents such as a judgment or contractual in nature. If the parties are not represented by counsel and a lawyer mediator drafts the agreement, there is some concern that the parties will have an expectation that the mediator is reviewing the agreement in terms of legal sufficiency. It is uncertain whether this is part of the mediator's role. Currently, in most instances mediators see it as beyond the scope of their role, and therefore, require that the parties have the agreement reviewed by their own counsel before finalization.

For the non-lawyer, some issues are simpler, while others more difficult. The non-lawyer mediator will probably not be expected or required to look at the agreement in terms of its legal sufficiency, but rather draft specifically what the parties request. His drafting is essentially the memorialization of the agreement. On the other hand, the non-lawyer, if engaged in writing or drafting settlement decrees, might be viewed as engaged in the practice of law. This very issue has been raised in the context of divorce mediation in Tennessee, with two conflicting results within two years of each other.[33]

Non-lawyers, as a practical matter, have been mediating cases for many years, in many programs affiliated with the justice system and bar associations. It is common in the vast majority of these programs that the mediator draft the agreement. It is doubtful at this time that issues of the unauthorized practice of law for drafting agreements will be raised. In most cases, the mediator is serving in a scrivener role. If however, a non-lawyer mediator is unclear about an issue, it is recommended that he advise the party to obtain independent legal counsel before finalizing the agreement.

31. These will be examined further in Chapters 14 and 15, infra.

32. However, these issues were raised in the mid-eighties in terms of ethical opinions. The question of whether mediation is the practice of law was answered both in the affirmative and the negative. See Nancy H. Rogers & Richard A. Salem, A Student's Guide to Mediation and the Law, 117–121 (1987).

33. Id.

C. ENFORCEABILITY

In many of the community mediation models, the issue of technical enforceability of the mediated agreement is rarely raised. The theory is that individuals who take part in agreement formation have ownership in it; therefore they are likely to comply with the terms. Research has supported this. It has been demonstrated that not only are disputant satisfied with the agreement, but they perceive the outcome as significantly fairer than a court determination.[34] Consequently, there is much greater likelihood that they will follow the terms.[35] Yet some agreements, particularly those which must be performed over time, contain compliance provisions. These may include a third party who will monitor compliance.[36] In litigation, this party is often assumed to be the court.

BARNETT v. SEA LAND SERVICE, INC.
United States Court of Appeals, Ninth Circuit, 1989.
875 F.2d 741.

* * *

Appellant contends that the district court erred as a matter of law by not allowing the introduction of evidence that a settlement had been reached during the mediation session. We review questions of law *de novo*. *United States v. McConney*, 728 F.2d 1195 (9th Cir.) cert. denied, 469 U.S. 824, 105 S.Ct. 101, 83 L.Ed.2d 46 (1984).

Local Rule 39.1 of the Western District of Washington sets forth procedures for mediation, arbitration and special masters. The parties to the instant dispute participated in mediation under this rule. The provision which lies at the heart of the appellant's first contention is Local Rule 39.1(d)(3), which provides as follows:

> *Proceedings Privileged.* All proceedings of the mediation conference, including any statement made by any party, attorney or other participant, shall, in all respects, be privileged and not reported, recorded, placed in evidence, made known to the trial court or jury, or construed for any purpose as an admission against interest: No party shall be bound by anything done or said at the conference unless a settlement is reached, in which event the agreement upon a settlement shall be reduced to writing and shall be binding upon all parties to that agreement.

Although the parties entered into mediation, the appellees refused to sign a settlement agreement prepared by the appellant after the mediation took place. At trial, the district judge refused to allow testimony by

---

34. Janice A. Roehl & Royer F. Cook, *Mediation in Interpersonal Disputes: Effectiveness and Limitations*, in Mediation Research: The Process and Effectiveness of Third Party Intervention 33 (Kenneth Kressel & Dean G. Pruitt, eds., 1989).

35. Id. at 34.

36. Moore, supra note 15, at 252.

the mediator as to whether a settlement had been reached. Appellant contends that a settlement was reached.

Appellees argue that there was a mutual mistake and no settlement was ever consummated. Appellee argues that under Local Rule 39.-1(d)(d), since no written settlement was consummated, none exists and therefore the district court was correct in not accepting evidence of a settlement.

We agree with the appellees' interpretation of the Local Rule. While appellant focuses on the language which provides that no party shall be bound unless a settlement is reached, we believe that the last phrase of Local Rule 39.1(d)(3) is controlling. It provides that once a settlement is reached it shall be reduced to writing and shall be binding upon the parties. We interpret this to mean that until a settlement is reduced to writing, it is not binding up the parties. When a settlement is not binding no evidence may be introduced under Local Rule 39.-1(d)(3). This ruling is reached only under the language of Western District of Washington Local Rule 39.1 and is not meant to be a general pronouncement on when binding settlements are reached in other cases, disputes, and forums.

* * *

RIZK v. MILLARD

Court of Appeals of Texas, Houston (14th Dist.), 1991.
810 S.W.2d 318.

Petition denied.

PAUL PRESSLER, JUSTICE.

This Petition for a Writ of Mandamus challenges an order entered by respondent striking relator's pleadings and granting a default judgment against him in *Wesley L. Snyder v. Fred E. Rizk*, Richard Muriby and George Howard in the 189th Judicial District Court of Harris County, Texas. Relator requests that this court command respondent to reinstate relator's answers, set aside the default judgment and set this case for trial on the issue of liability. The petition is denied.

Relator was a member of a joint venture organized to subsidize certain patents on inventions developed by the plaintiff. The plaintiff is an inventor who developed a unique series of laser gun sight systems which were issued patents in both the United States and in numerous other countries in the world. The plaintiff claimed that relator and two other members of the joint venture had agreed to provide unlimited financial support. The level of support failed to meet the plaintiff's expectations, and he subsequently brought suit for breach of contract alleging damages of $200,000 as "prosecution" fees for preventing third parties from infringing upon the patents. Relator counterclaimed seeking recovery of all sums paid to the plaintiff under the agreement.

At the request of the parties, on October 1, 1990, respondent entered an Order of Referral for Mediation. The mediation was conducted on December 18. An oral compromise was negotiated and an initial draft of the settlement agreement was reduced to writing, but it was not signed by either the relator or the plaintiff. The mediator brought all parties into a conference room and repeated the terms of the settlement agreement asking each individual and his counsel to affirm, in the presence of each other, the specific terms of the agreement. All parties indicated that they agreed to the terms of the settlement agreement. No reservations or contingencies were orally expressed.

There is a difference of opinion between the parties as to why the settlement agreement was not signed the same evening it was drafted. According to the respondent, the agreement was not reduced to writing that night solely because counsel for the relator asked if he could attend his son's baseball game. Respondent points to the relator's deposition testimony where relator states that he made no statement that evening qualifying his agreement to the settlement. Relator claims that he equivocated at the conclusion of the mediation stating that he would have to obtain financing to meet his obligation before signing any settlement agreement. Relator's deposition does state that he had no intention of signing the compromise that day.

Relator later advised his counsel that he would be unable to meet his obligations under the compromise. Relator contacted the plaintiff, so informed him, and suggested the case be set for trial. The plaintiff responded that relator's actions violated the compromise and that he would seek all available remedies including a continuation of the litigation, a new lawsuit for breach of the compromise, and costs and expenses of the mediation as sanctions.

After hearing, on proper motions, respondent granted the plaintiff's Motion for Sanctions and on its own motion struck relator's pleadings and entered a default judgment for the plaintiff as to liability. Relator timely filed a Motion for Rehearing with a request for a hearing. Prior to the hearing, relator filed his petition for mandamus requesting that the respondent be directed to reinstate relator's pleadings, set aside the default judgment, and set the matter for trial on the issue of liability. This court stayed the scheduled hearing on the damages.

While a trial court has broad discretion in ruling on certain interlocutory matters, an appellate court's discretion is more confined in exercising its mandamus power. *Street v. Second Court of Appeals*, 715 S.W.2d 638, 639 (Tex.1986). Mandamus will issue only to correct a clear abuse of discretion or the violation of a ministerial duty imposed by law when there is no other adequate remedy at law by direct appeal. *Johnson v. Fourth Court of Appeals*, 700 S.W.2d 916, 917 (Tex.1985); *Central Freight Line, Inc. v. White*, 731 S.W.2d 121, 122 (Tex.App.—Houston [14th Dist.] 1987, orig. proceeding). Generally, to obtain mandamus a relator must establish three elements: 1) a clear right to the relief sought; 2) a clear violation of a legal duty or gross abuse of discretion by the respondent; and, 3) the lack of any other adequate remedy. *Dallas County by Com'rs Court v. Mays*, 747 S.W.2d, 842, 844 (Tex.App.—Dallas 1988), rev'd on other grounds not [sic]; *Mays v. Fifth Court of Appeals*, 755 S.W.2d 78 (Tex.1988). There must be a demand made to the respondent for performance of the relief sought and a refusal to perform after demand. *Hawthorne v. La–Man Constructors, Inc.*, 672 S.W.2d 255, 258 (Tex.App.—Beaumont 1984, no writ).

Respondent claims that this court has no jurisdiction because relator's petition is insufficient under Tex.R.App.P. 121 which requires that relator file a certified or sworn copy of the relevant order. Tex.R.App.P. 121(a)(4). In the appendix attached to the petition relator incorporated the trial court's order sanctioning relator and relator's attorney verified the petition with his sworn affidavit pursuant to Tex.R.App.P. 121(a)(2)(F). This is sufficient to comply with the requirement of Rule 121. *Progressive Insurance Companies v. Hartman*, 788 S.W.2d 424, 427 (Tex.App.—Dallas 1990, orig. proceeding). This court has jurisdiction under Tex.Gov't Code Ann. § 22.221(b) (Vernon Pamph.1991).

Relator argues that mandamus should issue because respondent's order constituted a gross abuse of discretion and is void. Relator contends that the unsigned settlement agreement was unenforceable and relator had an absolute right to revoke his consent to it under Tex. R.Civ.P. 11 since that rule, entitled Agreements to be in Writing, states:

> Unless otherwise provided in these rules, no agreement between attorneys or parties touching any suit pending will be enforced *unless it be in writing, signed and filed with the papers as part of the record* or unless it be made in open court and entered of record.

In *Kennedy v. Hyde*, 682 S.W.2d 525 (Tex.1984), the Texas Supreme Court held that Rule 11 is a *minimum* requirement for enforcement of all agreements concerning pending suits, including, but not limited to, agreed judgments. *Id.* at 528. As a general rule, compliance with Rule 11 is a prerequisite for any judgment enforcing an agreement on a pending suit. *Id.* at 529 (emphasis added).

In *Quintero v. Jim Walter Homes*, 654 S.W.2d 442 (Tex.1983), the supreme court stated that:

> A judgment based upon an agreement of the attorneys, cannot be rendered by a court when consent of one of the parties thereto is wanting. [citation omitted] The power to render an agreed judgment depends upon the "substance of the consent" at the time judgment is rendered. [citation omitted] Therefore, *a party has the right to revoke his consent at any time before the rendition of judgment.* [citation omitted] When a trial court has knowledge that one of the parties to a suit does not consent to a judgment, the trial court should refuse to sanction the agreement by making it the judgment of the court.

Id. at 444 (emphasis added); *see Burnamam v. Heaton*, 150 Tex. 333, 240 S.W.2d 288, 291 (1951); *Samples Exterminators v. Samples*, 640 S.W.2d 873, 874 (Tex.1982). Here, since the settlement agreement had not been signed or filed as part of the record pursuant to Tex.R.Civ.P. 11, relator had the right to revoke his consent.

Relator also claims that since there was no pending motion to strike the pleadings before the trial court, he had no notice and that constituted a deprivation of due process. In *Zeb Manufacturing Co. v. Anthony*, 752 S.W.2d 687 (Tex.App.—Houston [1st Dist.] 1988, orig. proceeding), there was no motion for sanctions under Tex.R.Civ.P. 215 pending and the trial court struck relator's pleadings *sua sponte*. The *Zeb* court held:

> Without a motion before the trial court that asked for sanction of discovery abuse, the relator had no notice that the hearing scheduled on other discovery motions would result in respondent's spontaneous striking of its pleadings. Notice is essential for the proper imposition of sanctions. [Citation omitted] Under these circumstances, the trial court's order is void.

752 S.W.2d at 690. Here, relator likewise had no notice that his pleadings might be stricken.

Relator further argues that respondent had no authority to impose discovery sanctions under Tex.R.Civ.P. 215 for what the respondent believed was a willful and deceptive violation of good faith during mediation. Relator contends that there was no lack of good faith, but even if there were, the order was beyond the court's power. Respondent granted sanctions under Tex.R.Civ.P. 215. It claims these sanctions are available under the court's inherent authority pursuant to Tex.Gov't Code Ann. § 21.001. Respondent's theory was that mediation is a discovery tool and violation of the trial court's order for referral of mediation is therefore subject to Rule 215.

Repudiation of an unsigned settlement agreement forged in mediation is not subject to discovery sanctions under Tex.R.Civ.P. 215. The options available to a party are either filing suit on the agreement asserting that it is a valid agreement or, continuing with the original suit. *Browning v. Holloway*, 620 S.W.2d 611 (Tex.Civ.App.—Dallas 1981, writ ref'd n.r.e.).

Relator's reluctance or refusal to sign a binding agreement the same day it was drafted is not a breach of good faith in mediation. Oral representations in arbitration are non-binding and privileged. Furthermore, there is no legal precedence for extending the court's inherent power to imposition of Tex.R.Civ.P. 215 sanctions without a violation of discovery.

Respondent asserts that mandamus is improper because relator has an adequate remedy at law. His motion for rehearing has not yet been heard. There was no hearing set on relator's motion for rehearing. At most, respondent merely denied relator's request for an immediate hearing on his motion. This court is confident that had the motion been set for hearing properly with the requisite notice sent to all parties affected, respondent would have heard the motion. The default judgment on liability is an interlocutory judgment and the relator's motion for rehearing can still be heard by the respondent. Thus, an adequate remedy at law remains available to the relator.

The petition for writ of mandamus is denied.

* * *

COLLEEN BENNETT v. LLOYD BENNETT
Supreme Court of Maine, 1991.
587 A.2d 463.

* * *

Lloyd first contends that the provisions of 19 M.R.S.A. § 665 (Supp. 1990) required the trial court to grant his motion to compel Colleen to sign and submit to the court the alleged agreement of the parties. We disagree. Section 665 provides: [t]he court may, in any case under this subchapter, at any time refer the parties to mediation on any issues. Any agreement reached by the parties through mediation on any issues shall be reduced to writing, signed by the parties and presented to the court for approval as a court order. When agreement through mediation is not reached on any issue the court must determine that the parties made a good faith effort to mediate the issue before proceeding with a hearing * * * The provisions in section 665 governing the requirements of an agreement reached through mediation explicitly assure the court of the parties' consent to and willingness to be bound by the terms of their agreement. Absent such a signed, written agreement being submitted to it, the court makes a determination of the issues presented by an action for divorce based on the evidence adduced by the parties at the time of the trial of that action.

* * *

His contention is that because Colleen did not sign the alleged mediated agreement between the parties, section 665 mandates that the court order Colleen to sign the document and submit it to the court for its approval. To read such a mandate into the language of section 665 would of necessity require the trial court to engage in the time-consuming process of exploring what transpired between the parties during the course of the mediation in order to determine if they had reached any agreement and, if so, the actual terms of that agreement. Clearly, this is contrary to and would undermine the basic policy of the mediation process that parties be encouraged to arrive at a settlement of disputed issues without the intervention of the court. Accordingly, the trial court properly denied Lloyd's motion requesting that the court order Colleen to sign and submit to the court for its approval the alleged agreement of the parties.

* * *

———

Some state statutes which address the enforceability of mediated agreements acknowledge the contractual nature of such agreements. Other statutes work to modify existing contract law.

MINN. CIVIL CODE (1988).

§ 572.35.   Effect of mediated settlement agreement

Subdivision 1.   General.

The effect of a mediated settlement agreement shall be determined under principles of law applicable to contract. A mediated settlement agreement is not binding unless it contains a provision stating that it is binding and a provision stating substantially that the parties were advised in writing that (a) the mediator has no duty to protect their interests or provide them with information about their legal rights; (b) signing a mediated settlement agreement may adversely affect their legal rights; and (c) they should consult an attorney before signing a mediated settlement agreement if they are uncertain of their rights.

Subdivision 2.   Debtor and creditor mediation.

In addition to the requirements of subdivision 1, a mediated settlement agreement between a debtor and creditor is not binding until 72 hours after it is signed by the debtor and creditor, during which time either party may withdraw consent to the binding character of the agreement.

* * *

UTAH CODE ANN. (1991).

§ 78–31b–5 ADR agreement enforcement

(1) An agreement reached through ADR procedures is enforceable as a contract among the parties if the agreement:

   (a) includes an acknowledgement that the agreement is enforceable as a contract; and

   (b) is executed in writing.

(2) This section applies to ADR conducted either through court referral or independent of the court.

(3) The ADR provider shall encourage the parties to the dispute to obtain individual legal advice and legal review of the agreement before signing it.

———

Questions may also arise with regard to the ability or duty of a court to review or revise a mediated agreement.

N.C. GEN. STAT. § 50–13–1 (1992).

(g) Any agreement reached by the parties as a result of the mediation shall be reduced to writing, signed by each party, and submitted to the court as soon as practicable. Unless the court finds good reason not to, it shall incorporate the agreement in a court order. If some or all of the issues as to custody or visitation are not resolved by mediation, the mediator shall report that fact to the court.

IN THE MATTER OF THE MARRIAGE OF AMES

Court of Appeals of Texas, Amarillo, 1993.
860 S.W.2d 590.

* * *

In the first of four points of error, Raymond contends that the trial court erred in entering its decree of divorce on the basis of the settlement agreement because he had repudiated the agreement. We disagree. In its order of mediation, the trial court stated that "[t]his case is appropriate for mediation pursuant to Tex.Civ.Prac. & Rem.Code §§ 154.001 *et seq.*" Chapter 154 of the Texas Civil Practice and Remedies Code is entitled "Alternative Dispute Resolution Procedures." Section 154.071(a) states:

> If the parties reach a settlement and execute a written agreement disposing of the dispute, the agreement is enforceable in the same manner as any other written contract.

Tex.Civ.Prac. & Rem.Code Ann. § 154.071(a) (Vernon Supp. 1993). We interpret this statute to mean, *inter alia*, that a party who has reached a settlement agreement disposing of a dispute through alternative dispute resolution procedures may not unilaterally repudiate the agreement.

* * *

If voluntary agreements reached through mediation were non-binding, many positive efforts to amicably settle differences would be for naught. If parties were free to repudiate their agreements, disputes would not be finally resolved and traditional litigation would recur. In order to effect the purposes of mediation and other alternative dispute resolution mechanisms, settlement agreements must be treated with the same dignity and respect accorded other contracts reached after arm's length negotiations. Again, no party to a dispute can be forced to settle the conflict outside of court; but if a voluntary agreement that disposes of the dispute is reached, the parties should be required to honor the agreement.[1]

Raymond argues strenuously, however, that section 154.071(a) does not apply in this case. Raymond maintains that section 154.071(a)

---

1. We are aware of the cases in which it has been held that a valid consent judgment cannot be rendered unless consent exists at the time the court undertakes to make the agreement the judgment of the court. *Vineyard v. Wilson*, 597 S.W.2d 21, 23 (Tex. Civ.App.—Dallas 1980, no writ); *Burna-* *man v. Heaton*, 150 Tex. 333, 338–39, 240 S.W.2d 288, 291 (1951). These cases are inapplicable to agreements reached pursuant to alternative dispute resolution procedures described in chapter 154 of the Texas Civil Practice and Remedies Code.

conflicts with Tex.Fam.Code Ann. § 3.631(a) (Vernon 1993), and that the Family Code provision is controlling.

* * *

Even though section 3.631(a) is the more specific statute in this case, the Family code provision expressly states that an agreement may be repudiated prior to rendition of the divorce *"unless it is binding under some other rule of law."* Pursuant to section 154.071)(a) of the Practice and Remedies Code, the settlement agreement is binding. Raymond could not unilaterally repudiate the agreement.

* * *

In his third point of error, Raymond, in the alternative, argues that if the agreement was not repudiated, the trial court erred in dividing the community property because the court's division differed significantly from the settlement agreement.

We agree with Raymond that there are several provisions of the divorce decree that are not found in the settlement agreement.

* * *

In her motion for rehearing, Nancy Jo Ames, appellee, concedes that the trial court's division of community property contains terms and provisions that are not found in the settlement agreement. Nancy now agrees with our conclusion that the court's judgment should have embodied the exact terms of the settlement agreement, said agreement being the only evidence before the court.

* * *

Rather, we are confronted with a decree of divorce that contains terms and provisions that were never agreed to by the parties. A trial court has no power to supply such terms and conditions. *Matthews v. Looney,* 132 Tex. 313, 317, 123 S.W.2d 871, 872 (1939). A final judgment founded upon a settlement agreement must be in strict compliance with the agreement. *Vickrey v. American Youth Camps, Inc.,* 532 S.W.2d 292, 292 (Tex.1976).

Therefore, the motion for rehearing is overruled.

* * *

QUESTIONS FOR DISCUSSION

12–1. Should there be a change in the Rules of Civil Procedure to provide for enforcement of mediated agreements, as distinguished from settlement agreements in the course of litigation? Does the mediation process offer additional safeguards to negotiation which should be taken into consideration when confronted with enforcement issues?

12–2. Are there occasions where sanctions should be imposed upon a party for reneging on a mediated agreement prior to its finalization by the court?

12–3. Should mediated agreements include a liquidated damages clause?

12–4. What should be the role of the referring court in reviewing a mediated agreement? See, for example, Kasper v. Board of Election Commissioners, 814 F.2d 332 (7th Cir.1987), where a trial court's refusal to enter a consent decree was affirmed.

12–5. A mediation has been underway in Columbus, Ohio for six hours. The dispute involves a suit by Woodrow and Sandra Bucki against Bea Fast, their architect, for alleged design defects in their home. The Buckis' primary allegation surrounds the pool area in the rear of their home. The pool was to be an exact replica of Ohio Stadium. Not only does it not look like Ohio Stadium, but, even worse, it resembles the stadium in Ann Arbor, Michigan. Fast, who, received a master's degree from the University of Michigan, disputes the claim and suggested in his deposition, that the Buckis might have spent too many hours at the V.C. watching re-runs of games.

Before the mediation, the Buckis' demand was $450,000.00 in actual damages for fixing and changing the design of their pool and an additional $2,000,000.00 in punitive damages for Fast's reckless conduct.

By the fifth hour of mediation, the Buckis were willing to accept $90,000.00 to fix the pool and a public apology by Fast at the 1995 Michigan–Ohio State football game in Columbus.

Fast, at mediation, agreed to the public apology. However, the insurance representative possessed only $25,000.00 in settlement authority. He requested three days to run trips to see if $90,000.00 could be raised. Fast's counsel, Will V. Reen has advised the mediator, in a separate caucus, that he would like three days to see if his client would respond favorably to the final proposal.

The Buckis were represented by Bruce Hayes. Hayes is outraged by his clients' willingness to even consider accepting $90,000.00 especially since the case is to be tried by a jury in Columbus. Nonetheless, Hayes tells the mediator that the three days are agreed to by the Buckis against his advice.

The mediator rejoins the parties in a joint session and confirms that Fast's counsel has three days to respond to the proposal; however, no written agreement is made. The mediation ends at 5:00 p.m. on Thursday.

On the following Tuesday, Fast's carrier agrees to pay the $90,-000.00. Such "agreement" is communicated by Reen to Hayes at about 1:00 p.m. that day. Hayes responds that no agreement has been reached because the offer was not make "in three days." Reen contends three days meant three *business* days and files a motion with the court to enforce the verbal agreement. Reen further subpoenaed the mediator Newt Badger, to attend the hearing. Reen has also suggested that Badger's failure to reduce the "non-agreement" to writing may be mediator negligence.

(a) As Reen, what are your arguments for enforcement of the agreement. What are your other alternatives?

(b) As Hayes, what is your position?

(c) As Badger, do you attend the hearing? What does your testimony consist of?

(d) As the referring court, Judge Bruin, make your ruling on the issue of enforceability of the agreement.

Chapter Thirteen

CLOSURE AND FOLLOW-UP

Once the mediation is over, there may be an initial tendency on the part of the mediator, the parties, or the attorneys to rush out the door. However, formal closure to the mediation is important. In fact, it is suggested that in addition to the agreement, a formal or symbolic activity that signifies the termination of the conflict should occur.[1] Interestingly, lower animals have devised regular communication patterns which symbolize the end of a conflict has ceased, whereas human beings have not.[2] While most parties will assume, based on the written agreement, that the conflict has ended, it is appropriate that an additional symbol of conflict termination take place.

In business and legal disputes, handshaking combined with exchanging the executed agreement are the most common rituals. In other cultures, a meal is often held to signify the end of a dispute. Concluding the mediation with a champagne toast might be appropriate in some cases, although the mediator should use her discretion. In a large neighborhood dispute over deed restrictions, for instance, a backyard barbecue or block party has been known to take place. These types of procedures, which can also indicate a peaceful resolution, enhance the likelihood of compliance with the agreement.

Even if the closure activities are not this elaborate, and in most instances they are not, the mediator must be certain that the parties have achieved formal closure. In fact, complaints have been lodged against mediators who have not permitted time for the parties to complete closing remarks. Therefore, the mediator must see closure as a specific stage in the process, which is not to be ignored. However, closure can take very different forms depending on the relationship of the parties, context of the dispute, and whether an agreement has been reached.

---

1. Christopher W. Moore, The Mediation Process: Practical Strategies for Resolving Conflict 253 (1986).

2. Id. at 260.

A. CONCLUDING THE MEDIATION

Most mediations are set for a time certain. Whether this increment of time is set in terms of hours, days, or weeks, participants have an understanding of a time frame. Rarely do mediations continue indefinitely until an agreement is reached.[3] Where the time is not definite, reaching the agreement is the primary indication that the process is ending. In those cases which do not achieve settlement, the mediator must, nevertheless, close the session. This is a distinct stage of the process.

1. CLOSURE WITH FORMAL MEDIATED AGREEMENT

In cases where agreement is reached, writing and signing the agreement is not necessarily the final part of the process. In some cases, all take place simultaneously. Execution of the agreement can take place at the session. It is then possible that the agreement, closure, and implementation stages are contemporaneous. However, this situation is not very common. The majority of mediated agreements will result in a written document. Some closing remarks and rituals may occur while the mediator is drafting the agreement.

The mediator must remember that at all times before, during, and after the mediation she is a neutral third party. After an agreement is reached, written, signed, and distributed, the mediator should still maintain neutrality. This includes refraining from providing business cards to, or soliciting business from, either the parties or the attorneys.[4] Sometimes, particularly in cases where parties are not represented, the parties try to continue discussions about a point made in the mediation. The mediator should refrain from doing so. Not only will a post-mediation private conversation demonstrate a lack of neutrality, it may also cause the other party to question the mediator's neutrality during the session. When this occurs, the other party may then want to rescind the agreement. In other cases, in a later action for breach of contract or failure to comply with the mediated agreement, there may be an attempt to claim the mediator's lack of neutrality as a basis for invalidation of the agreement.[5]

In closing, the mediator should make sure that: 1) the parties have exchanged any necessary information such as addresses and telephone numbers; 2) everyone has a copy of the agreement; 3) any follow-up between the parties or the mediator is clear and specific; and 4) that all dates, times, and places are clarified, and preferably in writing. This includes situations where there is an agreement to provide further information. After the signing of the agreement by all present, a copy is

---

3. Exceptions include the case of *international disputes*, such as those in the Middle East. Mediations of *class actions* also often lack deadlines.

4. An exception would be in the instance where the party inquires about the mediator's services for other mediations in the future. In most instances, the mediator should still remain completely *neutral* in her remarks and information provided.

5. While this is an extreme case, it is a possibility, and thus the mediator should avoid even the appearance of *bias*. Also see Chapter 14, infra, for further discussion of relevant *ethical considerations*.

distributed to each party. The participants usually shake hands as a common means of bringing the mediation to final termination.

2. CLOSURE WITHOUT FORMAL AGREEMENT

In many cases, the mediation will be closed without a formal agreement. Sometimes this is done with all participants together; and at other times, while the mediator is meeting separately with the parties. Cases where there is no substantive agreement, but rather an agreement to continue negotiations or schedule a follow-up mediation,[6] differ from cases where termination results and no further negotiations, either between the parties directly or with the mediator's assistance, are expected.

In many cases, the reason for termination of the mediation will be obvious to the parties. As participants, they observe firsthand the stalemate. If no agreement is reached, the mediator need not explain to the parties in detail why the mediation is being terminated. She should explain only that it has reached an impasse, and should do so in a positive manner. Many times mediators declare impasses to motivate the parties forward.[7] As the term impasse has become more widely used, it has developed a negative connotation. The mediator, even in cases where an impasse has been declared, should positively reinforce any progress that was made during the mediation and encourage the parties to continue their negotiation. However, it is recognized that in rare instances continued negotiation would be futile and should not be recommended.

In most cases, the parties will be amicable when leaving. In those occasional instances where there is concern about the safety of the party, or where the mediation was volatile and face to face confrontation should be avoided, the mediator should take care to assure that the parties leave at different times. This might include meeting with one party separately while the other exits. It is imperative that neutrality be maintained at this time as well.

The mediator should be careful in recommending that the parties reschedule. Certainly all attempts to achieve a settlement should be made prior to the parties proceeding to trial or taking other action. However, there might be a tendency on the part of the mediator to recommend rescheduling the mediation, motivated by self-interest in reaching an agreement. In most instances, the rule of thumb when considering whether to reschedule the mediation is to ask the question: Can something tangible be achieved by meeting again? Only if the answer is affirmative and specific should another session be scheduled.

---

6. The case of agreements to follow-up with mediation activity is discussed in § B, infra in this chapter.

7. See supra Chapter 10, § C.

B. POST MEDIATION FOLLOW-UP

In instances where the mediation terminates and an agreement is not reached, some mediators continue the session by negotiating with both sides by telephone in order to achieve a settlement. While this should not be discouraged, the mediator should take care in how this is approached. She should not continually harass the parties in the hopes that this would motivate them to settlement. In fact, some complaints have been lodged against mediators who continuously called the attorneys at least once a day for several weeks following the mediation. This type of follow-up is not recommended. In cases of unsolicited follow-up, it is suggested that initial telephonic communication be made by conference call, although if the mediation was conducted in a private session format, the telephone calls may be conducted separately as well.

In other instances, while the mediation does not result in final settlement of the case, the parties may agree to return to mediation at a later date. A specific time may be predetermined at the mediation. For example, where one or both of the parties need additional information or time to retrieve data, the mediator should write a memorandum or agreement to reflect such, along with the time and place of the next meeting. In other instances, where there is not a definite time, and the session is not scheduled with the same mediator, a written agreement to continue is acceptable, though not necessary.

In cases of both rescheduling and follow-up, the mediator should have specific objectives in mind. Perhaps additional information is required. Perhaps the parties just need time to think about an offer or proposal on the table. A break may be necessary to allow one of the parties to obtain professional advice. In all cases the mediator should close the session with the goals and objectives clearly understood by all participants.

Chapter Fourteen

ETHICAL CONSIDERATIONS

The term ethics as applied to mediation is almost impossible to define and dissect. This is not because a wide range of definitions are not available, but rather is due to the inherent variability of the process and the participants. An example of a generic definition of ethics is: "[t]he discipline of dealing with what is good and bad and with moral duty and obligation".[1] Ethical is also defined as "conforming to accepted professional standards of conduct".[2] An example of the legal definition provides "of or relating to moral action, conduct, motive or characteristics conforming to professional standards of conduct." [3]

A discussion of ethics in mediation necessarily includes a variety of other considerations. There is clear overlap between ethics and standards of practice. Distinguishing ethical behavior from a particular standard of practice for a mediator can be very difficult. Issues surrounding confidentiality and neutrality are often considered ethical in nature. In many situations these are, in fact, termed "ethical considerations".[4] But, there have been attempts, at least, to distinguish standards of practice from ethics.[5] A consideration of qualifications for mediators also includes ethical ramifications. Some of this cross-over discussion is no doubt due to the fact that the mediation "profession" is currently at a point where all issues are in the process of development and are ripe for examination. Perhaps as more of these issues mature, the lines between these matters will become more defined.

Notwithstanding such difficulties, most educators, trainers, and practitioners alike agree that a definitive code of ethics is not only advisable, but at this stage in the development of the mediation practice, a necessity.

1. Merriam Webster's Collegiate Dictionary 398 (10th ed. 1993).

2. Id.

3. Black's Law Dictionary 553 (6th ed. 1990).

4. See, for example, Robert A. Baruch Bush, *The Dilemmas of Mediation Practice:* *A Study of Ethical Dilemmas and Policy Implications*, A report on a study for the National Institute of Dispute Resolution (1992).

5. Jay Folberg & Alison Taylor, Mediation: A Comprehensive Guide to Resolving Conflicts Without Litigation 250 (1984).

Equally important in the developing world of mediation practice are ethical guidelines for those participating in the mediation, most often the disputing parties and their attorneys. Ethical considerations for the court or agency that is referring the matter to mediation may also be appropriate. Moreover, certain ethical duties and obligations might be established to guide the organizations or agencies that administer mediation programs. At this time, the only significant development in this regard has been the ethics of the mediator. However, as the use of mediation increases, it is likely that some consideration will be given to the others as well.

A. MEDIATOR ETHICS

Ethical codes and guidelines have historically been established in a variety of professions. A major obstacle in determining ethics for mediators is that mediation has yet to be formally established as a profession. Assuming movement in that direction, the development of ethical standards appears to be occurring contemporaneously with the creation of the profession. Additional problems face the mediator. There is a built in inconsistency in the development of "standards" for mediators. The entire premise of mediation is its lack of rigidity. Mediation is a flexible process, and that flexibility is one of mediation's key benefits. There are no definitive standards of competency and, in fact, testing for mediators in the traditional sense is not advised. In order to encompass the variety of mediator styles, it would seem that ethics must likewise possess elasticity. Yet, flexibility is not normally a component of ethics. Moreover, setting and enforcing guidelines of any nature seem almost antithetical to the mediation process. But, because of the impact mediators can have on individual lives, there is a need for some type of guidance concerning certain mediator actions. The challenge is creating guidelines which are sufficiently specific in directing mediator conduct, while simultaneously allowing for some flexibility in the process.

1. HISTORICAL OVERVIEW

The early development of ethical considerations for mediators was primarily for programs at the community level. In most of these programs the mediators were volunteers from a variety of disciplines. Mediation was, and still is, an unregulated field; yet many of the participants looked for a set of standards by which to guide the actions of the mediator.

At the conclusion of a mediation, frequently one mediator would ask another, "Should I have done that?" The question often could have been be rephrased, "does that seem unethical?" General, informal discussions between mediators would follow. These discussions led to the conclusion, primarily by the staffs and boards of these centers, that a code of ethics or at least a set of guidelines was needed to provide some answers for the mediators.

It was recognized early on that because mediation is an interdisciplinary field, it was unlikely that any existing ethical guidelines or standards which govern behavior of another profession would be directly applicable in the mediation context. Not only is there a question of whether mediators wear the specific hat of their primary profession during the mediation, but also whether the ethical considerations and guidelines of other professions have relevance in mediation.

For instance, most ethical standards include discussions of avoidance of impropriety, fraud, conflicts, dishonesty, etc. There is little doubt that these would be applicable in mediation. On the other hand, lawyers also have specific duties premised on adversarial conduct. Ethics for social workers are geared toward a therapeutic approach. The practice of mediation requires skills and behaviors different from the other professions. Consequently, many of the ethical standards of other professions are not suitable as standards for mediators. Moreover, many of the ethical considerations important in other professions are in direct conflict with the role of a neutral mediator. Although codes of ethics existed historically for arbitrators, particularly in labor and more recently commercial areas, these are not useful for mediators. Despite the difficulties, there have been many attempts to create a code of ethics for mediators. Several are in existence, and efforts continue.

An early leader in the ethics effort has been the Center for Dispute Resolution (now CDR Associates) in Boulder, Colorado. In 1982 CDR Associates pioneered the effort to create a code of ethics by creating a Code of Professional Conduct for Mediators. The Code was intended to be applicable to all types of mediators, and it was subsequently adopted by the Colorado Council of Mediators in 1982,[6] and later by a number of similar organizations.

In a similar vein, the interdisciplinary association, Society of Professional in Dispute Resolution, (SPIDR) has enacted ethical standards. SPIDR is a primary dispute resolution organization with a large number of mediator members from a vast array of professional backgrounds. The code adopted by the SPIDR board of directors in 1986 purports to govern all neutrals, including mediators.

Also, in 1986 the Supreme Court of Hawaii established guidelines for both public and private mediators. Indicative of the previously discussed problems in differentiating ethics and standards of practice, the guidelines were entitled Standards for Private and Public Mediators in the State of Hawaii.[7]

Many dispute resolution centers, likewise, have developed a code of ethics. In Texas, for example, all 12 centers worked in conjunction with one another, so that there is consistency among all centers in the state. While the Hawaii Code is statewide and applicable to all mediators, in

---

6. Christopher W. Moore, The Mediation Process: Practical Strategies for Resolving Conflict 299 (1986).

7. *In the Matter of the Standards for Private and Public Mediators in the State of Hawaii*, (Order of the Supreme Court of Hawaii, 1986).

contrast, the Texas model governs only those volunteer mediators in the centers. Certain practitioners have attempted self-regulation. Since many mediators practice in the divorce area, the Academy of Family Mediators enacted a specific code of Standards of Practice for Family and Divorce Mediation.

As the use of mediation spread into the courts, additional concerns arose. Most of the mediators were lawyers, and some assumptions were made that the lawyer's code of ethics would apply. Yet it soon became apparent that the fundamental differences in the roles of the advocate and mediator prevent wholesale adoption by mediators of the lawyer's code of professional responsibility. Initial attempts were then made to modify the Model Rules of Professional Conduct to provide guidance for the lawyer mediator. But there have not been any general changes thus far. However, changes have occurred in the family law area. Most lawyer mediators worked initially in the divorce area, and in 1984, the ABA adopted standards with regard to the lawyer mediator in family law matters.[8] Some state and local bar associations through their ethics committees, have also attempted to address the need for guidelines for the lawyer mediator. The result has been a segregation of the interests of lawyer mediators from those of non-lawyer mediators. Most individuals within the field believe that a code of ethics applicable to all mediators is preferable.

2. CURRENT CODES

Currently, there are probably at least one hundred various codes of mediator ethics, many of which include the broader consideration of standards of conduct. Mediators' duties may be determined by the type of case, the background of the mediator, the agency in which the case is mediated, or the place of referral, such as a court. With a number of codes in existence, it is very difficult, at any given time, for the mediator to determine exactly what code of ethics should be followed. Fortunately, in most instances the code provisions are essentially consistent, although cases of inconsistency do exist. Certain codes are narrow in focus. Other codes of ethics are more expansive and cover practice issues, since in reality it may be difficult to distinguish between the two.

In addition to advances made at local levels, many larger groups of mediators, such as the Academy of Family Mediators and the National Association of Social Workers, have enacted ethical guidelines for mediators. These organizations request that all members follow their code. In essence, implicit in membership is an agreement to conduct mediations in accordance with the ethical standards. However, these standards are purely aspirational. There is no method of inquiry or determination of violation of an ethical guideline. Moreover, proving ethical violations is complicated by the confidential nature of mediation.

---

8. Standards of Practice for Lawyer Mediators in Family Disputes, (Adopted by the House of Delegates of the American Bar Association, August 1984).

Some of the more widely distributed codes identified as ethical in nature are as follows: SPIDR's Ethical Standards of Professional Conduct; Association of Family & Conciliation Courts' Model Standards of Practice for Family and Divorce Mediation; Standards for Mediators in the State of Hawaii; Colorado Council of Mediators and Mediation Organizations' Code of Professional Conduct for Mediators; Texas Dispute Resolution Center Directors Councils' Code of Ethics for Volunteer Mediators; Oregon Mediation Association's Standard of Mediation Practice; and Standards of Professional Conduct for Certified and Court–Appointed Mediators in Florida. These codes cover a number of issues, and, as their titles indicate, most are considered a code of conduct which incorporates ethical guidelines. Only a few purport to provide exclusively "ethics".

A number of practice areas are consistently found with in these codes. These include issues of conflicts of interest, the mediator's role, impartiality, confidentiality, providing professional advice, fees, fairness of agreement, qualifications, training, advertising, and continuing education.[9] Other areas which some of these codes include are the mediator's responsibility to the courts, self-determination of the parties, interests of outsiders and absent parties, separate caucuses, and use of multiple procedures.

3. ISSUES SURROUNDING THE USE OF A CODE OF ETHICS

There are several considerations which present challenges to both the creation and implementation of a code of ethics for mediators. These include the interdisciplinary nature of the field, the inherent flexibility of the process, lack of enforcement authority and even problems as basic as defining the process to be regulated.

Mediation is, by definition, a flexible process. This is usually emphasized in training and teaching mediation. Due primarily to this flexibility, the process has wide applicability and has been effective in the resolution of an extremely wide array of disputes. The difficulty in defining the process and precisely how it works contributes to the complications in determining ethics and standards of practice. Moreover, it is feared that if rigid standards are established, then the ability of a mediator to be pliant will be extinguished.

Mediators currently come from all walks of life. Until the profession is established by some form of licensure or regulation, the ability to impact all mediators inclusively is impossible. Many are volunteers and arguably should not be overburdened by regulation. On the other hand, to establish a standard of ethics which would exclude volunteers may send a message of a two-tiered approach to competency in mediation services.

Another consideration involves the situation where the individual mediator is bound to comply with other professional ethics. This may be

---

9. Many of these topics will be examined in § 4 of this chapter, though the latter four are seen as part of mediator competency, and hence included in Chapter 15, infra.

due to their primary profession, that is, their training, background, education and licensure prior to becoming a mediator, whether this be doctor, lawyer, accountant, or therapist. While in most situations there will be more consistency than conflict, in the event of conflict, how will a decision be made concerning which code controls?

Just as troublesome in the creation of ethical guidelines is the determination of who is to enforce them. Some argue that the mere existence of ethical standards, in and of itself, is sufficient enforcement. Individual mediators can voluntarily abide by them. Others, however, stress that there must be outside enforcement of the guidelines. In essence, these should be more than guidelines and reach the level of standards.[10] The majority of the current codes of ethics were established as guidelines for mediators. In reality, no sanctions exist for mediator violations. Whether a mediator knowingly violates, admits to a violation, or a violation is determined by an outside entity,[11] rarely do sanctions exist. It is currently uncommon for the mediator to be prohibited from practicing mediation with the entity which enacted the standards. Although the specific means of application of established ethical guidelines is yet to be determined, the institution of enforcement mechanisms should include the types of penalties which are appropriate for violations.

Another consideration is how to introduce ethical codes to new mediators, and even experienced mediators. In many instances, there is no training requirement for mediators. Furthermore, training and educating mediators is far from standardized.[12] There is no consistency with regard to course content and it is difficult to ascertain whether trainings actually include ethical components. Although some mediator membership organizations provide ethical guidelines for their members, it is difficult, if not impossible, to determine whether the mediators are familiar with them. There is no standard testing of mediators. Consequently, many mediators may not even be aware of the existence of ethical guidelines or standards.

4. AREAS FOR ETHICAL CONSIDERATION

The variety of ethical issues facing mediators is considerable. The difficulty in determining which issues to address in a code of ethics is evidenced by the number of codes in existence.

---

10. This is the position of at least one Associate Justice of the Florida Supreme Court. When the Florida Supreme Court was enacting certification procedures, it was deemed necessary to establish an enforcement body. The Supreme Court of Florida was the first entity to assume the role of a regulating authority for the mediator profession. More recently, the State of Utah has provided that the Division of Occupational and Professional Licensing is authorized to deny or revoke certification of a dispute resolution provider. Utah Code Ann. § 58–39a–6 (1993). By the time this work is published, it is likely that a few other states will have enacted similar provisions.

11. This outside entity could be an organization of mediators, a mediation program or a referring court or agency.

12. This will be examined in Chapter 15, infra.

An attempt to determine what issues mediators face in practice was made in the State of Florida. Research included interviews with over 80 mediators, both lawyers and non-lawyers. Program and private practice mediators were included, and the cases were from the family, civil litigation and community fields of practice. The mediators were asked specifically to describe situations presented in the course of their experience which appeared as "ethical dilemmas".[13] The findings indicated concern about issues of: confidentiality, conflicts of interest, competency, preserving impartiality, informed consent, preserving self-determination, provision of counseling and legal advice and avoiding harm and abuse in the process.[14] Some of these admittedly overlap with standards of practice.

A survey of the literature and current draft codes reveals a number of primary issues which present ethical concerns for mediators. These include confidentiality and neutrality which have been previously discussed.[15] The others are:

    a. Conflicts of Interest

    b. Impartiality

    c. Role of the Mediator Versus Self–Determination

    d. Providing Professional Advice

    e. Advertising/Fees

In matters of conflicts of interest which are, admittedly related to impartiality, the issue is just how neutral the mediator must be. For instance, should a mediator serve in a case where one of the parties is a former client if the matter is totally unrelated to that of the prior representation? Can a mediator mediate a case involving a former partner? A former roommate? Once a mediator serves in the neutral role, is he forever barred from providing services (legal, accounting, etc.) to that individual?[16]

Additional situations present even more debate surrounding the necessity for impartiality and freedom from bias. For example, if a mediator is divorced, should he be prohibited from mediating divorce cases? Should this bar last during the pendency of the divorce or forever? Likewise, if a mediator has been in a car accident, should he, for any period of time, refrain from mediating automobile accident cases? Impartiality and neutrality are often defined as "having no interest in the outcome." Yet, if a mediator is an advocate for settlement, it can be argued that he does have an interest in the outcome. This is especially difficult in those cases where a settlement will result in additional business for the mediator.

13. Bush, supra note 4 at 6.

14. Id. at 9.

15. *Neutrality* is the subject of Chapter 7, supra, while Chapter 11, supra, addresses *confidentiality*.

16. See *Heelan v. Lockwood*, 143 A.D.2d 881, 533 N.Y.S.2d 560 (1988).

Self-determination of the parties, many claim, is at the very basis of the mediation process. Yet many mediators coerce parties into a settlement, claiming to have superior understanding of the best options for resolution of the matter. This occurs more often in court-annexed mediation. The degree of mediator directiveness determines whether the parties' settlement is self-determined.

Considerations of party self-determination, mediator neutrality, and professional advice are linked. These affect the role of the mediator in instances where a party is uninformed or uneducated about a matter. Should the mediator provide that information or advice, whether it be legal, financial, technical or therapeutic in nature?

At least two competing ethical considerations impact this issue. These are the mediator's duty to be neutral, and the obligation to achieve a fair, fully informed settlement.[17] Once a mediator provides advice or information to a party, his role can be viewed as that of an advocate. However, if the mediator is to empower the parties to exercise self-determination, it may follow that the mediator must ensure that decisions are made with complete information and understanding.[18] Often this information and understanding is in terms of the law. Should the mediator provide this information? Many view the duty of the mediator not to directly provide the information, but rather to advocate that the parties obtain independent legal counsel.[19] Often, however, doing so results in increased cost to the disputants. In these instances, some mediators will provide the needed legal information. Others view providing any advice as unethical.

Mediator advertising and fee schedules have also caused some concern in the field. The general opinion is that the only guidance which should be provided to mediators is that fees be reasonable and advertising truthful and not misleading. Prohibitions against contingency fees are also common. This ban is based upon the premise that a mediator cannot have an interest in the outcome of the case. A minority view exists, and a few practicing mediators bill on a contingency basis.

5. JOINT CODE

As more mediator organizations develop, so do the various codes of ethics and guidelines they promulgate. Many individuals in the mediation field belong simultaneously to a number of these organizations. In an attempt to consolidate and perhaps establish a definitive code of ethics, the three largest organizations of dispute resolution practitioners, (SPIDR) Society of Professionals in Dispute Resolution, AAA (American Arbitration Association) and the ABA (American Bar Association) have joined together in an effort to create such a code. They have formed a joint committee with representatives from each organization who are

17. These issues were addressed in Chapter 7, supra.

18. Robert A. Baruch Bush, *Efficiency and Protection, or Empowerment and Recognition?: The Mediator's Role and Ethical Standards in Mediation*, 41 Fla. L. Rev. 253, 278 (1989).

19. Id. at 280.

working together in the drafting of a code for all mediators in civil matters. It is hoped that the code will be finalized by early 1995 and distributed to all members of each organization. The goal is the creation of a genuinely national interdisciplinary code. Efforts have been made to obtain input from a wide array of providers as well as consumers of mediation services.[20]

Until, however, specific codes are adopted, or programs and courts institute mandatory ethical guidelines, many questions will remain unanswered for the practicing mediator. Determining what to do when faced with an ethical dilemma may be disconcerting for a mediator. Each mediator should be familiar with the primary codes of ethics relating to his practice. When specific issues are not addressed by the code, individual choices must be made.

B. ETHICS FOR THE ADVOCATES AND PARTIES

In the development of the mediation process, it is natural that the primary focus of ethics be on the mediator and his activities. The concern, initially, was that the mediator, as facilitator and conductor of the process, was perhaps in a position to reach too far and coerce the parties into an agreement. This was particularly true when the general public was unaware of the specifics of mediation and had no idea or expectations of the process. They were at the "mercy," as it were, of the mediator. In an attempt to protect the parties, ethical standards of practice developed.

However, the mediator is not the only participant in the mediation session. In fact, often it is the participants, whether the parties or their representatives, who have the more active roles in the mediation. Hence, it is not surprising that these participants should have ethical guidelines to follow. In fact, as previously described,[21] some of the recent abuses or misuses of the process have been committed by the participants. Therefore, general guidelines for those participants should be examined, particularly as the roles of the parties' and their representatives develop.[22]

The parties might be bound by certain ethical guidelines associated with their primary profession. For example, professionals such as accountants and physicians often participate in mediation as parties in negotiating past due accounts, often in small claims courts. These professionals may also find their way to the mediation table in response to a claim of malpractice. Ethical concerns may arise in the course of the mediation, and could even be the subject of the dispute. For instance, doctors have specific ethical guidelines which must be adhered

---

20. The most recent draft is included as Appendix C, infra.

21. See Chapter 11, supra.

22. The particular role of the attorney advocate in mediation is now being exam-

ined. See, for example, Eric R. Galton, Representing Clients in Mediation (1994).

to when dealing with a patient. It is likely that these guidelines continue to be operable in the mediation session.

Many times the party in a mediation will be accompanied at the session by a representative. In most cases this will be an attorney. In some matters, particularly in the family area, a therapist may attend the mediation with his client. It can be assumed that individuals will abide by the ethical guidelines already established for their profession. In the majority of cases, these guidelines will be appropriate. However, those ethics were not determined with the mediation practice in mind. For instance, there may be a conflict between the primary role of the attorney in the courtroom and that of the attorney in the mediation. The obligation of the attorney to zealously represent his client means something very different in trial than it does in mediation. Moreover, attorney advocates may have duties in mediation not otherwise considered. Determining the fairness of a mediated agreement is one example. In the case of therapists, they may be bound to inject an opinion regarding the interests of the children during custody mediation. As mediation develops, increased involvement of these representatives may indicate or even necessitate a closer examination of their roles. Since there have been no changes to date, it can be assumed that the current operative standard of ethics remains that of the representative's primary profession. For example, the conduct of an attorney advocate in mediation would be examined using the lawyer's code of professional responsibility as if he were participating in a more traditional negotiation.

There are also issues, ethical in nature, which affect representatives prior to the mediation. One concern is the duty of a lawyer to inform a client about the mediation option. In the legal profession, there is still some debate,[23] although most would allege that it has been settled. The attorney clearly has a duty, which has been legally established, to inform a client of settlement offers.[24] Argument has been made that this legal obligation should be expanded to discussing legal strategy, in particular settlement options, and ADR with the client.[25] Some state and local bar associations and Supreme Courts, including those in Texas and Colorado, have enacted ethical obligations in the form of professional mandates which direct an attorney to inform a client about ADR, when appropriate. While companion requirements for other professionals such as therapists and accountants have not been established, it is conceivable that they too, should inform and refer their clients to the mediation process where appropriate.

23. See Frank E. A. Sander & Michael L. Prigoff, *Should There be a Duty to Advise of ADR Options*, 76 A.B.A.J. 50 (Nov. 1990).

24. See, *Rizzo v. Haines*, 520 Pa. 484, 555 A.2d 58 (1989).

25. Robert F. Cochran, Jr., *Legal Representation and the Next Steps Toward Client Control: Attorney Malpractice for the Failure to Allow the Client to Control Negotiation and Pursue Alternatives to Litigation*, 47 Wash. & Lee L. Rev. 819 (1990).

C. ETHICAL CONSIDERATIONS FOR REFERRING AGENCIES OR ENTITIES

In many instances, the agency or entity which refers parties to mediation is the court. Others may include institutions such as schools, universities and business organizations. As these entities establish comprehensive dispute resolution programs,[26] some ethical responsibilities may accompany this development. These may involve obligations such as duties of the judge in the process of case and mediator selection. The courts, particularly, have been active in referring cases to mediation. In some instances the referral process can be conducted in such a way that the appearance of impropriety is clear. For example, if the majority of cases which are referred to mediation are sent to the judge's former law partner or son-in-law, ethical issues arise. Concern for the court's role in mediation resulted in the promulgation of standards which define the specific role of the court.[27] While only aspirational in nature, it is hoped that all state courts voluntarily adopt these standards. The standards which touch upon ethical concerns include a requirement for the court to determine that a mediator to whom a case is referred is competent; that the case is properly referred to mediation; and that the court does not receive confidential information from the mediator.

Another concern in the area of case referral which raises ethical issues is referral fees. If individuals or entities refer cases to a specific mediator, can the fee be split? In the alternative, would it be proper for the mediator to provide a referral fee to the person or agency which refers a case?

D. ETHICS FOR ORGANIZATIONAL PROVIDERS OF MEDIATION SERVICES

Organizational providers of mediation services include dispute resolution centers and statewide offices of dispute resolution. These are non-profit entities. There are also fee-generating private providers of these services. Both types of organizations employ administrative staff. In the not-for-profit area, agencies are publicly funded with the expectation that they will assist citizens in locating a mediator who will help resolve their disputes. These organizations should also abide by ethical standards, including those of impartiality and confidentiality. Likewise, conflicts of interest should be avoided. Some of these organizations have voluntarily applied the appropriate standards of mediator ethics to the manner in which they conduct business.

Private providers of mediation should not be exempt from any established ethical guidelines. When discussed, ethical issues such as

---

26. See Chapter 16, infra on Dispute Systems Design.

27. See National Standards for Court–Connected Mediation Programs, Center for Dispute Settlement and Institute of Judicial Administration, (1992). Executive summary, Appendix D, infra.

conflict of interest, impartiality, advertising and fees have been traditionally considered only in application to the individual mediator. Extending application to the administrative organization may be proper, particularly in light of recent proposed changes with regard to law firms. Recently a committee of the Association of the Bar of the City of New York has recommended that law firms be liable for ethical violations of their lawyers.[28] The reasoning is that the entity, the firm, should have ethical obligations. Moreover, there are some matters over which the law firm has control, and it is the organization which should be responsible.[29] Similarly a private provider of mediation services should be held ethically accountable. The mediation organization should be responsible for the actions of its mediators which it can control, as well as be obligated to ethical standards in its own right.

QUESTIONS FOR DISCUSSION

14–1. The local court has referred to you a commercial litigation case for mediation. You recognize that the firm representing the defendant is where your ex-spouse is working, but do not see the name on the pleadings or correspondence. Should you disclose this to anyone? Who? Assume that you do not disclose this information, and much to your surprise, s/he arrives at the mediation representing the defendant. What should you do?

14–2. As a lawyer, you resign from your sixty lawyer firm to begin a full-time mediation practice. Should you be barred from serving as a mediator in all cases where your former partners and associates represent a party?

14–3. You are an accountant for Sam Walt who is involved in a heated business dissolution. A variety of business and tax consequences concern your client. Moreover, of the five partners in this seven million dollar enterprise, two are related to Sam. One is a brother, and the other an aunt. These family issues have made the disputing parties even more tense. The attorney for Sam, has not mentioned ADR or mediation. You are familiar with the mediation process, having attended a mediation with a client in a real estate matter. What do you do?

14–4. You have a Ph.D. in clinical psychology with emphasis on child development and are in private practice as a therapist. You have been seeing Ralph, a ten year old child for the past four months. Ralph has demonstrated behavioral problems. You now learn that Ralph's parents have just filed for divorce. Each parent has called you. It appears that both have employed aggressive attorneys, as each attorney has called to schedule your deposition.

(a) How do you respond to the request for your deposition?

28. Henry J. Raske, *Promoting Better*   **29.** Id.
Supervision, 79 A.B.A.J. 32 (1993).

(b) Should you discuss mediation as an alternative for the divorce process? Should you initiate discussions with the lawyers? With Ralph's parents? With the court?

Chapter Fifteen

QUALITY CONTROL

The issue of quality control for mediators may seem, at first glance, a very simple endeavor—even unnecessary. After all, mediation is a voluntary process and the mediator doesn't make decisions. How can there be harm? Yet, the issue of quality control is a widely discussed and debated topic among mediators and other dispute resolution professionals. It seems as if the seventies were the time for experimentation with mediation; the eighties were the time of implementation of programs; and now in the nineties we confront issues of regulation of the field. In fact, the largest organization of dispute resolution professionals, SPIDR (Society of Professionals in Dispute Resolution), has its second commission reviewing the matter.[1] Matters of "quality" in mediation encompass many aspects of the mediator's work. As pointed out in the previous chapter, standards of conduct are related to, and overlap with, ethical considerations. The topic of quality control is even more expansive and it is similarly problematic, due to the variety of forms, functions and definitions of a mediator.

In this new and continually developing field of ADR, a variety of inquiries into matters of qualification, certification and evaluation of the mediator's work are now underway. Entities such as state and local bar associations, mediator organizations, and court administrative groups are beginning to examine these issues. Yet, except for the states of Florida and Utah which have enacted specific certification guidelines for mediators,[2] no other entity or organization has established strict regulations or licensing procedures.

Even though the profession is moving in the direction of quality control, debate about the need for regulation continues. Reasons advanced for the establishment of quality checks may serve the mediator, the profession and the public. For the mediator, qualifications provide guidance to those who are considering mediating as a career, standardization of training, enhancement of credibility with disputants, and a sense of professionalism. The establishment of qualifications will afford the mediation profession with legitimation of the field, preparation for

---

1. See § A infra.   2. See § D infra.

continued, organized growth of the mediation practice, and standardization of processes and procedures. The public will also benefit since marketing and education about the differences in mediation may be provided, controls will be maintained, and a basis for redress of problems will be created.[3]

On the other hand, a contrary view expresses strong reservations about the establishment of mediation qualifications. There is fear that such "limiting" qualifications will retard the growth of ADR use. Furthermore, it is alleged that research has yet to demonstrate a real nexus between the mediator's skill and a successful outcome. Moreover, what constitutes *success* in mediation has not been determined. Finally, qualifications can raise costs and certainly limit the mediator's work.[4] Even the SPIDR Commission has recognized that mandatory standards may provide inappropriate barriers to the field and limit the innovative quality of the profession.[5] Nonetheless, it appears that the profession is moving in the direction of establishing mediator qualifications. Determining specifically what those qualifications should entail is currently the focus of discussion. Research, including a test design project is ongoing, with additional inquiry strongly advocated.[6]

Many ways exist to ensure quality control in the practice of mediation. Such methods may be used separately or in combination with one another. Most existing quality control techniques have been tried in community or court-annexed programs. Quality control methods include: initial selection of individuals to become mediators; mediator training and education; testing and evaluation of competencies of the mediator, which may also be included in a certification process; regulation by a certification or licensing procedure; enactment of standards of conduct which must be followed; and establishment of liability. These elements, if correctly put into practice can enhance the quality of the mediation practice.

An initial impediment to implementation of the foregoing methods is the identification of a source which will make ultimate judgments of competency and quality. What entity should control mediator regulation? In court connected programs, many strongly urge the courts to take this role.[7] In community centers, funding agencies or the boards of directors of the non-profit managing entities have assumed some respon-

---

3. Peter R. Maida, Why Qualifications? Qualifications Sourcebook Compendium (Society of Professionals in Dispute Resolution, Commission on Qualifications 1993).

4. Christine Carlson, Why the Practice of Mediation Should Not be Overregulated From the Perspective of a State Program Manager, Qualifications Sourcebook Compendium, (Society of Professionals in Dispute Resolution, Commission on Qualifications 1993).

5. Society of Professionals in Dispute Resolution, Report of the SPIDR Commis-

sion on Qualifications, (hereinafter referred to as Report) (1989).

6. Margaret L. Shaw, Selection, Training and Qualification of Neutrals, A working paper for the National Symposium on Court–Connected Dispute Resolution Research (September 1993).

7. Center for Dispute Settlement and the Institute of Judicial Administration, Standards for Court–Connected Mediation Programs (hereinafter referred to as National Standards (1992).

sibility for mediator quality. In other programs, and in the case of the marketplace, who should assume the role of regulation and enforcement of standards is undetermined. Options range from the consumer to the mediator to a state agency.

With such a variety of entities attempting to assure quality control, there can be little consistency. One suggested option is for each state to create a board of licensure or regulation for mediators similar to the state boards of other professions. The search for answers to such issues continues.

A. BACKGROUND

Complaints about mediators, though few and far between, have begun to surface. As more individuals participate in the process, there is fear that complaints will increase. In 1988, SPIDR, as the primary interdisciplinary organization of mediators and third party neutrals, established a commission to examine issues surrounding the quality of neutrals. It was recognized that the task was not a simple one. SPIDR acknowledged both that there is no single way to promote quality in any professional practice and that a number of options are currently used. The current methods included: free market; disclosure requirements; public and consumer education; "after the fact" controls, such as malpractice lawsuits; rosters; voluntary standards; codes of professional ethics; mandatory standards for neutrals; mandatory standards for programs; and improvements in training for neutrals, including apprenticeship programs.[8] A report entitled The Commission on Qualifications was published in 1989 and provided general recommendations.

The Commission, striving to reach an appropriate balance between competing concerns, adopted three central principles:

A.   that no single entity (rather, a variety of organizations) should establish qualifications for neutrals;

B.   that the greater the degree of choice the parties have over the dispute resolution process, program or neutral, the less mandatory the qualification requirements should be; and

C.   that qualification criteria should be based on performance, rather than paper credentials.[9]

The Commission recognized that the knowledge, skills and techniques needed to practice mediation competently may change depending upon a number of variables. The context of the dispute and its resolution, the particular process used, the issues involved in the case, and the institutional setting can all impact the mediator's actions. Therefore, there was no single entity to certify general dispute resolution competency.

8. Report, supra note 5 at 1.   **9.** Id. at 2.

The second principle attempted to balance the use of a free market-place with mandatory programs. SPIDR specifically recommended that:

1. When parties have free choice of the process, program, and neutral, no standards or qualifications should be established that would prevent any person from providing dispute resolution services, as long as there is full disclosure of the neutral's relevant training and experience, the fees and expenses to be charged, and any financial or personal interest or prior relationship with the parties that might affect the neutral's impartiality.

2. Where public or private entities operate programs that offer no choice of process, program or neutral, an appropriate public entity should set standards or qualifications for such programs and for neutrals, in accordance with the principles set forth in this Report and make such standards and qualifications available to the parties.

3. When parties have some, but not a complete, choice of process, program or neutral, each program offering such services should establish clear selection and evaluation criteria and make such information available to the parties, together with its rules governing confidentiality, the means by which complaints may be lodged, and all relevant "full disclosure" information concerning the neutral selected for the particular case.[10]

The third principle, performance-based qualifications, included specific recommendations of performance-based testing, continuing education for the neutrals, and establishing qualifications for trainers.

The concern with this SPIDR report was that it raised more questions than it answered. In other words, it was just the beginning. The guidelines were not definitive, and since the report, a more detailed analysis is in progress. Moreover, to complicate matters even further, some states, in direct contravention of the third principle, have enacted statutes which qualify mediators by the mere possession of a college or graduate degree.

A second SPIDR commission on qualifications has been appointed to follow the work of the first. This second commission is expected to present a final report in December of 1994. In its work, the second commission has attempted to distinguish and define with some precision the terms surrounding these issues of quality control. These are as follows:

Certification:

Certification is an explicit recognition that a person has completed a specific level of education or training or has achieved a particular level of skill in performing certain functions. Certification can be granted by public or private professional or educational bodies. In cases where certification has been granted by a public body, the right to practice may

10. Id.

be a consequence. Other times the right to use a professional title accompanies certification.[11]

Certification: a process whereby an individual is tested and evaluated in order to determine his mastery of a specific body of knowledge or some portion of a body of knowledge. As individuals are certified by groups expert in a certain field, it is voluntary.[12]

Licensure:

Licensure is permission to practice a particular activity, function, or profession. Licenses are generally granted by public authorities based on prescribed levels of education, experience, or performance. Licensure usually also carries with it a fee.[13]

Licensure is a process applied to individuals, granted by a political body to people who meet predetermined qualifications. It gives them the right to engage in a particular occupation or profession, use a particular title or perform a specific function. It is required.[14]

Regulation:

Regulation is the administration, direction, supervision, control or management of an activity usually by a public authority. Generally administrative regulations are established by public bodies through open hearings and implemented through published rules and procedures.[15]

Often these terms are used interchangeably but as the mediation profession advances in its quest for certainty, specificity in determining each quality control element becomes necessary.

B. QUALIFICATIONS

There are a number of ways by which an individual is selected to become a mediator. The term qualification, in this context, refers to the characteristics of an individual prior to participating in mediation training or education. These include the individual's educational background and any other acquired skill or training. Qualifications also include general innate tendencies, such as personality, communication abilities and conflict management style.

Some programs, courts and statutory schemes provide that a college or graduate degree is required of all a mediators. Some specifically require additional training,[16] while others determine that a degree itself

11. Adapted from an early publication of the National Institute for Dispute Resolution and a 1991 report from the New South Wales Law Reform Commission in Society of Professionals in Dispute Resolution, Commission on Qualifications, Qualifications Sourcebook Compendium (hereinafter referred to as Compendium.

12. Taken from an Information Background Kit provided by American Society of Association Executives to SPIDR, in Compendium, supra note 11.

13. Compendium, supra note 11.

14. Taken from an Information Background Kit, in Compendium supra note 10.

15. Society of Professionals in Dispute Resolution, supra note 11.

16. See Fla.R.Civ.Proc. 10.010 (1992); V.T.C.A., Civ.Prac. & Rem.Code § 154.052 (Supp. 1993) which, while recommending specific training, allow the court to waive the requirement; and Utah Code Ann. § 30–3–27 (1993).

establishes sufficient competency.[17] As a practical matter, most, if not all, mediators in court-connected programs possess college degrees, and the majority have received graduate degrees, most often a law degree.

Mediation trainers, educators and administrators have not reached consensus on which characteristics constitute necessary "qualifications". Many assert that it is a combination of factors which indicate the individual's appropriateness for mediation training. In fact, preliminary research indicates that initial, innate qualities, such as one's predisposition for conflict management, are more important in determining a mediator's effectiveness than training or prior experience.[18]

Assuming that a determination of pre-training qualifications is necessary regardless of subsequent training or education, the problem of how these qualifications may be assessed remains. In the case of the requirement of a degree only, it is simple. In other instances, assessment of appropriate characteristics can be difficult. Several programs hold initial screening interviews before accepting individuals into training. Others require potential mediators to "audition" by conducting mock mediations. Some trainers require a number of years experience in a given field, primarily law. Pre-training appraisal via psychological inventories may also be used. One example is the Meyers–Briggs type indicator.[19]

Many of the factors used to determine mediator qualifications are subjective in nature, and consequently, some trainers claim they are unfair, particularly as applied. Moreover, if mediation skills can be taught, there should be no necessity for initial screening. However, most professions have initial qualification requirements which must be met before a student can enter a professional school. If mediation is to be established as a "profession", pre-training qualifications must be defined and implemented.

C. TRAINING AND EDUCATION— TESTING AND EVALUATION

There is wide variation in the training and education of mediators.[20] While there was early consensus that some type of training or education for mediators was necessary and such was conducted, there was no consensus on the content of that training. Some programs and courts require nothing more than a three to four hour orientation to the mediation process. This is particularly true where the requirement is a degree, particularly the law degree, as the indicator of mediator competency. Other programs and projects recognize that specific training and

---

17. See Mich.Comp.Laws § 552.513(4) (1989).

18. Shaw, supra note 6 at 14.

19. For an in-depth examination of the use of Meyers–Briggs in teaching negotiation, see Don Peters, *Forever Jung: Psychological Type Theory, the Meyer–Briggs Type Indicator and Learning Negotiation*, 42 Drake L. Rev. 1 (1993).

20. For an in-depth examination of training issues see Joseph B. Stulberg, *Training Interveners for ADR Processes*, 81 Ky. L. J. 977 (1992–93).

education in the mediation process is necessary. The majority of training programs range from a minimum of sixteen [21] hours to the maximum standard of a forty hour training.[22]

In most other professions, in order to be licensed or certified, at least one year of schooling or education is necessary. Currently the most training or education required to "become a mediator" is forty hours, although additional hours are sometimes required in specialty areas, especially in family matters.[23] There has recently been a development of both undergraduate and graduate degree programs in conflict resolution which require a minimum of a year of study. If a mediation profession is established, it seems likely that the forty hour requirement will increase. However, preliminary research has not indicated that those who have more training necessarily perform better than mediators with less.[24]

Even in the instances where there is agreement as to the number of hours of required mediation training or teaching, there is no regulation as to the form of that education. There is diversity in both the method and content of training. Some mediation training programs consist of no more than viewing videotapes of mediations. Others consist primarily of lectures. Some training programs encourage continuous participation by the trainee. Most educators recognize that it is a combination of activities that provides the best learning experience. Most of the ongoing forty hour trainings do, as a rule, have a combination of these activities, although each will vary in the proportion devoted to each. For mediators who will work in court programs, it is recommended that the training includes role-playing with feedback.[25] Although some instructors and trainers voluntarily share information and methodology, currently no standards for those who teach and train in the mediation process exist.

An even greater difficulty for the mediation trainer is the determination of whether a trainee has "passed" the course. How will successful completion be determined? Some mediation courses and trainings, particularly those in law schools or other educational institutions administer tests to the students. These range from traditional written examinations to performance based assessments. Court-based programs have experimented with performance based testing,[26] but have found the time and effort involved in doing so overwhelming. Others continue to test the evaluation process.[27]

---

21. For example, Columbus, Ohio Night Prosecutor Program, (1980), Washington D.C. Multi–Door Training Agenda, (1992), and New Orleans Civil Courts Pilot Project (1993).

22. See, for example, V.T.C.A., Civ.Prac. & Rem.Code § 154.052 (Supp. 1993); Fla. R. Civ. Proc. 10.010 (1992).

23. See V.T.C.A., Civ. Prac. & Rem. Code § 154.052(b) (Supp. 1993) and Fla. R. Civ. Proc. 10.010(b) (1992).

24. Shaw, supra note 6 at 13.

25. National Standards, supra note 7 at 6–4.

26. Brad Honoroff, et al., *Putting Mediator Skills to the Test*, 6 Negotiation J. 37 (1990).

27. Christopher Honeyman, *On Evaluating Mediators*, 6 Negotiation J. 23 (1990).

In addition, there are different times at which the evaluation or testing can be conducted. In fact, a number of trainers test mediators within a year of training, since it has been noted that experience itself increases the mediator's skills.[28] Therefore, some programs include an apprenticeship requirement. Other methods of evaluation which have been used include settlement rates, user perceptions, including satisfaction, and opinions of judges, attorneys and peers.[29]

Most training programs, whether at the volunteer community or the professional mediator level, do not provide a formal evaluation of the trainee at the conclusion of the session. Most, however, evaluate the trainees during the training and provide direct feedback; some is provided in informal conversation, while other programs use more sophisticated tools, including forms and charts for evaluation. Few training programs will directly tell a trainee that he did not "pass" the mediation training. Since there is currently no licensure, even if individuals do not receive letters or certificates of completion, they may still mediate.

Many programs,[30] courts[31] and even some states[32] have continuing education requirements for mediators. Because of the infancy of the field, and its rapid change and expansion, regardless of a requirement, active mediators will find it a necessity to continue the educational process.

D. REGULATION; CERTIFICATION; AND LICENSURE

It is very difficult to predict just what the regulation of a mediation profession through a certification or licensure process will be, and who will administer it. In many professions, regulation is achieved by a board and is administered on a state-wide basis. Such boards have not been established in the mediation profession, although the Supreme Court of Florida has attempted to fill that role; and in Utah, the job has been delegated to the State Division of Occupational and Professional Licensing.[33] Mediators are still attempting to determine who the certifying or regulatory authority should be.

There is currently no type of licensure required for mediators. The term "certification" or "certified mediator" is widely mentioned, although the "certification" procedure consists, in most instances, of the receipt of a certificate which provides that the individual has completed a specific number of hours in mediation training. The certificate, itself has no bearing on the individual's competency as a mediator.

---

28. Shaw, supra note 6 at 17.

29. Id.

30. For example, many Dispute Resolution Centers require all volunteer mediators to complete a number of hours of "continuing *mediator* education" to remain active with the center.

31. See Local Rule 22, United States District Court, Southern District of Texas (1991).

32. Fla. R. Civ. Proc. 10.120(b) (1992).

33. Utah Code Ann. § 58–39a–2 (1993).

Some regulations exist in specific programs. For instance, many community based centers regulate mediators by allowing them to mediate only in a team or co-mediation format. In other instances, regulation is accomplished by a staff person or experienced mediator observing the mediators. Some mediator trade organizations have been formed which attempt self-regulation by enacting specific requirements for membership.

In 1992, the Supreme Court of Florida became the first organization in the United States to enact comprehensive guidelines for mediator certification and decertification.

PROPOSED STANDARDS OF PROFESSIONAL CONDUCT FOR CERTIFIED AND COURT–APPOINTED MEDIATORS
[May 28, 1992].

PER CURIAM.

In 1989 we appointed the Florida Supreme Court Standing Committee on Mediation and Arbitration Rules and directed the committee to propose procedural rules and to recommend standards of professional conduct. We adopted procedural rules for mediation and arbitration in *In re Amendments to Florida Rules of Civil Procedure*, 563 So.2d 85 (Fla.1990). The committee submitted its report on standards of conduct and disciplinary rules for mediators in November 1991,and we requested written comments from interested persons. The Court has received several comments and suggested changes. After considering the committee's proposal and those comments and suggestions, we adopt the rules set out following this opinion as the Florida Rules for Certified and Court–Appointed Mediators, rules 10.010 through 10.290. Florida Rule of Civil Procedure 1.760 is hereby repealed and readopted as rule 10.010 . . .

* * *

These changes will be effective immediately on the filing of this opinion.

* * *

PART I. MEDIATOR QUALIFICATIONS

RULE 10.010 GENERAL QUALIFICATIONS

(a) **County Court Mediators**. For certification a mediator of county court matters must:

(1) Complete a minimum of 20 hours in a training program certified by the Supreme Court;

(2) Observe a minimum of four county court mediation conferences conducted by a court certified mediator and conduct four county court mediation conferences under the supervision and observation of a court certified mediator; and

(3) Be of good moral character; or

(4) Be certified as a circuit court or family mediator.

(b) **Family Mediators**. For certification a mediator of family and dissolution of marriage issues must:

(1) Complete a minimum of 40 hours in a family mediation training program certified by the Supreme Court;

(2) Have a masters degree or doctorate in social work, mental health, behavioral or social sciences; or be a physician certified to practice adult or child psychiatry; or be an attorney or a certified public accountant licensed to practice in any United States jurisdiction; and have at least four years practical experience in one of the aforementioned fields; or have eight years family mediation experience with a minimum of ten mediations per year;

(3) Observe two family mediations conducted by a certified family mediator and conduct two family mediations under the supervision and observation of a certified family mediator; and

(4) Be of good moral character.

(c) **Circuit Court Mediators.** For certification a mediator of circuit court matters, other than family matters, must:

(1) Complete a minimum of 40 hours in a circuit court mediation training program certified by the Supreme Court;

(2) Be a member in good standing of the Florida Bar with at least five years of Florida practice and be an active member of the Florida Bar within one year of application for certification. This paragraph notwithstanding, the chief judge, upon written request setting forth reasonable and sufficient grounds, may certify as a circuit court mediator a retired judge who was a member of the bar in the state in which the judge presided. The judge must have been a member in good standing of the bar of another state for at least five years immediately preceding the year certification is sought and must meet the training requirements of (c)(1);

(3) Observe two circuit court mediations conducted by a certified circuit mediator and conduct two circuit mediations under the supervision and observation of a certified circuit court mediator; and

(4) Be of good moral character.

(d) **Special Conditions.** Mediators who have been duly certified as circuit court or family mediators before July 1, 1990, shall be deemed qualified as circuit court or family mediators pursuant to these rules.

PART II. STANDARDS OF PROFESSIONAL CONDUCT

RULE 10.020   PREAMBLE

(a) **Scope; Purpose**. These rules are intended to instill and promote public confidence in the mediation process and to be a guide to mediator conduct. As with other forms of dispute resolution, mediation must be built on public understanding and confidence. Persons serving as mediators are responsible to the parties, the public, and the courts to conduct themselves in a manner which will merit that confidence. These rules apply to all mediators who are certified or participate in court-sponsored mediation and are a guide to mediator conduct in discharging their professional responsibilities in the mediation of Circuit Civil, and Family and County Court cases in the State of Florida.

(b) **Mediation Defined**. Mediation is a process whereby a neutral third party acts to encourage and facilitate the resolution of a dispute without prescribing what it should be. It is an informal and nonadversarial process with the objective of helping the disputing parties reach a mutually acceptable agreement.

(c) **Mediator's Role**. In mediation, decision-making authority rests with the parties. The role of the mediator includes but is not limited to assisting the parties in identifying issues, reducing obstacles to communication, maximizing the exploration of alternatives, and helping the parties reach voluntary agreements.

(d) **General Principles**. Mediation is based on principles of communication, negotiation, facilitation, and problem-solving that emphasize:

(1) the needs and interests of the participants;

(2) fairness;

(3) procedural flexibility;

(4) privacy and confidentiality;

(5) full disclosure; and

(6) self determination.

RULE 10.030 GENERAL STANDARDS AND QUALIFICATIONS

(a) **General**. Integrity, impartiality, and professional competence are essential qualifications of any mediator. Mediators shall adhere to the highest standards of integrity, impartiality, and professional competence in rendering their professional service.

(1) A mediator shall not accept any engagement, perform any service, or undertake any act which would compromise the mediator's integrity.

(2) A mediator shall maintain professional competence in mediation skills including, but not limited to:

(A) staying informed of and abiding by all statutes, rules, and administrative orders relevant to the practice of court-ordered mediation;

(B) if certified, continuing to meet the requirements of these rules; and

(C) regularly engaging in educational activities promoting professional growth.

(3) A mediator shall decline appointment, withdraw, or request technical assistance when the mediator decides that a case is beyond the mediator's competence.

(b) **Concurrent Standards**. Nothing herein shall replace, eliminate, or render inapplicable relevant ethical standards, not in conflict with these rules, which may be imposed upon any mediator by virtue of the mediator's professional calling ...

* * *

PART III. DISCIPLINE

RULE 10.160 SCOPE AND PURPOSE

These rules apply to all proceedings before all panels and committees of the Mediator Qualifications Board involving the discipline or decertification of certified mediators or non-certified mediators appointed to mediate a case pursuant to Florida Rules of Civil Procedure 1.700–1.750. The purpose of these rules is to provide a means for enforcing the Florida Rules for Certified and Court–Appointed Mediators.

RULE 10.170 PRIVILEGE TO MEDIATE

Certification to mediator confers no vested right to the holder thereof, but is a conditional privilege that is revocable for cause ...

* * *

RULE 10.190 MEDIATOR QUALIFICATIONS BOARD

(a) **Generally**. The mediator qualifications board shall be composed of 3 standing divisions that shall be located in the following regions: ...

... Other divisions may be formed by the Supreme Court based on need.

(b) **Composition of Divisions**. Each division of the board shall be composed of the following members:

(1) three circuit or county judges;

(2) three certified county mediators;

(3) three certified circuit mediators;

(4) three certified family mediators, at least 2 of whom shall be non-lawyers; and

(5) three attorneys licensed to practice law in Florida who have a substantial trial practice and are neither certified as mediators nor judicial officers during their terms of service on the board, at least one of whom shall have a substantial divorce law practice.

* * *

RULE 10.220   COMPLAINT COMMITTEE PROCESS

(a) **Initiation of Complaint**. Any individual wishing to make a complaint alleging that a mediator has violated one or more provisions of these Rules shall do so in writing under oath. The complaint shall state with particularity the specific facts that form the basis of the complaint.

* * *

RULE 10.240   SANCTIONS

(a) **Generally**. The panel may impose one or more of the following sanctions:

(1) imposition of costs of the proceeding;

(2) oral admonishment;

(3) written reprimand;

(4) additional training to be completed;

(5) restriction on types of cases which can be mediated in the future;

(6) suspension for a period of up to one year; or

(7) decertification or, if the mediator is not certified, bar from service as a mediator under Florida Rules of Civil Procedure.

(b) **Decertified Mediators**. If a mediator has been decertified or barred from service pursuant to these rules, the mediator shall not thereafter be certified in any circuit nor assigned to mediate a case pursuant to Florida Rule of Civil Procedure 1.700 nor be designated as mediator pursuant to Rule 1.720(f) unless reinstated.

(c) **Decision to be Filed**. Upon making a determination that discipline is appropriate, the panel shall promptly file with the center a copy of the decision including findings and conclusions certified by the chair of the panel. The center shall promptly mail to all parties notice of such filing, together with a copy of the decision.

(d) **Notice to Circuits**. The center shall notify all circuits of any mediator who has been decertified or suspended if an appeal has not been filed pursuant to the Florida Rules of Appellate Procedure.

(e) **Reinstatement**. A mediator who has been suspended or decertified may be reinstated as a certified mediator. Except as otherwise provided in the decision of the panel, no application for reinstatement may be tendered within 2 years after the date of decertification. The reinstatement procedures shall be as follows:

(1) A petition for reinstatement, together with 3 copies, shall be made in writing, verified by the petitioner, and filed with the center.

(2) The petition for reinstatement shall contain: ...

(3) The center shall refer the petition for reinstatement to the appropriate division for review.

(4) The division shall review the petition with or without hearing and, if the petitioner is found to be unfit to mediate, the petition shall be dismissed. If the petitioner is found fit to mediate, the division shall notify the center and the center shall reinstate the petitioner as a certified mediator; provided, however, if the decertification has continued for more than 3 years, the reinstatement may be conditioned upon the completion of a certified training course as provided for in these rules.

————

But once certified or licensed, what is to guide the mediator's conduct on a day to day basis?

E.   STANDARDS OF CONDUCT

Acceptance and adherence to common standards of practice is often an element in the definition of a profession.[34] What are termed *standards of conduct* within each profession varies. Many published standards of conduct include specific ethical considerations. As examined here, however, standards of conduct address the mediator's activities in a practical sense. Standards provide guidance to the mediator about skill and practice actions as opposed to ethics, which cover moral, or right and wrong, issues. These standards of conduct operate in some instances to regulate the practice, not in the sense of who may practice, but in terms of expectations of mediator conduct.

One problem in the enactment of these standards is that there are many stylistic differences in mediators. While some styles are seen by the majority of mediators as standard, other mediators may have difficulty conforming to specific patterns of action. The enactment of standards might imply that only some mediator styles will be deemed proper.

For instance, Folberg and Taylor [35] identified a number of distinct mediation styles. They did so recognizing that there can be overlap, that the distinctions are not always clear, and that often a single mediator will blend styles or attempt to combine several styles resulting in a hybrid style. Perhaps the true mediator is a chameleon. Nonetheless, some of the more common of these styles follow.

1. **Labor Mediation**: The labor style uses separate meetings between the mediator and each side to explore minimum settlement positions, procedural traditions, and regulations. In the traditional model, each side had experienced representatives as participants representing others, rather than having all decision makers present. Thus a frequent requirement is ratification of the agreement.

34. Jay Folberg & Alison Taylor, Mediation: A Comprehensive Guide to Resolving Conflicts Without Litigation 258 (1986).

35. Id. at 130–145.

2. **Therapeutic Mediation**: While mediation proponents allege that mediation generally has a therapeutic value, this type of mediation is usually conducted by one with specific training in the psychotherapeutic or mental health field. In this process, emphasis is placed on understanding the underlying conflict and resolving the emotional aspects of the matter. The parties' psychological acceptance of the solution is often stressed by the mediator.

3. **Legal Mediation**: In legal mediation, the focus is on the dispute and little attention is paid to the underlying conflict. This style of mediation usually involves a legally trained mediator who discusses certain views of what the law is, and the legal parameters within which the parties' positions may be stated. The tendency is to focus only on the "legal" solutions as possible outcomes. The mediator may also provide legal analysis.

4. **Supervisory Mediation**: This mediation technique involves a mediator with some inherent authority, either assumed by the mediator or provided by the parties. There is a realization that if the parties do not arrive at their own settlement, the mediator may use this authority to decide for them.

5. **Muscle Mediation**: In describing this style, an admonition to refrain from its use is included. The muscle mediator is not a mediator in the classic sense of the word, since the mediator's role is to direct the parties to what their "best voluntary resolution" might be. This directing nature runs contrary to normal mediation practice.

6. **Scrivener Mediation**: The scrivener mediator reports thoughts and ideas expressed by others and does little else. One of the most passive styles of mediation, the scrivener mediator relies on the ability of the parties to resolve their own conflicts. No active intervention is provided. The mediator's presence provides a safe and peaceful setting, an expectation of reasonableness and presence of someone who can clarify and record the agreement. This style is often used intermittently with the others.

7. **Structured Mediation**: This is the most rigid form of mediation; it is used primarily in divorce cases where the mediation takes place over a period of time. A set of rules specify such things as goals to be accomplished at each session, the role of the mediator, the session lengths, ordering of the issues, permissible conduct between sessions and use of outside attorneys or consultants.

8. **Shuttle Mediation**: This brand of mediation involves separate caucus sessions that are connected by a "shuttling" mediator. Techniques taken from the labor field are used to narrow issues and explore positions.

9. **Crisis Mediation**: This is a formal mediation which is used in disputes which are "active"; that is, the parties are in the process of disputing. The mediator intervenes in the crisis in an attempt to reach

a calming point; thereafter the underlying cause of the crisis is explored in an attempt to obtain a resolution.

10. **Team (Co) Mediation**: This involves the use of two or more mediators simultaneously. This is particularly useful where the conflicts are multi-dimensional and require expertise of various types. Teams of mediators specifically trained in relevant fields save time, promote trust and more quickly narrow issues. However, there are disadvantages as well, including additional cost, scheduling difficulties, inability of the mediators to work as a team and confusion of the parties.

Although court-connected mediation was previously identified as a distinct style,[36] it has now developed to the point where there is attention focused specifically on the styles of mediators in pending litigation. Distinct styles of mediators in Florida's court program were studied, and three approaches to mediation were identified. These were "trashing", "bashing" and "hashing it out".[37]

The "trashing" methodology involved tearing apart the cases in a legal sense. Thereafter the mediator assists in building the case back with a more realistic settlement figure on the table. Direct communication between the parties is discouraged.[38] This process resembles a case evaluation approach to dispute resolution.

The "bashing" technique was the second style identified in the study. Rather than engage in case evaluation aimed at getting the parties to offer more realistic monetary figures, bashers focus on the actual settlement offers. Generally, they then "bash" away at them until the parties agree to a figure somewhere in between the two original amounts. Mediators who bash permit direct communication.[39] Because of the distributive bargaining implicit in this style, the final settlement figure is predictably near the middle of the first offers.

The third style is "hashing it out". "Hasher" mediators take a more flexible approach to the process. Their styles and techniques vary depending on the needs and interests of the parties. Direct communication between the disputing parties is encouraged, permitting more party control of the process, and a focus on the interests and issues of the parties.[40]

Approaches to mediation have also been categorized as either problem-solving or predictive.[41] In predictive settlement procedures, the mediator attempts to affect the parties' concepts of what will happen at trial, thereby encouraging settlement. While there are other ADR processes such as neutral case evaluation, moderated settlement conference and summary jury trials which provide this evaluation, some mediators opt for this approach. In fact, evaluative mediation has been

36. Id.

37. James J. Alfini, *Trashing, Bashing and Hashing It Out: Is this the End of "Good Mediation"?*, 19 Fla. St. U. L. Rev. 47 (1991).

38. Id. at 67.

39. Id. at 69.

40. Id. at 72.

41. Craig A. McEwen, *Mediator as Predictor or Problem Solver*, 19 Fla. St. U. L. Rev. 77, 78 (1991).

labeled an emerging form, in which the mediation streamlines the exchange of information so to reduce the amount of time necessary for the parties to present positions.

Conversely, the problem solving approach does not rest on predicting what a court might do. The focus is not merely on arriving at a monetary settlement, but rather on the needs of the parties and their underlying interests. There is increased opportunity for integrative bargaining. Also in the problem solving approach, there is room for exploration of creative solutions.

Because of the variety in mediation practice, enacting standards is difficult. Unnecessary restrictions may be placed on the mediator's activities. Specific standards which dictate the mediator's activities may conflict among themselves. The mediator must decide which approach to follow. Moreover, some standards obligate the mediator to do that which he should not do—make a decision.[42] Implementation is also problematic. Who will be present to monitor the mediator's actions?

Most standards encompass areas such as neutrality, impartiality, and confidentiality.[43] Most of the standards that have been established to date require that the mediator abide by confidentiality. Many provide that the mediator remain neutral and impartial. However, exceptions are then carved out. One such exception is with regard to imbalances of power or knowledge. For instance, the Oklahoma Supreme Court Rules require, in court cases, that the mediator avoid the bargaining imbalances that one party may have in legal knowledge or negotiating skill. The mediator must provide assistance to one party if the other party is represented.[44] The mediator must recognize a power imbalance, which requires a judgment on the part of the mediator. Farmer-lender mediation programs often require mediators to provide expert advice ranging from legal aid to financial assistance[45] to the farm owner. These programs have pre-determined that the lender possesses an advantage.

Standards of conduct are difficult to define with precision. In many instances, the behavior chosen by the mediator at a specific time may be a matter of personal choice. She will need to make decisions on her own, unless otherwise dictated by the training or practice requirements of a program, project or court through which she is mediating.

F. MEDIATOR LIABILITY

One option to assure quality control in the profession is the "after the fact" control method of establishing liability through malpractice

42. See, for example, Code of Professional Conduct for Mediators, Oklahoma Supreme Court Rules and Procedures for the Dispute Resolution Act, which provides that the mediator shall terminate a session if a party is being *harmed*.

43. Since these matters were covered in previous chapters, they will not be examined in detail here.

44. Oklahoma Supreme Court Rules and Procedure for Dispute Resolution Act, Rule 12 (1992).

45. Iowa Code Ann. § 654A.1 (1993); Wyo. Stat. § 11–41–105(a), (b) (1993).

suits. Even though mediation is a new profession with a great number of unanswered questions, there have been a few cases filed against mediators. While the number is not large, it is anticipated that such filings will continue. At the end of 1993, a primary insurer of arbitrators and mediators [46] reported that the current number of claims against mediators and arbitrators average five per year. The majority of these involved either general negligence, conflicts of interest, or breaches of confidentiality. The remaining were divided among other theories of liability.[47] The mediator should examine the following issues raised in malpractice cases with a focus on how she might prevent such an occurrence.

1. CAUSES OF ACTION

A number of legal theories exist through which one can allege mediator malpractice. The theory with the broadest ramifications is general negligence. Depending on the nature of mediation practice, others include Deceptive Trade and Practices Act (DTPA), breach of contract, fraud, false imprisonment, libel, slander, breach of fiduciary duty, and tortious interference with a business relationship.

In fee generating mediations, the disputing parties qualify as consumers under the breach of contract or DTPA theories. The mediator should be cautious in advertising and guard against making promises or guarantees. It may be advisable to put any information provided to the parties in writing and design a method to verify what information was received by the parties.

Matters such as libel and slander may fall within a claim of breach of confidentiality. The extent of confidentiality in the mediation process is not clear. Confidentiality, in the legal sense, varies depending on the jurisdiction, type of mediation and nature of dispute.[48] Recognizing this variation, the Joint Code [49] proposes that the mediator's duty is only to meet the parties' expectations with regard to confidentiality. The code, by design, does not specify what those expectations should be. It is therefore very important that the mediator be explicit with regard to confidentiality provisions and provide these in written documents as well. The mediator must then be careful to abide by the specific confidentiality provisions.

In the area of general negligence, under current nebulous standards, an attorney would have difficulty in proving liability by a breach of duty. However, as previously pointed out,[50] there are a few standards which, for the most part, are consistent. These include duties to remain impartial and avoid conflicts of interest. Mediators should be knowl-

---

46. Complete Equity Markets, Inc.

47. Telephone conference with Gracine Huffnagle, January 3, 1994.

48. See Chapter 11, supra.

49. *Standards of Conduct for Mediators*, Joint work of ABA Section of Dispute Reso-

lution, American Arbitration Association, and Society of Professionals in Dispute Resolution, Draft Code, April 1994. See Chapter 14, supra, and Appendix C.

50. See § E this chapter, supra.

edgeable about those standards, and adhere to them. Where there is doubt about what the standard of practice is, the mediator must rely on her own judgment in making a decision. When there is a fine line, implementing a policy embracing "better safe than sorry" is advisable. As time passes, research and practice should determine more specifically what the operable standard of practice is within any mediation organization or entity. Once determined, violations of these standards will likely result in negligence.

2. DAMAGES

Even where a disputant is able to prove a breach of duty, thereby establishing liability against a mediator, in order to recover, damages must also be proven. In a truly consensual process such as mediation, there may be difficulty in establishing damages, particularly where the claim concerns the mediation process itself rather than a peripheral issue such as a slander claim. Admittedly in claims such as slander or tortious interference with a business relationship, the damages may involve events which occur outside of the mediation process. If liability under these theories is established, recovery against the mediator is probable. Likewise, in a case where the mediator provides professional advice, and the advice is incorrect, if the party shows that she relied upon such advice to her detriment, recovery against the mediator is likely. However, in claims against the mediator which turn on the elements of the process, establishing damages will be more difficult. Even if the mediator breached a duty with regard to performance in the mediation, the claimant must also establish that, but for those actions in the mediation, there would have been a better outcome to the case. What this better outcome would be will rely on speculation, and proving it may be a difficult task.[51] To date, there has not been a reported case where a plaintiff has successfully prevailed on this issue.

G. IMMUNITY

1. POLICY CONSIDERATIONS

There are a number of situations where a mediator may be immune from liability. One of the older dispute resolution devices, arbitration, has historically provided immunity for the arbitrators. Immunity was initially premised on the fact that the arbitrator was an extension of the court or judge, and as such, should be given immunity.[52] Extension of this immunity to mediators has not been unequivocally established. In fact, some argue that the mediator's role is so dissimilar to that of the

---

51. See, for example, *Lange v. Marshall*, 622 S.W.2d 237 (Mo.App. 1981), where a claim was made against a lawyer acting in a mediative role in a divorce action, and the plaintiff was unable to establish damages.

52. Judicial immunity was first established in Bradley v. Fischer, 80 U.S. 335, 20 L.Ed. 646 (1872), based upon the need for independence and freedom to act in the administration of justice. This was first extended to arbitrators in the United States in *Jones v. Brown*, 6 N.W. 140 (Iowa 1880), which noted the similarity between a judge and arbitrator.

court, that a new common law immunity premised along the lines of judicial and arbitral immunity is unlikely.[53] Yet a few courts have begun to address this issue directly, and a number of states have enacted statutes providing immunity for the mediator.

If immunity is absolute, or sufficiently broad, the consumer of mediation services will have no recourse for any damage resulting from participation in mediation. Since mediation is such a new field, essentially without regulations, rules or standardized procedures, there must be a way to guard against abuse of the process and the parties by the mediator. Furthermore, mediators resemble service providers who have not traditionally been protected by immunity.[54] These include lawyers and therapists. Conversely, mediators, particularly those who volunteer, need to do so without fear of having to expend time and money in the defense of malpractice claims. A compromise between these two considerations has resulted in enactment of immunity statutes aimed primarily at protection of the pro bono mediator.

2. STATUTORY PROVISIONS

A survey of statutes show that at least nineteen states provide some immunity for mediators. These include: Arizona, Colorado, Florida, Iowa, Maine, Minnesota, Oklahoma, Utah, Washington, Wisconsin, and Texas.

Most of these statutes provide for immunity in the volunteer or pro bono setting, often under specific programs or conditions. There has yet to be a statute which provides blanket immunity for all mediators in all actions. Nearly all of the statutes provide a qualified immunity and include an exception for wanton and willful misconduct.

For instance in Colorado, the Dispute Resolution Act limits the liability of mediators to willful or wanton misconduct.[55] In Iowa, statutory immunity covers both informal dispute resolution as well as the farm mediator. In Iowa all mediators, employees, and agents of a center as well as members of a dispute resolution center's board are protected from liability. The immunity does not extend if there is bad faith, malicious purpose, or wanton and willful disregard of human rights, safety or property.[56] In Iowa farmer-lender mediation, members of a farm mediation staff, including a mediator, employee or agent or member of the board of the service is not liable for civil damages for a statement or decision made in the process of mediation unless the member acts in bad faith, with malicious purpose, or in a manner exhibiting willful and wanton disregard of human rights, safety, or property.[57] In Washington, employees and volunteers of a dispute resolution center are immune from suit in any civil action based on any proceedings or other official acts performed in their capacity as employ-

53. Nancy H. Rogers & Craig A. McEwen, Mediation: Law, Policy & Practice 190 (1989).

54. Id.

55. West's Colo. Rev. Stat. Ann. § 13–22–305(6) (Supp.93).

56. Iowa Code Ann. § 679.13 (1987).

57. Iowa Code Ann. § 13.16(1) (1994).

ees or volunteers, except in cases of wilful or wanton misconduct.[58] The Supreme Court of Georgia did not wait for the legislature, and instead established by court order immunity for all neutrals in a court-annexed or court-referred program.[59]

3. CASE LAW

In a few instances, the courts have addressed this issue.

HOWARD v. DRAPKIN
Court of Appeal, Second District, 1990.
222 Cal.App.3d 843, 271 Cal.Rptr. 893.

* * *

Defendant Robin Drapkin ("defendant"), a psychologist, performed an evaluation of plaintiff and her family and plaintiff now claims that defendant acted improperly in carrying out that task.

In this appeal we are asked to determine whether the alleged wrongful actions of which plaintiff complains were performed in such a context that defendant can claim (1) common law immunity as a quasi-judicial officer participating in the judicial process or (2) statutory privilege under Civil Code section 47, subdivision (2) ("section 47(2)")[1] for a publication in a judicial proceeding. We conclude that defendant, acting in the capacity of a neutral third person engaged in efforts to effect a resolution of a family law dispute, is entitled to the protection of quasi-judicial immunity for the conduct of such dispute resolution services. We also find that the litigation privilege provided for in section 47(2) applies to the facts of this case. We therefore affirm the dismissal of plaintiff's complaint.

* * *

With respect to defendant's alleged non-disclosures, plaintiff asserts that defendant (1) failed to divulge her lack of expertise in the area of child and sexual abuse, (2) failed to disclose that she and Robert had a prior professional relationship in that they had spoken and participated together in professional seminars and (3) failed to disclose that she was a close personal friend of the wife of one of the partners in the law firm which represented Robert in the underlying action.

* * *

This appeal raises the issue of the availability of (1) quasi-judicial immunity by reason of defendant's involvement as a neutral dispute-resolving participant in the judicial process and (2) the absolute privilege

---

58. West's Rev. Code Wash. Ann. § 7.75.100 (1992).

59. Rule 6.2 Alternative Dispute Resolution Rules, Supreme Court of Georgia, March 9, 1993.

1. Civil Code section 47, subdivision 2 provides in relevant part that with certain exceptions for dissolution of marriage proceedings, "A privileged publication or broadcast is one made—... [P] 2. In any ... (2) judicial proceeding...."

under the provisions of section 47(2), as a complete bar to plaintiff's actions.

* * *

The concept of judicial immunity is longstanding and absolute, with its roots in English common law. It bars civil actions against judges for acts performed in the exercise of their judicial functions and it applies to all judicial determinations, including those rendered in excess of the judge's jurisdiction, no matter how erroneous or even malicious or corrupt they may be.

* * *

The rationale behind the doctrine is twofold. First, it "protect[s] the finality of judgments [and] discourag[es] inappropriate collateral attacks." (*Forrester v. White*, supra, 484 U.S. 219, 225, 108 S.Ct. 538, 543.) Second, it "protect[s] judicial independence by insulating judges from vexatious actions prosecuted by disgruntled litigants."

* * *

Under the concept of "quasi-judicial immunity," California courts have extended absolute judicial immunity to persons other than judges if those persons act in a judicial or quasi-judicial capacity. Thus, court commissioners "acting either as a temporary judge or performing subordinate judicial duties ordered by the appointing court" have been granted quasi-judicial immunity.

* * *

Plaintiff seeks to establish that California's version of common law judicial and quasi-judicial immunity is applied only to public officials (judges, grand jurors, prosecutors, commissioners, etc.). If that were so, then arbitrators would not be protected by common law quasi-judicial immunity. We believe that in California, it is not so much one's status as a public official which has generally been the litmus test for judicial immunity but rather the above-referenced analysis of "functions normally performed by judges." It just so happens, that with the exception of arbitrators, and sometimes referees (*Park Plaza Ltd. v. Pietz* (1987) 193 Cal.App.3d 1414, 1418–1419, 239 Cal.Rptr. 51), such functions have usually been performed by public officials.

* * *

We are persuaded that the approach of the federal courts is consistent with the relevant policy considerations of attracting to an overburdened judicial system the independent and impartial services and expertise upon which that system necessarily depends. Thus, we believe it appropriate that these "nonjudicial persons who fulfill quasi-judicial functions intimately related to the judicial process" (*Myers v. Morris*, supra, 810 F.2d at p.1466–1467) should be given absolute quasi-judicial immunity for damage claims arising from their performance of duties in connection with the judicial process. Without such immunity, such persons will be reluctant to accept court appointments or provide work product for the courts' use. Additionally, the threat of civil liability may affect the manner in which they perform their jobs. (*Moses v. Parwatikar* (8th Cir.1987) 813 F.2d 891, 892, cert. den. 484 U.S. 832, 108 S.Ct. 108, 98 L.Ed.2d 67.)

* * *

In arguing for extensions of immunity to the category of persons who function apart from the courts in an attempt to resolve disputes, defendant and amicus emphasize that in this day of excessively crowded courts and long delays in bringing civil cases to trial, more reliance is being placed by both parties and the courts on alternative methods of dispute resolution. Along traditional lines, the provisions of article VI, section 22 of the Constitution, which allow the Legislature to provide for the appointment by trial courts of officers such as commissioners, references and masters (*Tagliavia v. County of Los Angeles*, supra, 112 Cal.App.3d at 763, 169 Cal.Rptr. 467), are becoming ever more important. We have court commissioners (Code Civ. Proc., § 259) and voluntary and mandatory referees (Code Civ. Proc., § 638 et seq.). In addition, contracts for binding arbitration (Code Civ. Proc., § 1280 et seq.) and provisions for non-binding arbitration (Code Civ. Proc., § 1141.10 et seq.) help relieve court congestion. So also does Civil Code section 4607's provision for mandatory mediation of child custody and visitation disputes.

More recently, other aspects of alternative dispute resolution efforts are being used with greater frequency. There are voluntary settlement conferences which are conducted by volunteers working with the court through, for example, local bar associations. In addition, if it is necessary, the parties can choose a mediator or neutral fact-finder with the expertise to facilitate a resolution of their particular dispute. As amicus notes, mediation is traditionally a non-binding dispute resolution alternative. While most mediation is voluntary, some is compulsory, like that provided for in Civil code section 4607.

* * *

We therefore hold that absolute quasi-judicial immunity is properly extended to these neutral third-parties for their conduct in performing dispute resolution services which are connected to the judicial process and involve either (1) the making of binding decisions, (2) the making of findings or recommendations to the court or (3) the arbitration, mediation, conciliation, evaluation or other similar resolution of pending disputes. As the defendant was clearly engaged in this latter activity, she is entitled to the protection of such quasi-judicial immunity.

* * *

WAGSHAL v. FOSTER

United States District Court, District of
Columbia, 1993.
1993 WL 86499.

This federal civil action against a state-court-appointed mediator and his law partners, brought by a litigant who believes himself to have been wronged by the mediator in the course of court-ordered "alternative dispute resolution" ("ADR") proceedings, is presently before the Court on defendants' motion, in advance of answer, to dismiss or for summary judgment on the ground of judicial immunity.

* * *

In June, 1990, Jerome Wagshal brought suit in the Superior Court of the District of Columbia against the manager of real property owned by Wagshal ("The Sheetz case"). In October, 1991, the Honorable Richard A. Levie, the Superior Court judge to whom the case had been assigned, ordered a stay of discovery pending efforts to bring the case to settlement through the Superior Court's ADR program, and referred the case, over Wagshal's objection, to a "case evaluator." In the Superior Court ADR is mandatory.[1]

* * *

Wagshal then objected to the first case evaluator appointed as having a "conflict of interest," and Judge Levie accordingly appointed the defendant Mark W. Foster, Esquire, as a substitute on November 21, 1991.

* * *

Wagshal's counsel then interposed an objection to Mr. Foster as an evaluator, questioning Foster's neutrality once again on the basis of a perceived "conflict of interest," and, when Wagshal refused Foster's express request that Wagshal either waive the objection or make an issue of it before proceeding with evaluation, on February 19, 1992, Foster wrote to Judge Levie to recuse himself as an evaluator.

* * *

In a telephone conference call hearing on February 20, 1992, Judge Levie agreed with Mr. Foster's observations that the alleged conflicts of interest were "attenuated"—indeed, would have been of no consequence to him had he been asked for a ruling—but he acceded to Mr. Foster's recusal and excused him from further participation in the conference. Judge Levie then reiterated his determination to maintain the stay of discovery in place and to try once more with case evaluation.

* * *

1. The alternative dispute resolution program of the Superior Court is a formal division of the court established by order of its Chief Judge, known as the "Multi-Door Dispute Resolution Division," and offers mediation, arbitration, and case evaluation processes to litigants in lieu of trial and judgment. "Case evaluators" for cases such as the Sheetz case are members of the District of Columbia Bar, with at least five years of relevant litigation experience, who volunteer to serve without compensation, undergo required training, and are approved as such by the court.

For purposes of this case the functions of mediators and evaluators are indistinguishable.

A review of the case law, however, reveals that court-appointed mediators and their like have not been around long enough to have generated much in the way of precedent with respect to the extent to which they enjoy the immunity of the court whom they serve when they venture into a private controversy represented by a pending case, and in the course thereof, antagonize one or more of the parties. Other, more traditional agents of the judicial process have, however, historically been held to possess such immunity when they act in their official capacities,[2] and this Court concludes that court-appointed arbitrators, mediators, case evaluators, and others who are directly involved in ADR programs with express authority from the court may properly invoke the same protection, for similar reasons.

In the instant case it appears that Mr. Foster was discharging his duty to the Superior Court of the District of Columbia, and acting with the knowledge and approval of the judge by whom he had been appointed, in all the respects with which plaintiff finds fault with his performance. He therefore possesses that court's judicial immunity, and this complaint, and each count thereof must be dismissed as to all defendants.

For the foregoing reasons, it is, this 5th day of February, 1993,

ORDERED, that defendants' motion to dismiss or for summary judgment is granted, and the complaint is dismissed with prejudice.

If this trend continues and immunity is established for all mediators, and courts continue in their use of the process, will the result be a society without rules, procedures, standards, or regulation? Some fear that will occur as a result of ADR use.

H. QUALITY MEDIATION DOES NOT EXIST

There are some who would propose that it is impossible to establish quality in mediation. The only "quality" is no mediation. Although most mediators, participants and legal scholars support the use of

---

2. Judges have absolute immunity from damage liability for actions taken in their judicial capacity. *Forrester v. White,* 484 U.S. 219 (1988). This absolute immunity may be extended to other officials when their activities are integrally related to the judicial process and when they perform a judicial function as an officer of the court. *Schinner v. Strathmann,* 711 F.Supp. 1143 (D.D.C.1989) (psychiatrist appointed to determine defendant's mental competency to stand trial). See, e.g., *Imbler v. Pachtman,* 424 U.S. 409, 430 (1976) (prosecutors); *Crosby–Bey v. Jansson,* 486 F.Supp. 96, 98 (D.D.C.1984) (probation officer); *Simons v.* *Bellinger,* 643 F.2d 774 (D.C.Cir.1980) (court-appointed committee monitoring unauthorized practice of law); *Wolff v. Faris,* 1989 WL 84718, 1989 U.S. Dist. LEXIS 8520 (N.D.Ill. July 19, 1989) (conciliator in custody dispute); *Howard v. Drapkin,* 222 Cal.App.3d 843, 860 (1990) ("[A]bsolute immunity is properly extended to neutral third persons who are engaged in mediation, conciliation, evaluation or similar dispute resolution efforts."); *Austern v. Chicago Board Options Exchange, Inc.,* 898 F.2d 882, 886 (2d Cir.) (arbitrators), cert. denied, 111 S.Ct. 141 (1990).

mediation, some criticism of the process has been leveled. In general, these critics point out that the traditional legal system has more safeguards for the individual and for society than the mediation process. With the increased use of mediation, and other dispute resolution procedures, combined with a lack of protection for the consumers, a system may develop very unlike that which we currently know. While some may find this a favorable result, others have expressed grave concern.

One criticism is based on gender.[60] The primary focus of the critique is on mandatory mediation in custody disputes. The use of mediation is disapproved for these matters for a number of reasons. These include the fact that the woman will not have the opportunity to have blame assessed;[61] when the individuals are treated alike advantages are accorded to the husband;[62] there is an inability to express anger which is often necessary in custody cases;[63] the mediation process may contribute to prejudices;[64] lawyers who are protectors of rights are excluded;[65] and a direct confrontation with the soon to be former spouse may be intolerable.[66]

At first glance, these concerns as described appear to be valid. However, mediation is a flexible process, and each program, and in fact, each mediator, is different. Generalization to all mediation is misplaced.[67] For instance, where the parties agree to voluntarily participate in mediation, if the situation becomes uncomfortable, they can leave. Moreover, in the majority of programs, in direct contrast to the California model, the mediator is prohibited from making any report to the court, other than whether a settlement was achieved. Thus, the mediator makes no decisions, and maintains all of the information as confidential. Moreover, while lawyers are sometimes discouraged from attending mediation with their clients[68] rarely is their presence prohibited. In fact, an innovative area of law practice is developing known as mediation advocacy.[69]

Some have expressed fear that the informality of ADR fosters racial and ethnic prejudices.[70] Mediation is again compared with the courts, as courts are assumed to possess procedural safeguards which assist in preventing the demonstration of prejudice.[71] While pre-trial and trial procedures may, in theory, be structured to guard against explicit bias,

60. Trina Grillo, *The Mediation Alternative: Process Dangers for Women*, 100 Yale L. J. 1545 (1991).

61. Id. at 1560.

62. Id. at 1568.

63. Id. at 1572.

64. Id. at 1587.

65. Id. at 1597.

66. Id. at 1601.

67. See Joshua D. Rosenberg, *In Defense of Mediation*, 33 Ariz. L. Rev. 467 (1991).

68. This is usually in divorce cases or pre-litigation matters. The rationale is cost savings.

69. See Eric R. Galton, Representing Clients in Mediation (1994).

70. Richard Delgado et. al., *Fairness and Formality: Minimizing the Risk of Prejudice in Alternative Dispute Resolution*, 1985 Wis. L. Rev. 1359 (1985).

71. Id. at 1367.

in the real world these rules are manipulated. It has been demonstrated that in an informal setting such as mediation, individuals will more likely act on their prejudices than if they are placed in an environment where they must conform.[72] Consequently in the informal mediation environment, the chance of overt prejudice is increased.

Other related criticisms have also been leveled. While the mediation process provides safeguards for the private person, such as confidentiality, it may also be more intrusive. One example is in the request or expectation of shared information.[73] Although disclosure is encouraged in the mediation process, it is the rare situation where a mediator would *require* a party to reveal secret information. Most mediators can sense if a person is uncomfortable speaking about certain information, and will not pursue the subject. Moreover, the mediation process can actually assist in preserving confidential information, particularly when the process is conducted in a caucus format.

Probably the most common critique of the mediation process is that the public or social order is not served by its use. If cases settle, then issues will not be litigated. Consequently new public policies cannot be made. Some believe that this works specifically to the detriment of minorities.[74]

It is also argued that the courtroom is the preferred site for dispute resolution since imbalances between parties can be mitigated by judges.[75] In the mediation setting, if the mediator subscribes to complete neutrality and impartiality[76] and takes the parties as she finds them, the imbalance will not be corrected. In fact, it may carry over into the terms of settlement.

Some contend that a primary purpose of our legal system is to shape the world we live in; to determine societal standards. The job of the courts is not to make peace or determine rights for private parties, but rather enforce the Constitution and statutes, interpret values, and apply them to reality.[77] If all cases are settled in a private manner, then the purpose of the lawsuit has been rendered to that of resolving private matters.[78]

While some of these criticisms are valid, it is doubtful that in all cases our system is able to give force to values. Witness the noncompliance and disregard for courts that is prevalent. Even if it were to be assumed for the sake of argument only, that the poor, disadvantaged, and minority groups would fare better in adjudication, what are the realistic possibilities that members of those groups ever actually get to court? What should the balance be? For one percent of a group to find a resolution through adjudication or for ninety percent to conclude their disputing?

72. Id. at 1387.

73. Id. at 1397.

74. Id. at 1398.

75. Owen Fiss, *Against Settlement*, 93 Yale L. J. 1073, 1075 (1984).

76. See Chapter 7, supra.

77. Fiss, supra note 75, at 1085.

78. Id.

QUESTIONS FOR DISCUSSION

15–1. Florida Rule of Civil Procedure 10.240(e)(4) provides for the reinstatement of mediators. A key to being reinstated is a finding of "fit to mediate". What does this mean?

15–2. Other than a bar from service, the Florida standards do not provide any other sanction for an uncertified individual who violates these rules. Are other sanctions appropriate? What should they include?

15–3. While the current case law appears to provide immunity to neutrals, it does so only when they are mediating a pending case. In order to protect herself, should a mediator require the parties to file a lawsuit before serving as a mediator in a matter? What are other viable options?

15–4.[79] You are mediating the following divorce action. The parties have been married for over eighteen years. The husband, C. Vanderbilt Cabot–Lodge, has a combined J.D./MBA degree. He was in law practice for ten years, and thereafter went to work for a major corporation, where he now serves as CEO. Judy, his wife was only 19 when the couple married. The couple has three children, Jack and Jill who are in high school, and Joe who is three years old. The mediation is focused on the division of property.

The estate includes: a six bedroom homestead; a drug store, heavily indebted, that Vanderbilt spends 15 hours a week, managing; a record archives business, financed on debt, that he spends 10 hours a week managing; a six story office building he owns and manages, subject to first and second mortgages totalling more than the market value of the building; 38 different stocks, all bought on margin; tax free bonds pledged as security for other assets; a tract of land which used to be a chemical company dump site. The EPA is demanding $3,000,000 worth of environmental clean-up of that site; and inter vivos trust which Vanderbilt created to hold about a million dollars worth of assets immune from creditors. The couple appears before you without counsel, seeking a quiet, quick, confidential and inexpensive way to divide these properties. It is agreed that together the couple has only $3,000 readily accessible cash.

Vanderbilt brought the preceding list of properties to the mediation, and offers ideas as to valuation and how they should be divided. You assume from what he has said that these values are based largely on what he paid for the properties in the past, extending back 20 years.

Judy trusts his "business judgment", but you wonder whether he really knows the property values.

79. Used with permission, from Tom   in Mediation (1992).
Arnold, A Short Discussion of Ethics Issues

Whether he know the values or not, you believe that inherently, his figures must be biased, and that it is not in Judy's interest to rely on his valuation.

(a) What is the mediator's responsibility? For the process? For the agreement?

(b) Should you as the mediator urge both of them to get counsel?

(c) Should you recommend to either or both that appraised values of each property be obtained?

(d) Should you recess the mediation until further information is available?

(e) What if both of them really want the case concluded today and don't seem to care about fairness?

(f) Suppose Judy informs you privately that she has a rich, young lover she wants to marry next week. She will give up anything to get this over with today. Judy and Vanderbilt are nearly in agreement on accepting his values.

Is it proper for the mediator to intervene?

(g) Should the mediator consider the fairness of the potential agreement?

(h) Is a proposal to these parties that they employ counsel and experts to evaluate the property, a neutral act or an act favoring Judy? Does it destroy the integrity of the mediator's neutrality?

(i) Does proposing counsel and experts destroy the concept that the parties are free to make their own deal without mediator interference?

(j) Suppose you find Vanderbilt to be an engaging fellow, not really out of sorts with his wife, just too busy to give her the time and comfort she needs. And you find her to be a warm person, still much in love with her husband, but in need of a little attention.

Do you address this issue? To what degree? Do you suggest, recommend or urge that the parties seek a therapist?

Chapter Sixteen

SPECIALIZED APPLICATIONS OF MEDIATION

Earlier chapters examined mediation as a process for resolving conflict in a number of situations. The recent ADR movement [1] has primarily focused on the use of mediation in community-based programs and as an adjunct to the courts. Consequently, the increased use of mediation has been in the context of assisting individuals to resolve legal or quasi-legal disputes. Within these areas, a number of specialized applications of mediation has developed. In addition, mediation, along with its derivative and hybrid processes,[2] can be used to resolve a wide variety of conflicts.

It has been claimed that mediation can assist in the resolution of disputes from A to Z—from agricultural to zoning matters, and everything in between.[3] This chapter will highlight several of the diverse applications of mediation. Within many of these specialized areas, there are distinctive differences in the way the mediation process is conducted. As noted in the previous chapter, mediation styles differ.[4] Variations may result from the type of dispute mediated. In some of these specialized applications, there may also be specific modifications of the process. Comparisons between traditional, classic mediation and that employed in the specialized applications of the process is helpful in describing some of the diversity of mediation use. Mediators are urged to receive additional training prior to mediating in some specialized areas. In some instances, specialized training is mandatory. Moreover, where the mediation process is statutorily provided, specific rules may direct the mediator's actions.

The following description of the variety of areas where the mediation process is used is by no means exhaustive. A complete listing of all of the specific applications of mediation is impractical, if not impossible,

---

1. See Chronology, Chapter 2, § B, supra.

2. See Chapter 17, infra.

3. E. Wendy Trachte, Broadening the Scope of ADR: Developments from A to Z,

B–3, Alternative "Trial Notebook" South Texas College of Law and AA White Dispute Resolution Institute, November 1992.

4. Chapter 15, § E, supra.

since new uses are constantly discovered. Many of these specialized areas have developed without direction, while others are mandated by statute. For example, statutes exist which advocate mediation use in barber disputes,[5] matters involving mobile homes,[6] disputes between dentists and patients,[7] and cases concerning human skeletal remains in burial grounds.[8] This small sample demonstrates the expansive application of the mediation process. In the specific areas described herein, there has been, or currently is, a great deal of interest, and thus specific programs, projects, or practices have developed. That is not to say, however, that a general practice mediator might not encounter many of these disputes in practice.

A. AGRICULTURAL DISPUTES

A number of mediation programs have been created to focus on resolving disputes between farmers and lenders. These programs developed in the mid-eighties when the farmers were caught in a financial squeeze between high costs and low profits. Foreclosures were numerous and many believed that mediation could provide protection from immediate home loss for the farmer.[9] Iowa and Minnesota enacted mandatory programs while other states offered voluntary mediation.[10] Farm mediation programs differ from more traditional mediation projects in one important respect: the statutes and rules surrounding these programs presume an inherent imbalance of power between a farmer and a lender. In these programs, the farmer must be provided legal information, financial advice and the like prior to the mediation.[11] Such information and counsel is not provided directly by the mediator, but by the organization which administers the program. Nevertheless, it is viewed as a form of the mediation process which attempts to balance the parties' power.[12] In these mediations, the mediator may also assume a more active role in equalizing the parties positions.[13]

Mediation in the agricultural setting may also be observed in disputes between migrant farm workers and growers. These disputes involve parties with an ongoing relationship; it is in everyone's best interest to resolve them quickly. Also disputes along the chain of

---

5. Kan.Stat.Ann. § 65–1824 (1993).

6. West's Colo.Rev.Stat.Ann. § 38–12–216 (1990); Nev. Rev. Stat. 118B.024 (1993).

7. 59 Okla.Stat.Ann. § 328.60 (1994).

8. Mont.Code Ann. 22–3–804 (1993).

9. This occurred prior to the enactment of Chapter 12 of the Bankruptcy Code, which provides some protection in bankruptcy.

10. Comment, *Avoiding Farm Foreclosure through Mediation of Agricultural Loan Disputes: An Overview of State and Federal Legislation*, 1991 J. Disp. Resol. 335 (1991).

11. E.g., Iowa Code Ann. § 654A.7 (1988 & Supp. 1993)., Minn. Civ. Med. Act § 583.23 (1993).

12. See Chapter 7, supra for a more complete discussion of issues surrounding *power imbalances*.

13. For a detailed examination of farmer-lender mediation, see Leonard L. Riskin, *Two Concepts of Mediation in the FHMA's Farmer–Lender Mediation Program*, 45 Admin. L.Rev. 1 (1993) and Cheryl L. Cooper, *The Role of Mediation in Farm Credit Disputes*, 29 Tulsa L.J. 159 (1993).

commerce from the farmer to the grocer are ripe for mediation. As time progresses additional projects in this area will no doubt, develop.

B. FAMILY AND DIVORCE

Family and divorce mediation is one of the oldest "specialties" in the mediation profession. When the development of mediation and alternative dispute resolution took place in the seventies and early eighties, the focus was on cases involving divorce, and specifically child custody. Many of the pioneering state statutes and court programs were in the family and divorce area.

Divorce mediation differs from traditional or generic mediation.[14] "Generic" mediation, whether it be at a pre-litigation stage or in a pending lawsuit, is seen as a one time intervention. That intervention may last an hour or an entire day. But mediation is not thought of as an ongoing, continuous process. Furthermore, the mediation process is not normally segmented. However, because of the number of issues, and in particular the emotions involved in family law matters, the structure of the process in divorce mediation is extended over a period of weeks, and in complex cases, months. The actual sessions with the parties and the mediators are normally limited, generally to an hour, although some mediators extend the session to an hour and a half. The mediation typically takes from six to eight sessions, but it will continue until all property and custody issues are resolved.

In the divorce area, co-mediation is commonly used.[15] The mediation team usually consists of a therapist or other individual from the social and behavioral sciences and a lawyer. An accountant is sometimes included when the focus of the case is on asset division and financial matters. When the process was first used, divorce mediators met with the parties without their counsel present. Lawyers served primarily to review only the final agreement upon completion of the mediation. A number of issues were raised about the lack of representation during the process. Thereafter, it became general practice for the mediator to urge the parties to obtain legal and financial advice after each session. Currently in an increasing number of instances, lawyers attend each mediation session with their clients. In limited instances, an accountant or a therapist for a party may also attend. The children do not normally participate. It is important that the divorce mediator stress to the parties that he does not provide professional advice. Rather, the parties should be encouraged to obtain independent counsel.

14. For more information on divorce mediation, see Jay Folberg & Ann Milne, Divorce Mediation: Theory and Practice (1988) and John M. Haynes, Divorce Mediation (1981).

15. Co-mediation means two mediators, usually from different backgrounds. See Chapter 15, § E, supra.

C. SCHOOLS AND UNIVERSITIES

The use of mediation in schools and universities is one of the fastest growing areas of practice. Mediation can be used in schools and universities in a number of ways. The first and most common application is peer mediation programs. Peer mediation employs trained student mediators to resolve student disputes. When a dispute or conflict arises between students, instead of resorting to traditional forms of discipline, teachers refer the disputing students to a peer mediator. This mediator is a student who has been trained in mediation or conflict management skills.

There has been some experimentation with peer mediation in nearly every state. Peer mediation or conflict management programs have been implemented from elementary level schools to high schools and colleges. Some statutes require that school districts develop teaching outlines in the mediation and dispute resolution area.[16] The National Association of Mediation in Education (NAME) serves as a national clearinghouse for materials and information regarding peer mediation programs. At the university level, these programs are administered through offices of student affairs.

Administrative concerns in schools and universities provide another area in which the mediation process can assist in resolving disputes. These may occur within the educational institution itself as in conflicts between departments. In other cases, mediation can resolve conflicts between an outsider, such as a parent or other interested party, and the administration. Mediation in truancy cases has been specifically provided for in some states.[17] Another particular area in the education field where mediation is appropriate and statutorily recommended consists of disputes involving special education issues.[18]

D. HEALTH CARE ISSUES

Health care affects everyone. When individuals seek health care, a number of conflicts can arise. Mediation has been used in the health care industry in disputes over bills, treatment and allegations of medical negligence or malpractice. Some states mandate mediation before a malpractice suit can be filed.[19]

The mediation process can also benefit parties during the treatment phase of the patient-health care provider relationship. Because health care is so important, the time during which individuals are involved in treatment can be a very trying time, full of emotion and conflict. There are many opportunities for the use of mediation in these situations. Moreover, resolving disputes at an early stage in the patient-provider

---

16. Mich. Comp. Laws Ann. § 380.1167 (1993).

17. See Iowa Code § 299.5A (1993).

18. N.Y.–McKinney's Educ.Law § 4404–a (1992). For detail, see Linda Singer & Eleanor Nace, *Mediation in Special Edu-*cation: *Two States' Experiences*, 1 Ohio St. J. on Disp. Resol. 55 (1985).

19. Mont. Code Ann. 27–6–701 (1993). See also *Woods v. Holy Cross Hospital*, 591 F.2d 1164 (5th Cir. 1979).

relationship can prevent later conflict. Some states have recognized this and have provided statutory authority and mandate for mediation in these types of disputes. One state legislature has mandated a hospital mediation system for all disputes arising in the context of the issuance of orders not to resuscitate.[20]

Disputes over bills can be resolved to the benefit of all parties through mediation. Mediation saves time and money, which is important to the patient, the provider and third party payors such as insurance companies. In at least one state, disputes regarding in-patient reimbursement are referred to mediation.[21]

Mediation has also been very effective in assisting the resolution of medical negligence or medical malpractice cases. While the initial response to the growing number of medical malpractice cases was the creation of screening panels and use of arbitration,[22] mediation has become a viable alternative. Many states have statutes which advocate or mandate the mediation of medical malpractice cases before they can be brought to trial or sometimes even to the court house. Many malpractice cases are also mediated after a lawsuit is filed, particularly in those jurisdictions where pre-filing screening does not occur. Mediation has been effective in resolving a large number of these cases.[23]

Recognizing the role that ADR can play in the health care industry, the proposed Clinton Health Security Act includes major provisions on alternative dispute resolution.[24] The specifics of these ADR provisions have not yet been completed, but in essence, two broad areas have been designated for ADR use. These are pre-trial procedures for malpractice claims and a grievance procedure for disputes involving health insurance payment plans.

In other instances, those involved in the health care industry recognize that mediation can be helpful in resolving disputes within the work place, particularly hospitals. These institutions have implemented mediation procedures for dealing with intra-organizational disputes, which include mediation of issues such as physician privileges. Another area within the hospital where mediation has been determined appropriate and consequently implemented concerns issues of typical employee disputes, described below.

E.   EMPLOYMENT AND LABOR

The labor and employment area is historically seen as the birthplace of the mediation process. Mediation was not, however, used in individu-

---

20. N.Y.–McKinney's Pub. Health Law § 2972 (1993).

21. N.Y.–McKinney's Pub. Health Law § 2807–c (1993).

22. *Health Care Providers and Alternative Dispute Resolution: Needed Medicine to Combat Medical Malpractice Claims*, 4 J. Disp. Resol. 64, 66 (1988).

23. For a more detailed examination of particular factors involved in mediating these types of malpractice cases, please see Eric R. Galton, Representing Clients in Mediation (1994).

24. 4 World Arb. and Mediation Rep. 239 (1993).

al complaints, but rather in union or group matters. In the traditional labor mediation model, the mediator meets with representatives of each group and then is very active in formulating solutions with each representative negotiator.

Recently there has been an increased use of the mediation process to resolve individual complaints about employment issues, as well as to resolve intra-organizational disputes. Major corporations have designed entire dispute resolution systems through which employees may resolve their grievances.[25] Mediation can also be effective in resolving charges of discrimination in employment. Entities such as the Equal Employment Opportunity Commission (EEOC) are in the process of conducting pilot mediation projects in an attempt to resolve charges of discrimination in the work place. In employment cases, the actual mediation process used may vary. In the EEOC pilot, both the employer and employee must first agree to mediate. If a voluntary agreement to mediate is not obtained, the mediation does not take place. On the other hand, in programs which are established within organizations, this is not the case. In companies which have implemented a mediation program, it is implicit in the program's design that the responding party, the employer, will attend all mediations. One unsettled issue encountered in intra-organizational programs is with the choice of mediators; specifically, the use of an in-house or out-house mediator.

In mediating labor and employment cases, one of the most important aspects of the process is an initial issue determination. The primary issue is employment. The mediator must first determine whether continuation of employment is a possibility. The answer to that threshold question will likely shape the remainder of the mediation. If continued employment is agreed to, the mediation will likely take one direction. In the case where the relationship has been terminated, a different set of options will be explored.

F. PUBLIC POLICY MATTERS

Dispute resolution in the public sector raises a number of concerns very different from those in general or generic mediation. Public policy mediations can affect everyone in the community, and as such, may impose upon the mediator certain duties and obligations not otherwise found. The range of public policy mediation is quite expansive and includes general matters within government as well as specific environmental concerns. Governmental entities have begun to experiment with the mediation process, not only in the federal sector, but also at the state and local government levels.

1. GENERALLY

Mediation of public policy matters differs from traditional mediation in a number of ways. The most significant variation concerns confiden-

---

25. For a description of Dispute Systems Design, a new field of practice in ADR, see Chapter 17, § D, infra.

tiality. Unlike traditional mediation which generally operates under the cloak of confidentiality,[26] issues in public sector mediation are not private matters. Since most matters touch and concern a great number of individuals who cannot be present during the mediation process, it is imperative that discussions subsequent to the session take place. Many requirements are placed on public entities and organizations that represent "the people". These requirements may directly conflict with the tenets of mediation. Such potential conflicts can arise in the following instances: a duty to inform the public of decisions made during negotiations; the presence of the decision-maker when it is a body politic; and requirements for open meetings and public records.

In the context of mediation, most of these issues have not been resolved, and in fact, are only now being addressed. One alternative, when confronted with these issues, is to acknowledge that the mediation process in the public policy arena is quite different from the traditional process in a number of ways. Many of the safeguards and characteristics of mediation will differ when applied to public policy matters. A number of organizations have formed which deal exclusively with public policy matters. The MIT–Harvard Public Disputes Program at the Harvard Negotiation Project has been a longstanding leader in this effort.[27] Several states have initiated efforts to increase the use of mediation in these cases, and have created statewide offices for public policy disputes. These states include California, New Hampshire, Texas, Maine and Vermont.[28] These statewide offices assist state and local governmental entities in the implementation of mediation and other dispute resolution devices as integral parts of public service. Specialized training for those mediating in public policy matters is strongly advised. It is anticipated that as the use of mediation increases, some of the issues surrounding public sector mediation will be clarified.

2. ENVIRONMENTAL ISSUES

Matters of the environment effect all individuals. Moreover, these matters are complex and based in large part upon scientific principles. Consequently, litigation surrounding environmental cases can take years, perhaps even decades to resolve. Environmental law is a new area and as such, is in the process of development. Yet, early on it was recognized that ADR procedures could be effective in environmental concerns. The mediation process has been used successfully in a number of environmental cases.[29] It is important in environmental cases that the mediators have specific expertise and rely on the assistance of engineers and other experts to provide the necessary technical information. Moreover, as in other public policy matters, environmental concerns can be quite emotional for a number of people. It is important for

26. For a complete review of *confidentiality issues*, see Chapter 11, supra.

27. See Lawrence Susskind and Jeffrey Cruikshank, Breaking the Impasse (1987).

28. Peter S. Adler, *State Offices of Mediation: Thoughts on the Evolution of a Na-* *tional Network*, 81 Ky L.J. 1013, 1019 (1992–93).

29. Susskind and Cruikshank, supra note 27, at 162–175.

all members of the public who are affected to be provided an opportunity to participate in the mediation of these cases. Therefore, environmental mediations are not often resolved in one day or one session. They take place over a comparatively lengthy period of time.

Mediation in environmental disputes has often taken place after a complaint is made or a lawsuit has been filed. However, there is another form of the mediation process which can be utilized in enacting rules and regulations with regard to environmental matters. The mediation process derivative is regulatory negotiation or "reg-neg".[30] Through the reg-neg process a rule-making authority negotiates the passage of the rule with the affected parties prior to enactment of the rule.

3. THE FEDERAL SECTOR

In 1990, the United States Congress embraced ADR by enacting several pieces of legislation that have encouraged and urged the implementation and use of ADR within and by the federal government. The first was the Civil Justice Reform Act of 1990,[31] which required each federal district court to design a cost and delay reduction plan. The legislation encouraged the use of ADR in such plan. The ninety-four federal courts have submitted their plans and it appears that a majority have included ADR provisions. These provisions range from implementation of a complete and detailed court-annexed program to a simple statement which encourages the litigants to consider the use of ADR.

Also in 1990, Congress passed the Negotiated Rulemaking Procedure Act[32] and the Administrative Dispute Resolution Act.[33] The Administrative Dispute Resolution Act encourages each federal agency to establish a dispute resolution policy. It provides a broad grant of authority to the agencies to select a number of alternative dispute resolution methods.

Over the last decade, a number of federal agencies have encountered alternative dispute resolution. However, their actual use of ADR processes was very limited. There had not been a comprehensive, government-wide statement or emphasis on the use of these processes. In the early eighties, the Administrative Conference of the United States (ACUS) made recommendations for the use of ADR. One goal of the Administrative Dispute Resolution Act was to send a clear message to all federal agencies that the use of ADR processes is supported, recommended and urged by Congress.

The Act considers a variety of procedures to be used as alternatives to litigation including mediation, fact finding, mini-trial, arbitration, conciliation, or a combination thereof.[34] The Act also sets forth proce-

30. See § F 3 of this Chapter and Chapter 17, § A 3, infra.

31. 28 U.S.C.A. §§ 471–482 (1993).

32. 5 U.S.C.A. § 561 et seq. (Supp. 1993).

33. 5 U.S.C.A. § 571 et seq. (Supp. 1993).

34. 5 U.S.C.A. § 571(3) (Supp. 1993).

dures for confidentiality,[35] as well as determining who is eligible to serve as neutrals for both inter and intra-agency disputes.[36]

By enacting the Negotiated Rule–Making Act of 1990, Congress essentially codified much of what has been developed over the past few years, in legislative circles, known as negotiated rule-making or "reg-neg". The Negotiated Rule-making Act of 1990 specifically urges federal agencies to utilize the reg-neg process in their rule-making. Negotiated rule-making is neutral conflict assessment consisting of a three-step process. These steps include a determination of: (a) affected parties; (b) feasibility of process use; and (c) notice and meeting.[37]

The Federal Aviation Administration was the first federal agency to try a negotiated rule-making process in 1983.[38] The Animal and Plant Inspection Service of the U.S. Department of Agriculture has utilized the reg-neg process in regulating treatment of a killer sheep disease.[39] Vice President Al Gore's recent National Performance Review contains strong recommendations for the increased use of the reg-neg process by federal agencies.[40]

4. STATE AND LOCAL GOVERNMENTS

Many of the same dispute resolution practices encouraged by Congress are now the subject of experimentation within state and local governments. For example, the Texas Water Commission has implemented a pilot mediation program. While mediation has not been so thoroughly integrated at local government level as to affect policy making, no doubt there will be progress in that direction.

A number of states now have statewide offices of dispute resolution.[41] These efforts at dispute resolution on a larger scale were originally sponsored by NIDR (National Institute of Dispute Resolution) as a result of a need for coordinating the mediation of complex public policy disputes. Goals of these state offices include the statewide unification of services and a systematic approach to the mediation of governmental disputes.[42] Four of the initial six pilot states produced significant results. Each state varied in its approach to sponsorship and implementation. Nevertheless, the goals of education of government administrators, establishment of case referral procedures, and identification of mediators were achieved. Moreover, the primary goal of cooperative inter-agency work was realized.[43]

35. 5 U.S.C.A. § 574 (Supp. 1993).

36. 5 U.S.C.A. § 573 (Supp. 1993).

37. 5 U.S.C.A. § 563(a) (Supp. 1993). See Chapter 17, § A infra for more detail on the process.

38. Lawrence E. Susskind, et al., *When ADR Becomes the Law: A Review of Federal Practice*, 9 Negotiation J. 59, 61 (1993).

39. 3 World Arb. & Mediation Rep. 336 (1992).

40. 4 World Arb. & Mediation Rep. 215 (1993).

41. These include Ohio, Florida, Oregon, Hawaii, Minnesota, New Jersey, California, New Hampshire and Texas.

42. Adler, supra note 28, at 1017.

43. Id. at 1018.

G. GAY AND LESBIAN MATTERS

"There is no such thing as a gay divorce", declared one mediator brochure. Several issues surrounding the gay and lesbian community, legal as well as general conflict issues, cannot use traditional methods of dispute resolution. Some individuals have developed mediation practices specifically for such conflicts. One primary focus is often on issues surrounding the dissolution of relationships. Matters involving health care and claims of discrimination can also be assisted by the mediation process.

H. DISPUTES INVOLVING PERSONS WITH HIV

Many disputes and issues facing individuals who are HIV positive are not of the nature to be determined by a judge or jury. In many instances, both time and monetary resources are limited. Because of the medical prognosis of patients, proceeding through a lengthy litigation process would be futile. A speedy resolution is important. In addition, these persons often need or desire confidentiality. In these matters, the mediation process can usually provide confidentiality, particularly in cases before a lawsuit is filed. Efforts to develop programs focusing on the use of mediation in disputes concerning HIV positive individuals is in progress.

I. DISPUTES INVOLVING ATTORNEYS

The legal community has been very active in the promotion and implementation of mediation. Many complaints filed against attorneys by their clients resulted simply from lack of communication. Once the parties are able to better communicate, such disputes are often resolved. If the profession is to practice what it preaches, then the mediation of lawyer-client disputes should increase. The use of mediation in attorney-client matters is in its infancy. Many state and local bar associations are experimenting with pilot projects. Mediation between attorneys and clients can be used in disputes over skill in representation, fees, and law firm dissolutions. Mediation can assist in the resolution of legal malpractice claims as it does any professional negligence matter. More importantly, if resolution of an attorney-client dispute can be reached early, claims of malpractice may be prevented.

Many times dissatisfaction and claims of attorney malfeasance or malpractice arise out of a disagreement over attorney's fees. If fee disputes are handled expeditiously, the matter may be privately concluded. The use of ADR can be quite effective in resolving disputes over attorney's fees.[44]

Another distinct area in which disputes involving attorneys can be resolved is in the area of law firm dissolution. In fact, at least one bar

44. For elaboration, see Alan Scott Rau, *Resolving Disputes Over Attorney's Fees:* *The Role of ADR*, 46 SMU L.Rev. 2005 (1993). For a discussion of attorney-client

association has a mediation project specifically for these cases.[45] The Pennsylvania Bar Association provides mediation, and if the matter is not settled, subsequent arbitration of disputes involving law firms. The matters mediated include dissolutions or lawyer departures, internal disputes within firms, and fee disputes between lawyers of different firms.

J. CRIMINAL ARENA

Many of the first mediation practices evolved, at least tangentially, from within the criminal justice system. Some of these first mediation programs started within prosecutor or district attorney's offices.[46] These offices served as the referral source of cases for these programs. While in nearly all of the referred cases a formal criminal charge had not been filed, allegations of criminal activity had been made. Yet these cases were successfully mediated.[47] However, debate surrounds the propriety of mediation in criminal matters. Even more controversial are cases involving domestic or co-habitant violence.[48] Yet, research has demonstrated, particularly when the parties know each other, that mediation can be beneficial. Some jurisdictions have trained police officers to mediate "on the spot" when called to a domestic or neighborhood disturbance. Moreover, some programs have utilized police officers to refer the parties to mediation while on the scene. Rather than arresting the parties, the officer issues a ticket which mandates the citizen's appearance at mediation.

The foregoing examples involve mediation prior to the filing of a formal complaint or charge. Mediation after a complaint is filed is also possible. Participation in mediation can be part of the offender's probation or restitution in a case. These mediations are often called VORP (Victim–Offender Restitution Programs or Victim–Offender Reconciliation Programs).[49] Victim-offender mediation is focused on negotiating the terms of restitution to be provided to the victim by the offender. In

disputes and the use of ADR in general, see Kimberlee K. Kovach, *Resolving Disputes with Clients*, 18 Barrister 3, 54 (1991).

45. Penn. Bar Association–Lawyer Dispute Resolution Program Rules (1989).

46. For example, the Columbus, Ohio Night Prosecutor Program was located within the Columbus City Prosecutor's Office. The Houston Neighborhood Justice Center, now the Dispute Resolution Center, utilized the Harris County District Attorney's Office.

47. Research of these programs indicates an over eighty percent satisfaction rate. Royer F. Cook, et al., Neighborhood Justice Centers Field Test, Executive Summary Final Evaluation Report (1980).

48. For an in-depth discussion of these policy considerations and issues, see Karla Fisher, et al., *The Culture of Battering and the Role of Mediation in Domestic Violence Cases*, 46 SMU L. Rev. 2117 (1993); Nancy H. Rogers and Richard A. Salem, A Student's Guide to Mediation and the Law § 9.02 (1987).

49. This name was first given to the process by a juvenile probation department in Elkhardt, Indiana, where a probation officer recognized the mutual benefit that offenders and victims might gain by sitting and discussing the event with each other. See Stephen Wodpert, Victim–Offender Reconciliation Programs in Community Mediation: A Handbook for Practitioners and Researchers (Karen Grover Duffy, et al., eds., 1991).

many of these instances, where there is an ongoing relationship, other matters enter into the mediation as well. Studies have shown that both victims and offenders benefit from the process. Participants report not only satisfaction with the mediation process, but thereafter view the criminal justice system in a more favorable light.[50]

VORP mediation differs from traditional mediation in a number of ways. One is that the focus is on restitution rather than a broad, open-ended discussion of issues. Another is the specific selection criteria for those participating. For instance, most VORP programs deal only with property offenses and require that the offender have no more than two prior convictions. Recently, however, work has begun to utilize mediation in more violent cases, and even cases dealing with rape and murder. Disputes occurring within the confines of a prison system have also been referred to mediation for resolution. In fact, some state prisons have created mediation programs to handle prisoner complaints.

K. TRANSACTIONAL MATTERS

Mediation is a dispute resolution device. It is a process used to assist parties in resolving a dispute, and is often defined as such. Yet, it also has been defined as a process which assists parties in a negotiation. Many negotiations take place in a transactional context—in putting together a deal, a sale, a contract. Mediation can be quite effective in providing assistance to the negotiating parties in a transaction. For instance, in the negotiation of a complex contract or business arrangement, if the parties are unable to reach an accord on the specific terms, the assistance of a mediator may be beneficial. Additionally, in the negotiation of partnership documents or formation of a corporate entity, a neutral, third party mediator can provide structure to the negotiations. Unlike mediation in dispute resolution, in a transactional matter, the parties are clearly planning to work together, and the mediation process may have even greater long term benefit.

L. INTERNATIONAL AND CROSS-CULTURAL CONSIDERATIONS

Mediation in the international context can take a number of different forms. International disputes are usually thought of as those between people of different nations. These disputes may concern political or security issues, in which case the disputing parties are often groups. Disputes involving people from different nations also include economic and environmental matters. Here, the number of participants may be more limited. Mediation in security or political issues is usually

---

50. Mark S. Umbreit and Robert B. Coates, Cross–Site Analysis of Victim–Of-fender Mediation in Four States, 39 Crime and Delinquency 565 (1993).

conducted by an outside nation.[51]   The process differs in that the neutral mediator is not completely neutral but has relations with each country. Nonetheless, he does not favor either side.[52]   The mediator has three primary roles: communicator, formulator, and manipulator.[53]   It is the last role which clearly distinguishes this type of mediation from the more traditional process.[54]

What has become known as cross-cultural mediation is the mediation between individuals from different cultures.   The parties may be from the same nation or different nations.   Cross-cultural considerations are necessary as mediation use grows within the United States, as persons in conflict may be from a number of different cultures.   Often when disputes arise, people are unable to negotiate and reach agreements because of a lack of mutual understanding.   Mediation of cross-cultural disputes is particularly problematic because of the threshold difficulties associated with a lack of understanding and knowledge about the parties, their interests and cultural directives.   It is important that mediators intervening in cross-cultural disputes have sense of these additional issues.   As the mediator is attempting to facilitate communication and understanding, he must first realize these inherent, collateral issues.   As in many types of specialized applications of the mediation process, specific training is necessary.

Different cultures have varying concepts of the role of an intermediary in negotiation.   Some of the roles a mediator may assume include: providing assistance with the relationship, assisting in data collection or exchange, assistance with the process, and providing advice or decision-making.   While the first three may be seen as traditional mediation, the last is seen primarily in other ADR processes.   Therefore the mediator, before beginning the process, must be sure that he and the parties are clear about what his role is to be.

51.   Saadia Touval and I. William Zartman, Mediation in International Conflicts, in Mediation Research: The Process and Effectiveness of Third–Party Intervention, 118 (Kenneth Kressel, et al. eds., 1989).

52.   Id. at 126.

53.   Id. at 127.

54.   For additional information on International Mediation, see Mediation In International Relations: Multiple Approaches To Conflict Management (Jacob Bercovitch and Jeffrey Z. Rubin, eds., 1992).

Chapter Seventeen

PREVENTATIVE AND CREATIVE USES OF MEDIATION: DERIVATIVE, COMBINED AND HYBRID PROCESSES

In previous chapters the mediation process has been described and analyzed. The reader should now be able to clearly understand the process, and be developing basic skills. Different types and styles of mediation have been identified. As each mediator develops her skills, she is likely to adapt the style which best corresponds to her own personality, and moreover is best suited to assist the needs and desires of the parties. As such methods are developed, modifications will be made and additional styles of mediation will emerge.

Many processes resemble mediation, particularly in their theoretical basis. Yet, they are so distinct that different words are used to describe them. These are referred to as derivative processes and include consensus building, conciliation and regulatory negotiation.

Traditional mediation can also be combined with another process to form a combined process. Mediation is distinct in a combined process and either precedes or succeeds another process. An example is med-arb (mediation followed by arbitration). In other cases, the mediation process is blended into another ADR process to form a hybrid process. The mini-trial is one such product.

A. DERIVATIVE PROCESSES

1. CONCILIATION

The term conciliation is often used interchangeably with mediation. In some countries, conciliation is used more often than mediation. In many instances, the two terms have been traditionally confused. Some contend that no marked difference exists and the two should be used interchangeably. On the other hand, a closer examination reveals distinct differences.

Some see the primary difference between mediation and conciliation as resulting from the action of the neutral. In a conciliation, the parties are merely brought together to discuss matters, whereas in mediation, the mediator has a much more active role.[1]

"Conciliation" and "reconciliation" come from the same root word, and have nearly the same meaning. In the context of dispute resolution, conciliation often includes a reconciliation. The parties involved in a dispute or conflict not only come to a final resolution of that specific dispute, but they are able to reconcile their relationship. This is most effective in terms of individuals who have ongoing relationships. In some situations, a conciliation between the parties to a dispute can exist and yet, no specific agreement or resolution will have been reached. Both parties' emphasis is on the maintenance of their relationship, and through conciliation, they agree to continue negotiations rather than resolve the specific dispute. In fact, one element of the conciliation might involve walking away from the conflict.

In mediation, reconciliation between the parties is often an integral part of the process. However, reconciliation is not a necessary component. In many instances, particularly pending litigation cases such as personal injury matters, no previous relationship existed. The parties do not have a need, or a desire for reconciliation. A settlement agreement or resolution is mediated without a conciliation taking place. Mediators who mediate at the community level, in disputes such as those between neighbors, landlords and tenants, and the like, find that the combination of mediation with conciliation is the primary process used in these cases.

2. CONSENSUS BUILDING

The consensus building process is similar to mediation in its focus on assisting parties in a dispute to reach a voluntary, mutual, and satisfying agreement. Consensus building, however, is different in a number of ways. In most traditional mediations, there are two sides and two distinct views of the situation in conflict. Even though many lawsuits and disputes involve multiple parties, there are usually only three or four issues, divided among the group. In consensus building, there are a number of different groups with a variety of interests. Often coalitions are formed. While each group may have representatives at the mediation table, a great deal of intra-group negotiations takes place away from the table.

Traditionally, consensus building is used in large public policy disputes, such as disputes involving environmental issues. Therefore, the convener, as the neutral is often called in this process, attempts to find a number of issues upon which a consensus can be built. While at first glance such a process appears more difficult than a classic mediation, in many ways it is easier. Often a number of interests overlap.

1. Walter A. Maggiolo, Techniques of Mediation 13 (1985).

Some of the parties have shared goals. Consequently there is greater opportunity for integrative bargaining.

Unlike traditional mediation, consensus building is not a one time intervention. It takes place during a number of successive meetings, lasting weeks and even months. The pre-mediation phase is also quite lengthy. In fact, it is often the longest segment or phase of the process. As part of the pre-mediation or pre-negotiation stage of the process, the facilitator or convener may meet with the potential stakeholders in order to assess their position and determine the logistics. Furthermore, the convener meets with the interested or affected parties to help them choose their representatives for the consensus building process. Protocol for these meetings can be determined based on past experience and any individual need of a party. Protocol may even include, for instance, agreements about dealing with the media. The convener may also wish to talk to each party about agenda setting. Lastly, the mediator may engage in joint fact finding, and determine whether there are any consultants or advisors who may assist the process.[2] The actual negotiation, or mediation phase can then begin.

The mediation actually begins with the generation of options phase. In the pre-meeting stage, the issues have been identified and so the consensus building starts primarily with brainstorming options. Part of building a consensus includes a "packaging" stage, where the mediator will meet in a private session with each of the groups to determine what might be able to be bargained and packaged together.[3] If an agreement is reached, the mediator then writes an agreement and assists in binding the entire group. Because everyone participating in the process is a representative of others, the final phase before a final agreement is reached is the ratification phase. During this segment the actual participants go back to their constituencies and "sell" the agreement so that finality will be reached.[4] Lastly, in the consensus building process, often the neutral convener or mediator is involved in an implementation or post-negotiation phase as well.[5] This is not true in generic mediation. However, because of the magnitude of the dispute and its agreement, the parties may need assistance from the neutral, particularly if there are elected or appointed officials who must be consulted, or if there is a need for a monitor. The mediator is also involved if a need occurs for renegotiation of the agreement. Many of these mediations are public, and if an agreement is reached, it is published.

3. TEAM MEDIATION

Team mediators can actually be seen as part of the consensus building process. Team mediation generally means that there is more than one mediator. While two mediators are technically a team, most two mediator teams are referred to as co-mediators and act in tandem.

---

2. Lawrence Susskind and Jeffrey Cruikshank, Breaking the Impasse 142 (1987).

3. Id.

4. Id. at 143.

5. Id.

The lead role is exchanged evenly between the two. Co-mediators never separate; in a caucus format both of them meet with each side. It is necessary that the two mediators coordinate their actions and strategies. It is recommended that the co-mediators know each other and have an ongoing working relationship.

On the other hand, in team mediation the mediators act more independently. A team of mediators usually connotes several mediators. As with most teams, there will be a team leader, who is primarily responsible for the direction of the sessions. Each member of the team will work with an individual constituency. The team then exchanges information. Particularly when the number of parties is large, team mediation can save a great deal of time.

4. REG-NEG

Regulatory negotiation or reg-neg, as it is known, originated within the Administrative Conference of the United States,[6] and now its use is encouraged by statute.[7] Reg-neg[8] can be viewed as a specific form of consensus building. Regulatory negotiation is an attempt to shorten the rulemaking process for federal as well as state agencies.[9] Rather than the traditional method of enacting a rule, and thereafter sending it out for comment, in the reg-neg process, all interested or affected parties are contacted and invited to take part in the initial design of the rule. Discussions continue until all reach consensus about the content of the rule or regulation. The third party neutral, who acts much like a mediator, is called the convener and is responsible for each step in the process.

The first step is to determine who may be affected by the proposed legislation. Secondly, the convener determines whether it would be feasible to use negotiation among all of those affected to resolve any disputes. If the convener decided to use negotiation, notices of the meetings are published in the Federal Register. Rather than first publish the legislation and receive feedback, reg-neg is designed to obtain input during the drafting stages.

In the negotiation of regulations, the process appears to be very similar to consensus building. The difference is that reg-neg is more focused. In the consensus building process, usually there is an issue that needs closure, but the specifics of resolution are left to the parties involved. In regulatory negotiation, however, the goal is identified specifically at the beginning of the session; i.e., a draft of a regulation. The entire process therefore, is more limited. Likewise, in general consensus building, anyone with an interest may participate. In regulatory negotiation, the convener often limits the number of parties at the

---

6. Office of the Chairman, Administrative Conference of the United States, Negotiated Rulemaking Sourcebook, (hereinafter referred to as Sourcebook) (1990).

7. 5 U.S.C.A. § 561 (Supp. 1993).

8. See Chapter 16 § F supra for a discussion of the application of reg-neg.

9. At least two states recently enacted a negotiated rule-making statute. See 1993 Mont. Laws 400 (H.B. 317) & Idaho Code § 67–5206 (1993).

table from less than fifteen [10] to twenty-five.[11]   Moreover, only those parties who are directly affected by the proposed rule may attend the session.   Another distinction is that in regulatory negotiation the convener rarely does any follow-up.   Once a consensus is reached, the rule is implemented.

5. CONVENING CONFERENCES

A convening conference is a new process created by dispute designers.[12]   Mediative in nature, convening conferences are built upon the principle of consensus and collaborative problem solving, and have as their purpose the selection of the ADR process which will best assist in resolving a given dispute.[13]   In this process, the first step after a dispute is identified is a meeting with a neutral.   However, rather than focusing directly on the conflict, the disputing parties first confer about process options.   Many times the neutral may act as a technical consultant concerning ADR, and then use collaborative problem solving skills to assist the disputing parties in the selection of an appropriate ADR process.   Such conferences are the first step in resolution of the dispute.   It is suggested by its creators that a clause calling for a convening conference is an option to the more common automatic mediation or arbitration clause.   Using this process provides maximum flexibility along with an ability for the disputing parties to make early decisions about the process.

B. COMBINED PROCESSES

The mediation process may be combined with a number of other dispute resolution mechanisms in order to achieve a settlement.   The most common form is the med-arb process in which the parties first engage in the mediation process, and, if an agreement is not reached in a pre-determined amount of time or at the discretion of the mediator, an arbitration takes place.   A number of different forms of this process are now available.

In the original med–arb process, the neutral began the proceeding as a mediator, but with the understanding that any matter unresolved would be arbitrated.   Because the same individual served in both a mediative and adjudicative function, the process was criticized.   The criticism included the fact that since the mediator knew that a decision might have to be made, the mediator could not remain non-judgmental during the mediative phase.   Moreover, the type of presentations which should be made by the parties or their advocates differ drastically in

---

10. Philip J. Harter, *Negotiating Regulations: A Cure for Malaise*, 71 Geo. L. J. 46 (1982).

11. Sourcebook, supra note 6 at 37.

12. For an explanation of dispute systems design, see § D infra. The process of convening was first suggested by Karl A.

Slaikeu and Ralph H. Hasson, *Not Necessarily Mediation: The Use of Convening Clauses in Dispute Systems Design*, 8 Negotiation J. 331 (1992).

13. Id. at 332.

each process, and to be effective in one necessarily damages effectiveness in the other.

As a result, another form of med–arb developed. In this form, the parties attempt to mediate, and if a resolution is not achieved during the session, the parties begin arbitration with a different individual serving as the arbitrator. The difficulty in this form of med–arb is that it is repetitious and consequently more time-consuming and costly. A third form labeled co–med arb has been recently designed.[14] Because of the aforementioned criticisms of the med–arb process, this new process attempts to eliminate such dilemmas, yet still provide the benefits of both processes to the disputants. Specifically, the co–med–arb process consists of two neutrals simultaneously listening to the initial statements of the parties. The first neutral will then act as the mediator, leading a non-judgmental mediation session. Should that effort fail in completely resolving the matter, the second neutral will present the parties with a binding arbitration decision of those issues left undecided.

Traditional forms of med-arb dictate that the mediation process be conducted prior to the arbitration. A few practitioners have experimented with arbitration first, followed by mediation. The neutral provides a non-binding suggested arbitration award and then assists the parties in mediating their dispute. Such an approach is highly criticized because the mediator, having rendered an award, can no longer be impartial or neutral about the outcome of the case.

Just as arbitration has been combined with mediation, the evaluative ADR processes can also be merged. This can occur either before or after the mediation. In some cases, parties need certain information to assist them in the negotiation of a settlement. Evaluative processes, such as the moderated settlement conference, neutral case evaluation or the summary jury trial, could take place prior to the mediation. In other instances, parties could try mediation first. If the mediation does not result in a settlement due primarily to an inaccurate or incomplete evaluation or assessment of the case, the mediator may recommend that the parties participate in an evaluative process. After the evaluative process, the parties may choose to mediate again or negotiate a resolution without the assistance of a neutral.

C. HYBRIDS

The word "hybrid" indicates the actual merger of two different processes, which results in a composite. Rather than merely combining the mediation process with another process, there is true integration. If mediation is integrated with an evaluative process, the result is a completely new process, i.e., the mini-trial.[15] The mini-trial uses media-

---

14. For further elaboration of this concept, see 3 World Arb. and Mediation Rep. 21 (1992).

15. See Chapter 1, supra for a complete description of this process.

tion concepts not only in the facilitation of communication between the parties, but the neutral expert advisor may actually mediate. However, the form of mediation used may not be traditional. The neutral expert advisor first provides the parties with opportunity for direct negotiations. He then provides an evaluation, after which facilitated discussions resembling mediation take place. As the use of mediation continues to grow, additional opportunities to integrate it with the other processes will occur, and additional hybrid processes will result.

D. DESIGN ISSUES

The principles of mediation may actually be used in designing systems for dispute resolution. While it may be impossible to prevent disputes, it is possible to plan for their occurrence. The idea is essentially "planning for disputing." Providing "dispute systems design" is a new specialty in the ADR field. Major organizations, corporations, and businesses actually design, in advance, specific ways of dealing with disputes. Often, though not in all cases, the mediation process is included. The mediation process, or a form of it such as consensus building, can also be used in the actual design process.

Dispute resolution systems design requires five component parts: the assessment of the current system of dispute resolution; the determination of specific goals and objectives of a new system; the design of a plan for the new system; implementation of the new system; and evaluation.

In assessment of the current system, a dispute resolution consultant works with the organization to determine how disputes are currently resolved. Factors such as the cost for each type of dispute, in terms of money as well as loss of employee time, might be examined. Moreover, the effect of the current dispute resolution procedure is evaluated on the basis of its effect on public relations. A number of other issues can be examined in the assessment phase. These include an assessment of the skills of individuals involved in resolving disputes, the usual types of outcomes, and rate of recurrence of disputes.

In the next stage, the designer holds a meeting with the management team to determine exactly what the organization is hoping to achieve by designing a new dispute resolution system. In some instances, this may be no more than a savings of money. In other instances, it may include increased morale among the workers. Some companies will hope to focus on an enhanced public image. Whatever the objective, whether singular or multi-faceted, it can usually be achieved by a combination of processes. However, in order to design a workable plan that will meet the identified goals of the organization, it is important for the designer to encourage the organization to be very specific in determining what those objectives are. It is likely that the consultant will utilize the principles of collaborative problem solving and mediation in the effort to determine the objectives.

Once the goals are determined, the actual design of a plan will take place. This plan can be as complex or as simple as the participants deem appropriate. It might include a one-step process where, if a dispute occurs, the parties are immediately directed to one ADR process. In many instances, however, when the plan is designed, it is a multi-step plan. For instance, a first step after a dispute arises might be a convening conference including all parties in dispute.[16] In other instances it might be a private meeting of a party with staff from the human resources department. Another option is an initial mediation. If the first step is not successful in resolving the dispute, then the disputants go to the second tier or step. Here, a mediation, an evaluation or an arbitration may take place. If unsuccessful, the third step may include processes such as case evaluation, and ultimately litigation. As is apparent, the design of the plan is open to the creativity of the organization as well as the consultant.

Once the plan has been designed, it is then implemented. A very important segment of the implementation phase is education. Clearly those directly involved in the day to day operation of the dispute resolution plan must be educated in its use. Moreover, all members of the organization should be aware of the new plan. In essence, when integrating mediation into the culture of an organization, it is important to include everyone who is part of that culture or entity to assure that everyone understands the process.

Lastly, the evaluation and "loop-back" phase occurs. Any time a new plan is put into place, it should be evaluated. As evaluations are completed, re-designing may occur. A continuous evaluation and design loop results. Because of the novelty of systems design, it is recommended that at least initially, evaluations be made formally as well as informally. As dispute resolution practitioners, designers should integrate collaborative problem solving and decision making into the design process. Continued experimentation in this area is advancing the process.

E.   CONCLUSION

"A mind, once stretched by a new idea, never regains
its original shape."

— Oliver Wendell Holmes

Through the mediation process, it is hoped that the minds of mediators, lawyers, and disputants are stretched. If we, dispute resolution professionals, "walk the talk", the principles of mediation will become integrated into our professional and personal lives. New applications for the process will develop and new ways of disputing will emerge.

The field of dispute resolution generally, and mediation specifically, is in a state of constant change. Although it may now no longer be in

16. See § A, 5, supra.

the "embryonic" stage, it has not yet fully developed. Those involved in the mediation process have a great opportunity to fashion its future. It is up to all of us to continue to shape and form the principles and practice of mediation.

QUESTIONS FOR DISCUSSION

17–1. Revenue Realty

Plaintiff is Pat Smith, d/b/a Revenue Realty. Revenue Realty employed the defendant and counterclaimant, Tommy Thompson, as a realtor about three years ago. As part of employment, Thompson signed a covenant not to compete in the Denver area, which would be effective for three years from the date of termination. Revenue Realty has sued Thompson for violation of the covenant. The background of the case is as follows:

The covenant not to compete was part of a larger agreement which provided that Revenue Realty would provide the brokerage, office space, multiple listing service, and advertising to Thompson, while Thompson would be employed as a real estate agent. It also included a generous commission split of 50–50 along with the non-compete clause.

Problems began between Smith and Thompson about five months ago. Thompson "sold" a house to Frank and Betty Grey for $374,-500.00. However, the Greys did not qualify for financing. Thompson was then "let go" by Smith.

Thompson claims that the firing was caused by a refusal to tell the Greys not to reveal a $80,000.00 personal loan from Betty Grey's uncle (Buck Booth). Disclosure of that loan would result in the Grey's "debt/income" ratio being too high. Since the uncle's loan was a family matter, it would not be discovered in a typical credit check.

Smith asserts that the downturn in the economy has impacted the real estate market and that Revenue, like many other agencies, had to pare down its staff. About four weeks ago, Thompson was terminated by Smith. Two weeks ago, Smith learned that Thompson was, in fact, competing.

Suit was then brought by Revenue against Thompson to enforce the covenant not to compete; to collect monies owed on an expense account that Thompson charged; and for return of a 2 year old Lincoln Continental. Thompson has counter claimed for wrongful termination; withheld commissions of $27,400.00; and for a declaratory judgment voiding the non-compete clause.

The court at the preliminary injunction hearing has referred the case to ADR.

Appendix A

MATERIALS FOR MEDIATION ROLE PLAYS

GENERAL INSTRUCTIONS FOR ROLE PLAY PARTICIPANTS

It is imperative that when playing the role of the disputing party or advocate for a party that you are "in role". To get yourself ready, first become familiar with the content of the dispute. Then think about how you would feel and act, if truly in that situation. The emotions and reactions that you demonstrate during the role play should be consistent with the instructions provided to you and your own personality. Some of you may have a tendency, when involved in conflict, to react strongly while others have a more subtle approach.

It is important when learning about mediation that you understand the process, not only from the mediator's role but also from that of the participants. If you play the part of the participant realistically, it is much easier for you to feel that role and observe how the mediator's conduct, good or bad, affects you. Moreover, you are then able to provide more accurate feedback to the individual in the role of mediator.

MEDIATION PROCESS WORKSHEET

List highlights of the mediator's introduction.

Critique the opening statements:

(a) Party A

(b) Attorney A

(c) Party B

(d) Attorney B

(e) Others

What types of communication took place during the mediation?

What were the identifiable issues?

What were the interests of the parties?

What type(s) and styles of negotiation did you observe?

Additional Comments:

MEDIATION ANALYSIS

	D1	D2

Issues:

Interests:

Initial

Position:

Alternatives:

BATNA:

WATNA:

MEDIATION PROCESS FORM

Preliminary Arrangements

Mediator's Introduction

Opening Statements

Information Gathering

(Venting)

Issue Identification and Restatements

(Caucus)

Agenda Setting

Generation of Options

Negotiation

Agreement

Closure

A SLIPPERY GRAPE

On a beautiful Sunday after attending services at the Goodwill Church of The Rock, Vi Wynette decided to go grocery shopping for a prayer meeting that evening. Vi was shopping for ingredients to make a famous ambrosia salad which consisted of numerous fresh fruits, coconut, small colored marshmallows, mayonnaise, and several bottles of Big Red soft drink.

Vi entered the local grocery store, the Big Bag–N–Save, and proceeded to the soft drink aisle. After getting the Big Red, Vi headed for the fresh fruit section of the supermarket. Vi spied the grapes, and decided that they would make a wonderful addition to the salad. After selecting the grapes, Vi went toward the pineapple.

Suddenly, Vi heard a familiar voice, Lula May Thompson, a fellow member in the choir. Vi decided to backtrack to have a chat. As Vi moved the shopping cart around, the heel of the left shoe slid on a grape peel causing Vi to fall. Only a tight grasp on the cart prevented a total collapse.

Vi felt severe pain in the left knee and lower back, as well as a shooting pain in the right shoulder. Vi screamed out loudly, causing several customers and store personnel to rush over. The produce manager, Bob Weedon, appeared and as he picked Vi up, he exclaimed, "I've been telling them boys to keep this aisle clean. I knew someone would get hurt."

Vi was then taken by the ambulance to the local hospital for X-rays and observation. Upon release the following morning, only Advil was prescribed. Vi felt continuous pain and two days later asked the advice of Lula May. Lula May referred Vi to her chiropractor, Dr. Nelson. Vi saw Dr. Nelson on several occasions throughout the month. Nelson's diagnosis was that with constant adjustments, Vi's injury would be manageable and would not prevent further activities nor participation in the local bowling league.

Vi has hired an attorney and is seeking compensation for the injuries, medical bills, lost wages and mental anguish. Vi, through the lawyer, has indicated that $100,000.00 for medicals and past wages, plus $50,000.00 in mental anguish would settle the case. Big Bag has offered $5,000.00 in cash and $250.00 in super saver coupons.

The parties have agreed to try mediation before filing suit.

RUNS–N–ROSES

Plaintiff is a corporation operating under the name Rammel Properties, Inc. It owns several prime commercial properties, along with some not so prime retail strip centers throughout the city. The Chief Financial Officer and President of Rammel is Mr. William Fold, who is a majority stockholder.

The Defendant, Lee Brachy, is an individual. Brachy was a computer programmer who decided to take early retirement and change careers. Brachy chose to open a drive-through flower shop. Brachy and Rammel negotiated a lease agreement. During the negotiations, Brachy also negotiated certain build-out provisions with a leasing agent, Sue Storm. These included specific plumbing and thermostatic requirements. However, inadvertently these special build-outs were not reduced to writing.

Brachy entered into a franchise agreement with Runs–N–Roses Internationale' after reading in a magazine about this new concept founded in California. After signing the lease agreement, Brachy left her company and moved to California where she attended a three-month training session for a new career as a mobile florist. However, two months into the training, and six weeks prior to the Grand Opening of Runs–N–Roses # 38, the franchisor Runs–N–Roses Internationale' filed for Chapter 7 Bankruptcy. All bouquets were quickly liquidated. Brachy took this event as a divine indication that all is not well in the drive-through floral business, and has decided to forego a life-long ambition of self-employment. Brachy immediately informed Rammel that the shop would not be opening, and has been working off and on as a programmer.

Fold, as well as the leasing agent (who receives a commission of all lease agreements, are upset; additional money (loosely estimated to be several thousand dollars) was spent to outfit what was to be the drive-through area of the lease space. Because Brachy was told that the flowers must be kept at precise temperatures, special watering systems and temperature checks had been ordered.

Rammel has brought suit against Brachy for all sums due under the lease. Brachy has counterclaimed alleging that Rammel was the first to breach by not having the premises ready in accordance with the lease agreement. The court has referred the case to mediation.

THE BANKRUPTCY OF BETTER THAN A BONNET
General Information

Mr. Sal Salem owns 55% of the stock in Better Than A Bonnet (BTAB), a hat manufacturer in the Richmond, Virginia area. Mr. Salem, as the majority stockholder, is also the president of the corporation. Over the last ten years a substantial profit had been realized. About eighteen months ago, Sal convinced the Board of Directors to expand the company throughout the nation. However, at about the same time, due to the faltering economy and the scientific breakthrough in hair transplants, the hat market went into a steep decline. Due to pressures from creditors and under stress of a threatened divorce, Sal sought help. BTAB filed for bankruptcy protection under Chapter 11 about four months ago.

The primary creditor, Tokyo Mortgages, has the first lien on all of the equipment. Tokyo also claims personal guarantees of three individuals: Salem; Mr. Rocky Rico another stockholder and the corporate vice-president; and Mrs. Salem, whose great-grandfather founded Richmond Savings over one hundred years ago.

The remaining stockholders in Better Than a Bonnet consist of twelve family friends, who led by Rico, have instituted an adversary proceeding against Mr. Salem personally for breaches of fiduciary duty. They argue that Mr. Salem has fraudulently squandered company funds under the guise of business travel and entertainment. Additionally, The Felt Company (TFC), a Hong Kong direct supplier of raw materials for hat manufacture, has filed a Motion to Lift Stay, attempting to foreclose on BTAB in order to force the return of a large felt delivery.

Sally Salem, not an understanding woman, has filed for divorce. She claims one-half of all of the stock owned by her husband. Nearly twenty years ago, BTAB began as a sole proprietorship based on a wedding gift from Sally's father. The company incorporated a year later, and the stock was then distributed. Mr. Salem's interest presently is valued at approximately 1.2 million dollars.

Due to the number of related matters at a recent status conference, the Bankruptcy Court suggested that the primary parties try mediation. Present at the mediation are Sal, Sally, Rocky, Jako Datsu from Tokyo, and Charles Smith, the U.S. sales representative for The Felt Company. Each individual is accompanied at the mediation by an attorney.

Appendix B

CODE OF PROFESSIONAL CONDUCT

Preamble *

Mediation is an approach to conflict resolution in which an impartial third party intervenes in a dispute, with the consent of the parties, to aid and assist them in reaching a mutually satisfactory settlement to issues in dispute.

Mediation is a profession with ethical responsibilities and duties. Those who engage in the practice of mediation must be dedicated to the principle that all disputants have a right to negotiate and to attempt to determine the outcomes of their own conflicts. Mediators must be aware that their duties and obligations relate to the parties who engage their services, to the mediation process, to other mediators, to the agencies that administer the practice of mediation, and to the general public.

Mediators are often professionals (attorneys, therapists, and social workers) who have obligations under other codes of ethics. This code is not to be construed as a competitive code of behavior but as an additional guideline for professionals performing mediation. When mediating, professionals will be bound by the ethical guidelines of this code.

This code is not designed to override or supercede any laws or government regulations that prescribe responsibilities of mediators and others in the helping professions. It is a personal code of conduct for the individual mediator and is intended to establish principles applicable to all professional mediators employed by private, city, state, or federal agencies.

1. The Responsibility of the Mediator to the Parties

The primary responsibility for the resolution of a dispute rests on the parties themselves. The mediator should recognize at all times that the agreements reached in negotiations are voluntarily made by the parties. It is the mediator's responsibility to assist the disputants in

* *Note:* Drafted by Christopher W. Moore, Partner, Center for Dispute Resolution, and adopted by the Colorado Council of Mediation Organizations, January 1982.

reaching a settlement. At no time should a mediator coerce a party into agreement. The mediator should not attempt to make a substantive decision for the parties. Parties may, however, agree to solicit a recommendation for settlement from the mediator.

It is desirable that agreement be reached by negotiations without a mediator's assistance. Intervention by a mediator can be initiated by the parties themselves or by a mediator. The decision to accept mediation rests with the parties, except when mediation is mandated by legislation, court order, or contract.

Mediators will inform all parties of the cost of mediation services before intervention. Parties should be able to estimate the cost of the service in relation to that of other dispute resolution procedures.

Ideally, when costs are involved, the mediator should attempt to have parties agree to bear the costs of mediation equitably. When this is not possible, all parties should reach agreement as to payment.

2. Responsibility of the Mediator to the Mediation Process

Negotiation is an established procedure in our society as a means of resolving disputes. The process of mediation involves a third-party intervention into negotiations to assist in the development of alternative solutions that parties will voluntarily accept as a basis for settlement. Pressures that jeopardize voluntary action and agreement by the parties should not be a part of mediation.

The Mediation Process. Mediation is a participatory process. A mediator is obliged to educate the parties and to involve them in the mediation process. A mediator should consider that such education and involvement are important not only to resolve a current dispute but also to prepare the parties to handle future conflicts in a more creative and productive manner.

Appropriateness of Mediation. Mediation is not a panacea for all types of conflicts. Mediators should be aware of all procedures for dispute resolution and the conditions under which each is most effective. Mediators are obliged to educate participants as to their procedural options and to help them choose wisely the most appropriate procedures. The procedures should clearly match the type of outcome that is desired by the parties.

Mediator's Role. The mediator must not limit his or her role to keeping the peace or regulating conflict at the bargaining table. The mediator's role should be that of an active resource person whom the parties may draw on and, when appropriate, the mediator should be prepared to provide both procedural and substantive suggestions and alternatives that will assist the parties in successful negotiations.

Since the status, experience, and ability of the mediator lend weight to his or her suggestions and recommendations, the mediator should evaluate carefully the effect of interventions or proposals and accept full responsibility for their honesty and merit.

Since mediation is a voluntary process, the acceptability of the mediator to the parties as a person of integrity, objectivity, and fairness is absolutely essential for the effective performance of mediation procedures. The manner in which the mediator carries out professional duties and responsibilities will be a measure of his or her usefulness as a mediator. The quality of character as well as intellectual, emotional, social, and technical attributes will reveal themselves in the conduct of the mediator and in his or her oral and written communications with the parties, other mediators, and the public.

Publicity and Advertising. A mediator should not make any false, misleading, or unfair statement or claim as to the mediation process, its costs and benefits, or his or her role, skills, or qualifications.

Neutrality. A mediator should determine and reveal all monetary, psychological, emotional, associational, or authoritative affiliations that he or she has with any of the parties to a dispute that might cause a conflict of interest or affect the perceived or actual neutrality of the professional in the performance of duties. If the mediator or any one of the major parties feels that the mediator's background will have or has had a potential to bias his or her performance, the mediator should disqualify himself or herself from performing the mediation service.

Impartiality. The mediator is obligated during the performance of professional services to maintain a posture of impartiality toward all involved parties. *Impartiality* is freedom from bias or favoritism either in word or action. Impartiality implies a commitment to aid all parties, as opposed to a single party, in reaching a mutually satisfactory agreement. Impartiality means that a mediator will not play an adversarial role in the process of dispute resolution.

Confidentiality. Information received by a mediator in confidence, private session, caucus, or joint session with the disputants is confidential and should not be revealed to parties outside the negotiations. Information received in caucus is not to be revealed in joint session without receiving prior permission from the party or person from whom the information was received.

The following exceptions shall be applied to the confidentiality rule: In the event of child abuse by one or more disputants or in a case in which a mediator discovers that a probable crime will be committed that may result in serious psychological or physical harm to another person, the mediator is obligated to report these actions to the appropriate agencies.

Use of Information. Because information revealed in mediation is confidential and the success of the process may depend on this confidentiality, mediators should inform and gain consent from participants that information divulged in the process of mediation will not be used by the parties in any future adversarial proceedings.

The mediator is also obligated to resist disclosure of confidential information in an adversarial process. He or she will refuse to testify voluntarily in any subsequent court proceedings and shall resist to the best of his or her ability the subpoena of either his or her notes or person. This provision may be waived by the consent of all parties involved.

Empowerment. In the event that a party needs either additional information or assistance in order for the negotiations to proceed in a fair and orderly manner or for an agreement to be reached that is fair, equitable, and has the capacity to hold over time, the mediator is obligated to refer the party to resources—either data or persons—who may facilitate the process.

Psychological Well–Being. If a mediator discovers before or during mediation that a party needs psychological help, the mediator shall make appropriate referrals. Mediators recognize that mediation is not an appropriate substitute for therapy and shall refer parties to the appropriate procedure. Mediation shall not be conducted with parties who are either intoxicated or who have major psychological disorders that seriously impair their judgment.

The Law. Mediators are not lawyers. At no time shall a mediator offer legal advice to parties in dispute. Mediators shall refer parties to appropriate attorneys for legal advice. This same code of conduct applies to mediators who are themselves trained in the law. The role of an impartial mediator should not be confused with that of an attorney who is an advocate for a client.

The Settlement. The goal of negotiation and mediation is a settlement that is seen as fair and equitable by all parties. The mediator's responsibility to the parties is to help them reach this kind of settlement.

Whenever possible, a mediator should develop a written statement that documents the agreements reached in mediation.

A mediator's satisfaction with the agreement is secondary to that of the parties.

In the event that an agreement is reached that a mediator feels (1) is illegal, (2) is grossly inequitable to one or more parties, (3) is the result of false information, (4) is the result of bargaining in bad faith, (5) is impossible to enforce, or (6) may not hold over time, the mediator may pursue any or all of the following alternatives:

1. Inform the parties of the difficulties that the mediator sees in the agreement.

2. Inform the parties of the difficulties and make suggestions that would remedy the problems.

3. Withdraw as mediator without disclosing to either party the particular reasons for the withdrawal.

4. Withdraw as mediator but disclose in writing to both parties the reasons for such action.

5. Withdraw as mediator and reveal publicly the general reason for taking such action (bargaining in bad faith, unreasonable settlement, illegality, and so forth).

Termination of Mediation. In the event that the parties cannot reach an agreement even with the assistance of a mediator, it is the responsibility of the mediator to make the parties aware of the deadlock and suggest that negotiations be terminated. A mediator is obligated to inform the parties when a final impasse has occurred and to refer them to other means of dispute resolution. A mediator should not prolong unproductive discussions that result in increased time and emotional and monetary costs for the parties.

3. The Responsibility of the Mediator to Other Mediators

A mediator should not enter any dispute that is being mediated by another mediator or mediators without first conferring with the person or persons conducting such mediation. The mediator should not intercede in a dispute merely because another mediator may also be participating. Conversely, it should not be assumed that the lack of mediation participation by one mediator indicates a need for participation by another mediator.

In those situations in which more than one mediator are participating in a particular case, each mediator has a responsibility to keep the others informed of developments essential to a cooperative effort and should extend every possible courtesy to co-mediators.

During mediation, the mediator should carefully avoid any appearance of disagreement with or criticism of co-mediators. Discussions as to what positions and actions mediators should take in particular cases should not violate principles of confidentiality.

4. The Responsibility of the Mediator to His or Her Agency and Profession

Mediators frequently work for agencies that are responsible for providing mediation assistance to parties in dispute. The mediator must recognize that as an employee of such agencies, the mediator is their representative, and that he or she will not be judged solely on an individual basis but also as a representative of an organization. Any improper conduct or professional shortcoming, therefore, reflects not only on the individual mediator but also on the employer, and in so doing, it jeopardizes the effectiveness of the agency, other agencies, and the acceptability of the mediation process itself.

The mediator should not use his or her position for personal gain or advantage or engage in any employment, activity, or enterprise that will conflict with his or her work as a mediator.

Mediators should not accept any money or item of value for the performance of services other than a regular salary or mutually established fee, or incur obligations to any party that might interfere with the impartial performance of his or her duties.

Training and Education. Mediators learn their trade through a variety of avenues—formal education, training programs, workshops, practical experience, and supervision. Mediators have the responsibility to constantly upgrade their skills and theoretical grounding and shall endeavor to better themselves and the profession by seeking some form of further education in the negotiation and mediation process during each year in practice.

A mediator should promote the profession and make contributions to the field by encouraging and participating in research, publishing, or other forms of professional and public education.

Expertise. Mediators should perform their services only in those areas of mediation in which they are qualified either by experience or by training. Mediators should not attempt to mediate in an unfamiliar field or when there is risk of psychological, financial, legal, or physical damage to one of the parties due to the mediator's lack of experience.

A mediator is obligated to seek a co-mediator trained in the necessary discipline or refer cases to other mediators who are trained in the required field of expertise when he or she does not possess the required skills.

Voluntary Services. A mediator is obligated to perform some voluntary service during each year of practice to provide assistance to those who cannot afford to pay for mediation and to promote the field. It is left to the individual mediator to determine the amount and kind of service to be rendered for the good of the profession and of society.

Mediators should cooperate with their own and other agencies in establishing and maintaining the quality, qualifications, and standards of the profession. Mediators should participate in individual and agency evaluations and should be supervised either by an agency, a mutually established peer, or the professional organization's board of ethics. Mediators involved in any breach of this code of conduct should notify their agency of the breach. Mediators hearing of violations of this code of ethics should also report this information to their agency or the board of ethics.

5. Responsibility of the Mediator to the Public and Other Unrepresented Parties

Negotiation is in essence a private, voluntary process. The primary purpose of mediation is to assist the parties in achieving a settlement. Such assistance does not abrogate the rights of the parties to resort to economic, social, psychological, and legal sanctions. However, the mediation process may include a responsibility of the mediator to assert the interest of the public or other unrepresented parties in order that a particular dispute be settled, that costs or damages be alleviated, and that normal life be resumed. Mediators should question agreements that are not in the interest of the public or other unrepresented parties whose interests and needs should be and are not being considered. Mediators should question whether other parties' interests or the parties themselves should be present at negotiations. It is understood, however, that the mediator does not regulate or control any of the content of a negotiated agreement.

A mediator shall not use publicity to enhance his or her own position. When two or more mediators are mediating a dispute, public information should be managed by a mutually agreeable procedure.

Appendix C

JOINT CODE *

STANDARDS OF CONDUCT
Introductory Note

The initiative for these standards came from three professional groups: the American Arbitration Association, the American Bar Association, and the Society of Professionals in Dispute Resolution.

The purpose of this initiative was to develop a set of standards to serve as a general framework for the practice of mediation. The effort is a step in the development of the field and a tool to assist practitioners in it—a beginning, not an end. The standards are intended to apply to all types of mediation. It is recognized, however, that in some cases the application of these standards may be affected by laws or contractual agreements.

Preface

The standards of conduct for mediators are intended to perform three major functions: to serve as a guide for the conduct of mediators; to inform the mediating parties; and to promote public confidence in mediation as a process for resolving disputes. The standards draw on existing codes of conduct for mediators and take into account issues and problems that have surfaced in mediation practice. They are offered in the hope that they will serve an educational function and provide assistance to individuals, organizations, and institutions involved in mediation.

Mediation is a process in which an impartial third party—a mediator—facilitates the resolution of a dispute by promoting voluntary agreement (or "self-determination") by the parties to the dispute. A mediator facilitates communications, promotes understanding, focuses the

* Final Draft, 4/8/94. Not yet approved by each organization.

Drafting participants:

   Chair John D. Feerick and David Botwinik for the American Arbitration Association; James J. Alfini and Nancy H. Rogers for the American Bar Association; Susan Dearborn and Lemoine Pierce for the Society of Professionals in Dispute Resolution; Bryant G. Garth and Kimberlee K. Kovach, Reporters; and Frederick E. Woods, Project Staff Director (1994).

parties on their interests, and seeks creative problem solving to enable the parties to reach their own agreement. These standards give meaning to this definition of mediation.

I. Self–Determination: A Mediator Shall Recognize that Mediation is Based on the Principle of Self–Determination by the Parties.

Self-determination is the fundamental principle of mediation. It requires that the mediation process rely upon the ability of the parties to reach a voluntary, uncoerced agreement. Any party may withdraw from mediation at any time.

COMMENTS

• The mediator may provide information about the process, raise issues, and help parties explore options. The primary role of the mediator is to facilitate a voluntary resolution of a dispute. Parties shall be given the opportunity to consider all proposed options.

• A mediator cannot personally ensure that each party has made a fully informed choice to reach a particular agreement, but it is a good practice for the mediator to make the parties aware of the importance of consulting other professionals, where appropriate, to help them make informed decisions.

II. Impartiality: A Mediator Shall Conduct the Mediation in an Impartial Manner.

The concept of mediator impartiality is central to the mediation process. A mediator shall mediate only those matters in which she or he can remain impartial and evenhanded. If at any time the mediator is unable to conduct the process in an impartial manner, the mediator is obligated to withdraw.

COMMENTS

• A mediator shall avoid conduct that gives the appearance of partiality toward one of the parties. The quality of the mediation process is enhanced when the parties have confidence in the impartiality of the mediator.

• When mediators are appointed by a court or institution, the appointing agency shall make reasonable efforts to ensure that mediators serve impartially.

• A mediator should guard against partiality or prejudice based on the parties' personal characteristics, background or performance at the mediation.

III. Conflicts of Interest: A Mediator Shall Disclose all Actual and Potential Conflicts of Interest Reasonably Known to the Mediator. After Disclosure, the Mediator Shall Decline to Mediate Unless all Parties Choose to Retain the Media-

tor. **The Need to Protect Against Conflicts of Interest Also Governs Conduct that Occurs During and After the Mediation.**

A conflict of interest is a dealing or relationship that might create an impression of possible bias. The basic approach to questions of conflict of interest is consistent with the concept of self-determination. The mediator has a responsibility to disclose all actual and potential conflicts that are reasonably known to the mediator and could reasonably be seen as raising a question about impartiality. If all parties agree to mediate after being informed of conflicts, the mediator may proceed with the mediation. If, however, the conflict of interest casts serious doubt on the integrity of the process, the mediator shall decline to proceed.

A mediator must avoid the appearance of conflict of interest both during and after the mediation. Without the consent of all parties, a mediator shall not subsequently establish a professional relationship with one of the parties in a related matter, or in an unrelated matter under circumstances which would raise legitimate questions about the integrity of the mediation process.

COMMENTS

- A mediator shall avoid conflicts of interest in recommending the services of other professionals. A mediator may make reference to professional referral services or associations which maintain rosters of qualified professionals.

- Potential conflicts of interest may arise between administrators of mediation programs and mediators and there may be strong pressures on the mediator to settle a particular case or cases. The mediator's commitment must be to the parties and the process. Pressures from outside of the mediation process should never influence the mediator to coerce parties to settle.

IV. Competence: A Mediator Shall Mediate Only When the Mediator Has the Necessary Qualifications to Satisfy the Reasonable Expectations of the Parties.

Any person may be selected as a mediator, provided that the parties are satisfied with the mediator's qualifications. Training and experience in mediation, however, are often necessary for effective mediation. A person who offers herself or himself as available to serve as a mediator gives parties and the public the expectation that she or he has the competency to mediate effectively. In court-connected or other forms of mandated mediation, it is essential that mediators assigned to the parties have the requisite training and experience.

COMMENTS

- Mediators should have available for the parties information regarding their relevant training, education and experience.

- The requirements for appearing on a list of mediators must be made public and available to interested persons.

- When mediators are appointed by a court or institution, the appointing agency shall make reasonable efforts to ensure that each mediator is qualified for the particular mediation.

V. Confidentiality: A Mediator Shall Maintain the Reasonable Expectations of the Parties with Regard to Confidentiality.

The reasonable expectations of the parties with regard to confidentiality shall be met by the mediator. The parties' expectations of confidentiality depend on the circumstances of the mediation and any agreements they may make. A mediator shall not disclose any matter that any party expects to be confidential unless given permission by all parties or unless required by law or other public policy.

COMMENTS

● The parties may make their own rules with respect to confidentiality, or the accepted practice of an individual mediator or institution may dictate a particular set of expectations. Since the parties' expectations regarding confidentiality are important, the mediator should discuss these expectations with the parties.

● If the mediator holds private sessions with a party, the nature of these sessions with regard to confidentiality should be discussed prior to undertaking such sessions.

● In order to protect the integrity of the mediation, a mediator should avoid communicating information about how the parties acted in the mediation process, the merits of the case or settlement offers. The mediator may report, if required, whether parties appeared at a scheduled mediation.

● Where the parties have agreed that all or a portion of the information disclosed during a mediation is confidential, the parties' agreement should be respected by the mediator.

● Confidentiality should not be construed to limit or prohibit the effective monitoring, research or evaluation of mediation programs by responsible persons. Under appropriate circumstances, researchers may be permitted to obtain access to statistical data and, with permission of the parties, to individual case files, observations of live mediations and interviews with participants.

VI. Quality of the Process: The Mediator Shall Conduct the Mediation Fairly, Diligently and in a Manner Consistent with the Principle of Self–Determination by the Parties.

A mediator shall work to ensure a quality process and to encourage mutual respect among the parties. A quality process requires a commitment by the mediator to diligence and procedural fairness. There should be adequate opportunity for each party in the mediation to participate in the discussions. The parties decide when and under what conditions they will reach an agreement or terminate a mediation.

COMMENTS

- A mediator may agree to mediate only when he or she is prepared to commit the attention essential to an effective mediation.

- The mediator may only accept cases where they can satisfy the reasonable expectations of the parties concerning the timing of the process. A mediator should not allow a mediation to be unduly delayed by the parties or their representatives.

- The presence or absence of persons at a mediation depends on the agreement of the parties and mediator. The parties and mediator may agree that others may be excluded from particular sessions or from the entire mediation process.

- The primary purpose of a mediator is to facilitate the parties' voluntary agreement. This role differs substantially from other professional-client relationships. Mixing the role of a mediator and the role of a professional advising a client is problematic, and mediators must strive to distinguish between the roles. A mediator should therefore refrain from providing professional advice. Where appropriate, a mediator should recommend that parties seek outside professional advice, or consider resolving their dispute through arbitration, counselling, neutral evaluation, or other processes. A mediator who undertakes, at the request of the parties, an additional dispute resolution role in the same matter assumes increased responsibilities and obligations that may be governed by the standards of other professions.

- A mediator shall withdraw from a mediation when incapable of serving or when unable to remain impartial.

- A mediator shall withdraw from the mediation or postpone a session if the mediation is being used to further illegal conduct, or if a party is unable to participate due to drug, alcohol, or other physical or mental incapacity.

- Mediators should not permit their behavior in the mediation process to be guided by a desire for a high settlement rate.

VII. Advertising and Solicitation: A Mediator Shall Be Truthful in Advertising and Solicitation for Mediation.

Advertising or any other communication with the public concerning services offered or regarding the education, training, and expertise of the mediator shall be truthful. Mediators shall refrain from promises and guarantees of results.

COMMENTS

- It is imperative that communication with the public educate and instill confidence in the process.

- In an advertisement or other communication to the public, a mediator may make reference to meeting state, national, or private organization qualifications only if the entity referred to has a procedure for qualifying mediators and the mediator has been duly granted the requisite status.

VIII. Fees: A Mediator Shall Fully Disclose and Explain the Basis of Compensation, Fees and Charges to the Parties.

The parties should be provided sufficient information about fees at the outset of a mediation to determine if they wish to retain the services of a mediator. If a mediator charges fees, the fees shall be reasonable considering, among other things, the mediation service, the type and complexity of the matter, the expertise of the mediator, the time required, and the rates customary in the community. The better practice in reaching an understanding about fees is to set down the arrangements in a written agreement.

COMMENTS

- A mediator who withdraws from a mediation should return any unearned fee to the parties.

- A mediator should not enter into a fee agreement which is contingent upon the result of the mediation or amount of the settlement.

- Co-mediators who share a fee should hold to standards of reasonableness in determining the allocation of fees.

- A mediator should not accept a fee for referral of a matter to another mediator or to any other person.

IX. Obligations to the Mediation Process.

Mediators have a duty to improve the practice of mediation.

COMMENTS

- Mediators are regarded as knowledgeable in the process of mediation. They have an obligation to use their knowledge to help educate the public about mediation; to make mediation accessible to those who would like to use it, to correct abuses; and to improve their professional skills and abilities.

Appendix D

NATIONAL STANDARDS FOR COURT–CONNECTED MEDIATION PROGRAMS *

EXECUTIVE SUMMARY

1.0 ACCESS TO MEDIATION

1.1 Mediation services should be available on the same basis as are other services of the court.

1.2 Each court should develop policies and procedures that take into consideration the language and cultural diversity of its community at all stages of development, operation and evaluation of court-connected mediation services and programs.

1.3 To ensure that parties have equal access to mediation, non-judicial screeners should have clearly stated written policies, procedures and criteria to guide their discretion in referring cases to mediation.

1.4 Courts should take steps to ensure that *pro se* litigants make informed choices about mediation.

1.5 Courts should ensure that information about the availability of mediation services is widely disseminated in the languages used by the consumers of court services.

1.6 a. Courts should provide orientation and training for attorneys, court personnel and others regarding the availability, nature and use of mediation services.

   b. Prior to and at the filing of a case, courts should provide to the parties and their attorneys information regarding the availability of mediation.

1.7 In choosing the location and hours of operation of mediation services, courts should consider the effect on the ability of parties to use mediation effectively and the safety of mediators and parties.

* Center for Dispute Settlement and the
Institute of Judicial Administration.

2.0 COURTS' RESPONSIBILITY FOR MEDIATION

2.1 The degree of a court's responsibility for mediators or mediation programs depends on whether a mediator or program is employed or operated by the court, receives referrals from the court, or is chosen by the parties themselves.

   a. The court is fully responsible for mediators it employs and programs it operates.

   b. The court has the same responsibility for monitoring the quality of mediators and/or mediation programs outside the court to which it refers cases as it has for its own programs.

   c. The court has no responsibility for the quality or operation of outside programs chosen by the parties without guidance from the court.

2.2 The court should specify its goals in establishing a mediation program or in referring cases to mediation programs or services outside the court and provide a means of evaluating whether or not these goals are being met.

2.3 Program Management

   a. Information provided by the court to the mediator

      (1) When parties choose to go to mediation outside the court, the court should have no responsibility to provide any information to the mediator.

      (2) When a court makes a mandatory referral of parties to mediation, whether inside or outside the court, it should be responsible for providing the mediator or mediation program sufficient information to permit the mediator to deal with the case effectively.

   b. Information provided by the mediator or the parties to the court

      (1) If the program is court-operated, or if the case is referred to an outside program or mediator by the court, the program or individual mediator should have the responsibility to report information to the court, in order to permit monitoring and evaluation.

      (2) If the mediator or program is chosen by the parties without guidance from the court, the provider should have no responsibility to report to the court.

2.4 Aggregate Information

   Court-operated mediation programs and programs to which the court refers cases should be required to provide periodic information to the court. The information required should be related to:

   a. The court's objectives in establishing the program; and

   b. The court's responsibility for ensuring the quality of the services provided.

2.5 The court should designate a particular individual to be responsible for supervision, monitoring and administration of court-connected mediation programs.

2.6   Complaint Mechanism
      Parties referred by the court to a mediation program, whether or
      not it is operated by the court, should have access to a complaint
      mechanism to address any grievances about the process.

3.0   INFORMATION FOR JUDGES, COURT PERSONNEL AND USERS

3.1   Courts, in collaboration with the bar and professional mediation
      organizations, are responsible for providing information to the
      public, the bar, judges and court personnel regarding the media-
      tion process; the availability of programs; the differences between
      mediation, adjudication and other dispute resolution processes;
      the possibility of savings in cost and time; and the consequences
      of participation.

3.2   Courts should provide the following information:

   a.   To judges, court personnel and the bar:
        (1) the goals and limitations of the jurisdiction's program(s)
        (2) the basis for selecting cases
        (3) the way in which the program operates
        (4) the information to be provided to lawyers and litigants in
            individual cases
        (5) the way in which the legal and mediation processes inter-
            act
        (6) the enforcement of agreements
        (7) applicable laws and rules concerning mediation

   b.   To users (parties and attorneys) in addition to the information
        in (a):
        General information:
        (1) issues appropriate for mediation
        (2) the possible mediators and how they will be selected
        (3) party choice, if any, of mediators
        (4) any fees
        (5) program operation, including location, times of operation,
            intake procedures, contact person
        (6) the availability of special services for non-English speak-
            ers, and persons who have communication, mobility or
            other disabilities
        (7) the possibility of savings or additional expenditures of
            money or time
        Information on process:
        (1) the nature and purpose of mediation
        (2) confidentiality of process and records
        (3) role of the parties and/or attorneys in mediation
        (4) role of the mediator, including lack of authority to im-
            pose a solution
        (5) voluntary acceptance of any resolution or agreement

    (6) the advantages and disadvantages of participating in determining solutions

    (7) enforcement of agreements

    (8) availability of formal adjudication if a formal resolution or agreement is not achieved and implemented

    (9) the way in which the legal and mediation processes interact, including permissible communications between mediators and the court

    (10) the advantages and disadvantages of a lack of formal record

3.3   The court should encourage attorneys to inform their clients of the availability of court connected mediation programs.

4.0 SELECTION OF CASES AND TIMING OF REFERRAL

4.1   When courts must choose between cases or categories of cases for which mediation is offered because of a shortage of resources, such choices should be made on the basis of clearly articulated criteria. Such criteria might include the following:

    a.   There is a high probability that mediation will be successful in the particular case or category of cases, in terms of both the number and quality of settlements.

    b.   Even if there is not a high probability that mediation will be successful in the particular cases or category of cases, continuing litigation would harm non-parties, the dispute involves important continuing relationships, or the case, if not mediated, is likely to require continuing involvement by the court.

4.2   The following considerations may militate against the suitability of referring cases to mediation:

    a.   when there is a need for public sanctioning of conduct;

    b.   when repetitive violations of statutes or regulations need to be dealt with collectively and uniformly; and

    c.   when a party or parties are not able to negotiate effectively themselves or with assistance of counsel.

4.3   Courts should make available or encourage the availability of mediation to disputants before they file their cases in court as well as after judgment to address problems that otherwise might require relitigation.

4.4   While the timing of a referral to mediation may vary depending upon the type of case involved and the needs of the particular case, referral should be made at the earliest possible time that the parties are able to make an informed choice about their participation in mediation.

4.5   Courts should provide the opportunity on a continuing basis for both the parties and the court to determine the timing of a referral to mediation.

4.6   If a referral to mediation is mandated, parties should have input on the question of when the case should be referred to mediation, but the court itself should determine timing.

4.7   Courts should establish presumptive deadlines for the mediation process, which may be extended by the court upon a showing by the parties that continuation of the process will assist in reaching resolution.

5.0   MANDATORY ATTENDANCE

5.1   Mandatory attendance at an initial mediation session may be appropriate, but only when a mandate is more likely to serve the interests of parties (including those not represented by counsel), the justice system and the public than would voluntary attendance.   Courts should impose mandatory attendance only when:

   a.   the cost of mediation is publicly funded, consistent with Standard 13.0 on Funding;

   b.   there is no inappropriate pressure to settle, in the form of reports to the trier of fact or financial disincentives to trial; and

   c.   mediators or mediation programs of high quality (i) are easily accessible; (ii) permit party participation; (iii) permit lawyer participation when the parties wish it; and (iv) provide clear and complete information about the precise process and procedures that are being required.

5.2   Courts may use a variety of mechanisms to select cases for mandatory referral to mediation.   Any mechanism chosen should provide for an assessment of each case to determine its appropriateness for mediation, which takes into account the parties relative knowledge, experience and resources.

5.3   Any system of mandatory referral to mediation should be evaluated on a periodic basis, through surveys of parties and through other mechanisms, in order to correct deficiencies in the particular implementation mechanism selected and to determine whether the mandate is more likely to serve the interests of parties, the justice system and the public than would voluntary referral.

6.0   QUALIFICATIONS OF MEDIATORS

6.1   Courts have a continuing responsibility to ensure the quality of the mediators to whom they refer cases.   Qualifications of mediators to whom the courts refer cases should be based on their skills. Different categories of cases may require different types and levels of skills.   Skills can be acquired through training and/or experience.   No particular academic degree should be considered a prerequisite for service as a mediator in cases referred by the court.

6.2   Courts need not certify training programs but should ensure that the training received by the mediators to whom they refer cases includes role-playing with feedback.

6.3   Courts are responsible for determining that the mediators to whom they refer cases are qualified.   The level of screening needed to determine qualifications will vary depending upon the type of case involved.

6.4   Courts should orient qualified mediators to court procedures.

6.5 Courts should continue to monitor the performance of mediators to whom they refer cases and ensure that their performance is of consistently high quality.

6.6 Courts should adopt procedures for removing from their roster of mediators those mediators who do not meet their performance expectations and/or ensuring that they do not receive further court referrals.

7.0 SELECTION OF MEDIATORS

7.1 To enhance party satisfaction and investment in the process of mediation, courts should maximize parties' choice of mediator, unless there are reasons why party choice may not be appropriate. Such reasons might include:

a. there is significant inequality in the knowledge or experience of the parties.

b. the court has a particular public policy it is trying to achieve through mediation, which requires selection of a particular mediator or group of mediators.

c. party choice would cause significant and undesirable delay.

7.2 When a court determines that it should refer the parties to a private mediator who will receive a fee, the court should permit the parties to choose from among a number of providers.

8.0 ETHICAL STANDARDS FOR MEDIATORS

8.1 Courts should adopt a code of ethical standards for mediators, together with procedures to handle violations of the code.

Any set of standards should include provisions that address the following concerns:

a. Impartiality

b. Conflict of Interest

c. Advertising by Mediators

d. Disclosure of Fees

e. Confidentiality

f. Role of Mediators in Settlement

9.0 CONFIDENTIALITY

9.1 Courts should have clear written policies relating to the confidentiality of both written and oral communications in mediation consistent with the laws of the jurisdiction. Among the issues such a policy should address specifically are:

a. the mediators and cases protected by confidentiality;

b. the extent of the protection;

c. who may assert or waive the protection; and

d. exceptions to the protection.

9.2 Courts should ensure that their policies relating to confidentiality in mediation are communicated to and understood by the mediators to whom they refer cases.

9.3   Courts should develop clear written policies concerning the way in which confidentiality protections and limitations are communicated to parties they refer to mediation.

9.4   Mediators should not make recommendations regarding the substance or recommended outcome of a case to the court.

9.5   Policies relating to confidentiality should not be construed to prohibit or limit effective monitoring, research or program evaluation.

10.0   THE ROLE OF LAWYERS IN MEDIATION

10.1   Courts should encourage attorneys to advise their clients on the advantages, disadvantages, and strategies for using mediation.

10.2   Parties, in consultation with their attorneys, should have the right to decide whether their attorneys should be present at mediation sessions.

10.3   Courts and mediators should work with the bar to educate lawyers about:

    a.   the difference in the lawyer's role in mediation as compared with traditional representation; and

    b.   the advantages and disadvantages of active participation by the parties and lawyers in mediation sessions.

11.0   INAPPROPRIATE PRESSURE TO SETTLE

11.1   Courts should institute appropriate provisions to permit parties to opt out of mediation. Courts also should consider modifying mediation procedures in certain types of cases to accommodate special needs, such as cases involving domestic violence. Special protocols should be developed to deal with domestic violence cases.

11.2   Courts should provide parties who are required to participate in mediation with full and accurate information about the process to which they are being referred, including the fact that they are not required to make offers and concessions or to settle.

11.3   Courts should not systematically exclude anyone from the mediation process. Lawyers never should be excluded if the parties want them to be present.

11.4   Settlement rates should not be the sole criterion for mediation program funding, mediator advancement, or program evaluation.

11.5   There should be no adverse response by courts to nonsettlement by the parties in mediation.

12.0   COMMUNICATIONS BETWEEN MEDIATORS AND THE COURT

12.1   During a mediation the judge or other trier of fact should be informed only of the following:

    a.   the failure of a party to comply with the order to attend mediation;

    b.   any request by the parties for additional time to complete the mediation;

c. if all parties agree, any procedural action by the court that would facilitate the mediation; and

d. the mediator's assessment that the case is inappropriate for mediation.

12.2 When the mediation has been concluded, the court should be informed of the following:

a. If the parties do not reach an agreement on any matter, the mediator should report the lack of an agreement to the court without comment or recommendation.

b. If agreement is reached, any requirement that its terms be reported to the court should be consistent with the jurisdiction's policies governing settlements in general.

c. With the consent of the parties, the mediators' report also may identify any pending motions or outstanding legal issues, discovery process, or other action by any party which, if resolved or completed, would facilitate the possibility of a settlement.

12.3 Whenever possible, all communications with the judge who will try the case should be made by the parties. Where the mediator must communicate with the trial judge, it is preferable for such communications to be made in writing or through administrative personnel.

13.0 FUNDING OF PROGRAMS AND COMPENSATION OF ME-DIATORS

13.1 Courts should make mediation available to parties regardless of the parties' ability to pay.

a. Where a court suggests (rather than orders) mediation, it should take steps to make mediation available to indigent litigants, through state funding or through encouraging mediators who receive referrals from the court to provide a portion of their services on a free or reduced fee basis.

b. When parties are required to participate in mediation, the costs of mediation should be publicly funded unless the amount at stake or the nature of the parties makes participants' payments appropriate.

13.2 In allocating public funds to mediation, a court may give priority for funding to certain types of cases, such as family and minor criminal matters.

13.3 Where public funds are used, they may either: (a) support mediators employed by the court or (b) compensate private mediators. Where public funds are used to compensate private mediators, fee schedules should be set by the Court.

13.4 a. Where courts offer publicly funded mediation services, courts should permit parties to substitute a private mediator of their own choosing except in those circumstances under which the court has decided that party choice is inappropriate. Parties should have the widest possible latitude in selecting mediators, consistent with public policy.

b. Where parties elect to pay a private mediator, they should be
    permitted to agree with the mediator on the appropriate fee.

14.0 LIABILITY OF MEDIATORS

14.1 Courts should not develop rules for mediators to whom they refer
      cases that are designed to protect these mediators from liability.
      Legislatures and courts should provide the same indemnity or
      insurance for those mediators who volunteer their services or are
      employed by the court that they provide for nonjudicial court
      employees.

15.0 THE ENFORCEABILITY OF MEDIATED AGREEMENTS

15.1 Agreements that are reached through court-connected mediation
      should be enforceable to the same extent as agreements reached
      without a mediator.

16.0 EVALUATION

16.1 Courts should ensure that the mediation programs to which they
      refer cases are monitored adequately on an ongoing basis, evaluat-
      ed on a periodic basis, and that sufficient resources are earmarked
      for these purposes.

16.2 Programs should be required to collect sufficient, accurate infor-
      mation to permit adequate monitoring on an ongoing basis and
      evaluation on a periodic basis.

16.3 Courts should ensure that program evaluation is widely distribut-
      ed and linked to decision-making about the program's policies and
      procedures.

Topical Index

†